European Aristocracies and the Radical Right
1918–1939

Studies of the German Historical Institute London

GENERAL EDITOR: Hagen Schulze

European Aristocracies and the Radical Right 1918–1939

EDITED BY

KARINA URBACH

GERMAN HISTORICAL INSTITUTE LONDON

OXFORD
UNIVERSITY PRESS

OXFORD
UNIVERSITY PRESS

Great Clarendon Street, Oxford OX2 6DP

Oxford University Press is a department of the University of Oxford.
It furthers the University's objective of excellence in research, scholarship,
and education by publishing worldwide in

Oxford New York

Auckland Cape Town Dar es Salaam Hong Kong Karachi
Kuala Lumpur Madrid Melbourne Mexico City Nairobi
New Delhi Shanghai Taipei Toronto

With offices in

Argentina Austria Brazil Chile Czech Republic France Greece
Guatemala Hungary Italy Japan Poland Portugal Singapore
South Korea Switzerland Thailand Turkey Ukraine Vietnam

Oxford is a registered trade mark of Oxford University Press
in the UK and in certain other countries
Published in the United States
by Oxford University Press Inc., New York

British Library Cataloguing in Publication Data

Data available

Library of Congress Cataloging in Publication Data

Data available

ISBN 978-0-19-923173-7

1 3 5 7 9 10 8 6 4 2

Typeset by John Saunders Design & Production
Printed in Great Britain
on acid-free paper by
Biddles Ltd, King's Lynn

Foreword

The German Historical Institute London is situated within the vestiges of aristocratic remains. When looking out of the window, I can see the streets surrounding Bloomsbury Square with their many hotels, restaurants, and cafés named after the Duke of Bedford's family. To this day the Bedfords are great landowners in this area and ensure that we do not forget it.

Although the British aristocracy still exerts influence on the British 'sites of memory' and cleverly reinvented itself as national guardians of British heritage, its twentieth-century political legacy is less well known. The question of what happened to other European aristocracies after the Great War is even more obscure. This book seeks to remedy this and hopes to stimulate more research on the nobilities in the first half of the twentieth century.

In recent years the German Historical Institute has been interested in organizing conferences that not only cover German and British themes, but put things into a wider European perspective. The nobility as a truly European phenomenon therefore seemed an ideal subject for ourselves. Modernists, however, have thus far not done much research on the aristocracy. The organizer of this conference, Karina Urbach, who has already worked intensively on the British and German nobilities, was resourceful in finding speakers who encompass eleven countries and their nobilities in the interwar years: Austria, Belgium, Czechoslovakia, France, Germany, Great Britain, Hungary, Italy, the Netherlands, Romania, and Spain. Because we do not have a comprehensive picture of the aristocracy in many of these countries, discussion turned out to be refreshingly unconventional, with participants vehemently disagreeing with each other (most keenly within the German-speaking contingent). Emotions were ably channelled by distinguished chairmen and discussants: Professors Martin Baumeister (Munich), Derek Beales (Cambridge), T. C. W. Blanning (Cambridge), Robert Evans (Oxford), Dominic Lieven (London), Wolfram Pyta (Stuttgart), Richard Trainor (London), Dieter Weiß (Bayreuth), archivist Jesko Graf zu Dohna (Castell), and all Research Fellows of the German Historical Institute. I should like to thank Angela Davies for translation and for assistance in finalizing the manuscript for the press.

Hagen Schulze

Bloomsbury
August 2007

Contents

List of Tables   ix

1. Introduction   I
   KARINA URBACH

Part I: Western Europe

2. A Counter-Revolution *d'outre-tombe*: Notes on the
   French Aristocracy and the Extreme Right during
   the Third Republic and the Vichy Regime   15
   STEPHAN MALINOWSKI

3. Between *défence social* and Anti-Communism:
   The Belgian Aristocracy   35
   JAN DE MAEYER

4. Age of No Extremes? The British Aristocracy Torn
   between the House of Lords and the Mosley
   Movement   53
   KARINA URBACH

5. Distance and Attraction: Dutch Aristocracy and the
   Political Right Wing   73
   HANS DE VALK

Part II: Southern Europe

6. The Italian Aristocracy, the Savoy Monarchy, and
   Fascism   91
   JENS PETERSEN

7. Aristocracy, Fascism, and the Franco Dictatorship
   (1931–1945)   III
   CARLOS COLLADO SEIDEL

Part III: Central and Eastern Europe

8. 'Only a dictator can help us now': Aristocracy and the Radical Right in Germany   129
   ECKART CONZE

9. Genteel Nationalists: Nobles and Fascism in Czechoslovakia   149
   EAGLE GLASSHEIM

10. Nostalgic Agnostics: Austrian Aristocrats and Politics, 1918–1938   161
    LOTHAR HÖBELT

11. The Hungarian Aristocracy and its Politics   187
    IGNÁC ROMSICS

12. Aristocracy, Fascism, and the Social Origins of Mass Politics in Romania   201
    CONSTANTIN IORDACHI

Notes on Contributors   233

Index   237

List of Tables

3.1   The aristocracy in Belgium, 1830–1940   37

3.2   Chamber of Representatives: percentage of
       aristocratic members   38

3.3   Senate: percentage of aristocratic members   39

3.4   Composition of Belgian governments: percentage
       of aristocratic members   40

3.5   Provincial council of Antwerp: position of the
       aristocracy   40

3.6   Corps of provincial governors: number of aristocrats   41

3.7   Belgian army—general staff: percentage of
       aristocrats   41

3.8   Belgian army—infantry: percentage of aristocrats   41

3.9   Belgian army—cavalry: percentage of aristocrats   42

3.10   High finance and industry: ratio of aristocrats to
       total number of board members   43

3.11   Results of the elections to the Chamber of
       Representatives and Senate, 1936 and 1939   49

12.1   Distribution of the ownership of agrarian land in
       Romania, 1905   213

12.2   Distribution of the ownership of agrarian land in
       Romania, 1927   215

1
Introduction

KARINA URBACH

What do the post-war experiences of an impoverished Prussian
Junker have in common with those of a Florentine countess or a
politically influential British peer? How can one dare to compare
them and come to any useful conclusion about the nobility as
such in interwar Europe?

A noted philosopher has suggested one solution. In *Philosophical
Investigations* Ludwig Wittgenstein explained common features of
social groups in terms of 'family resemblances': 'We see a complicated network of similarities overlapping and criss-crossing:
sometimes overall similarities, sometimes similarities of detail. I
can think of no better expression to characterize these similarities
than "family resemblances"; for the various resemblances
between members of a family: build, features, colour of eyes, gait,
temperament, etc. etc. overlap and criss-cross in the same way.'[1]
Such an explanation would have appealed to nobles with their
own, very special concept of the family.[2]

I

The essays in this volume follow Wittgenstein by looking at the
'build and temperament' of the nobility of eleven different countries during a particularly testing time. A great help in tilling this
so far almost virgin soil are the works of early modernists.[3] Their

[1] Ludwig Wittgenstein, *Philosophical Investigations*, trans. Gertrude Anscombe (Oxford,
1967), p. 32e.
[2] For aristocratic family concepts see e.g. Andreas Gestrich, Jens-Uwe Krause, and
Michael Mitterauer (eds.), *Geschichte der Familie* (Stuttgart, 2003), 632 ff.
[3] See Ronald G. Asch, *Nobilities in Transition 1550–1700: Courtiers and Rebels in Britain and
Europe* (London, 2003); id. (ed.), *Der europäische Adel im Ancien Régime: Von der Krise der ständischen Monarchien bis zur Revolution (c.1600–1789)* (Cologne, 2001); M. L. Bush, *Rich Noble—
Poor Noble* (Manchester, 1988); id., *Noble Privilege* (Manchester, 1983); Walter Demel, *Der*

comparative studies on the aristocracy are encouraging as well as an example in terms of method. For them the noble houses of Europe are comparable: 'united by ideals of conduct and values which, in their different regional and national variations, still bear a certain resemblance to each other'.[4] This was also a result of the fact that contacts between nobles were much more frequent in the seventeenth and eighteenth centuries. Aristocratic mental maps and connections were truly international. Karl Heinrich Nikolaus Otto Prinz von Nassau-Siegen, for example, son of a German–Dutch family, was born in 1745 in France, became a *grande* of Spain, married a Polish countess, and worked as a Russian admiral until 1794.[5]

The process of incorporation of nations into states made such cosmopolitan biographies less common by the twentieth century, apart from the higher echelons of the aristocracy. Yet this does not mean that nobles did not still recognize each other as kindred spirits and in many cases as equals.

Historical research on aristocracies in the twentieth century, let alone a comparative approach on a European level, is, however, still in its early stages. In many countries, the fight against and cooperation with modernization since the nineteenth century, including the political alliances aristocrats formed in the twentieth century, are still neglected. Among modernists Dominic Lieven alone led the field,[6] followed by Hans-Ulrich Wehler, who more than fifteen years ago as an editor encouraged historians to turn from the history of the working classes and the bourgeoisie to the nobility. In his comparative study *Europäischer Adel 1751–1950* Wehler pointed out that research on the French, Italian, Russian, and Austrian nobility was all but non-existent.

Europäische Adel vom Mittelalter bis zur Gegenwart (Munich, 2005); J. Dewald, *The European Nobility, 1400–1800* (Cambridge, 1996); R. J. W. Evans, *The Making of the Habsburg Monarchy 1550–1700* (Oxford, 1979); H. M. Scott, *The European Nobilities in the Seventeenth and Eighteenth Centuries*, 2 vols. (London, 1995). See also the paper by Gerrit Walther, 'Wer gehörte dazu? Kriterien für Adel in der Frühen Neuzeit', given at the conference ' "The Rule of the Few"—Aristocratic Policy, Communication and "Noble" Lifestyle in Antiquity and Early Modern Times' held at the Zentrum für interdisziplinäre Forschung (ZIF, Centre for Interdisciplinary Research) at the University of Bielefeld, 1–3 March 2006. Conference report published in *ZIF Mitteilungen*, 3 (2006), 22–3.

[4] Asch, *Nobilities in Transition*, p. ix.
[5] Walter Demel, 'Der europäische Adel vor der Revolution: Sieben Thesen', in Asch (ed.), *Der europäische Adel im Ancien Régime*, 420.
[6] Dominic Lieven, *The Aristocracy in Europe 1815–1914* (London, 1992).

Although this has thankfully changed in respect of the Austrian nobility, many other countries are still a complete blank on the aristocratic map. This is because of historical fashions as well as very different national historical schools. Whereas British historians, for example, have always worked extensively on the nobility as a politically decisive group, and started to study the middle classes only twenty years ago, developments in Germany went in exactly the opposite direction.[7] Here, thanks to the projects of the Frankfurt and Bielefeld schools, the *Bürgertum* was at the centre of interest from the 1980s onwards. The nobility was seen as an irrelevant, declining group which after 1918 played a negligible walk-on part in German history and was treated in the context of the *Sonderweg* thesis. This changed with Heinz Reif, Eckart Conze, and Stephan Malinowski's work on the German aristocracy.[8] The latter two present their findings in this volume, with Malinowski for the first time turning his methodology to the French model. Eagle Glassheim is similarly a pioneer in his work on the aristocracy of Czechoslovakia, while Jens Petersen, quondam contributor to Wehler's study, reassesses his work on Italy a decade later.

All the other contributors to this volume had not previously specialized in the nobility and had to overcome great hurdles, including the lack of secondary literature and restricted access to archives. Hans de Valk, for example, faced the problem that in the egalitarian Netherlands elites had long ceased to be a politically correct endeavour to work on. He circumvented the lack of empirical research by turning to biography in his essay identifying three archetypical aristocratic figures. A similar lack of scholarly literature faced Jan de Maeyer for Belgium and Ignác Romsics who writes about the Hungarian nobility. Lothar Höbelt had an easier task with Austria. Here the works of Hannes Stekl and William D. Godsey have recently resurrected the Austrian aristocracy for the twentieth

---

[7] In Great Britain different historical schools opposed each other, seeing the nobility either as adaptable, politically strong, or, in Cannadine's sense, as an example of decline.

[8] Eckart Conze, *Von deutschem Adel: Die Grafen von Bernstorff im 20. Jahrhundert* (Stuttgart, 2000); id. and Monika Wienfort (eds.), *Adel und Moderne: Deutschland im europäischen Vergleich im 19. und 20. Jahrhundert* (Cologne, 2004); Stephan Malinowski, *Vom König zum Führer: Sozialer Niedergang und politische Radikalisierung im deutschen Adel zwischen Kaiserreich und NS Staat* (Berlin, 2003); Heinz Reif (ed.), *Adel und Bürgertum in Deutschland*, 2 vols. (Berlin, 2001); Monika Wienfort, *Der Adel in der Moderne* (Göttingen, 2006).

century.[9] In Eastern Europe studies—for example, on the Polish aristocracy—are only just emerging and could not be included in this volume. Some of the archival material has still not been catalogued because of a lack of funds; yet Constantin Iordachi overcomes such obstacles when he presents his research on the Romanian case. At least some south-eastern European archives are now technically accessible; something that cannot be said of the family archives of the Spanish nobility. In his chapter on Franco and the Spanish nobility Carlos Collado therefore had to piece together information from disparate aristocratic biographies and genealogical handbooks.

II

Apart from such very different starting positions, all the authors represented in this volume at first had to battle with the basic problem of defining their group. Lieven's verdict that 'everyone knows what aristocracy means until they have to write a book on the subject' remains valid to this day.[10] First of all the difference between 'aristocracy' and 'nobility' has never been properly analysed. British historians have used both terms interchangeably, though strictly speaking the term 'aristocracy' in Great Britain includes only the peerage and inner family. Lieven's own monograph is, however, entitled *The Aristocracy in Europe* and covers peerage *and* gentry in Germany, Russia, and England: 'To write a history purely of the peerage would . . . omit a key element in the story of how England's upper class confronted their rapidly changing society', he emphasizes.[11]

David Cannadine followed a similar line of argument.[12] During the conference on which this volume is based, T. C. W. Blanning opposed this and suggested that since 'aristocracy'

---

[9] Hannes Stekl and Marija Wakounig, *Windisch-Graetz: Ein Fürstenhaus im 19. und 20. Jahrhundert* (Vienna, 1992); Ralph Melville, *Adel und Revolution in Böhmen: Strukturwandel von Herrschaft und Gesellschaft in Österreich um die Mitte des 19. Jahrhunderts* (Mainz 1998); William D. Godsey, Jr., *Aristocratic Redoubt: The Austro-Hungarian Foreign Office on the Eve of the First World War* (West Lafayette, Ind., 1999); id., 'Nobles and Modernity: Review Article', *German History*, 20 (2002), 504 ff.

[10] Lieven, *Aristocracy in Europe*, p. xiii.

[11] Ibid.

[12] David Cannadine, *The Decline and Fall of the British Aristocracy* (London, 1996).

could be seen as a political term and did not cover the whole group, 'nobility' should be used as a more neutral word. This argument is also supported by the sources. When one types 'aristocracy' into the word search of the catalogue of the National Archives, London, the results are minimal. The word 'nobility' or 'nobles', however, results in an overwhelming array. In the following essays authors have tried to find their own adequate translations for their often very heterogeneous group. This was not just a problem of getting the terminology right. David Bell recently claimed that the French nobility, for example, was 'never a caste. It was a porous and untidy social category that incorporated hundreds of thousands of individuals, ranging from the grand aristocrats of Versailles to retired provincial aldermen.'[13]

As with studies of the bourgeoisie, the closer you look at a group the more blurred the picture becomes. In the case of the nobility, matters are complicated by the fact that in each country the distinctions that identify a noble as of the higher or lower nobility are very different. In Germany the age of the pedigree determines the social status of an aristocratic family (not necessarily the title), while in Great Britain hereditary peers are 'young', that is, they often have relatively short pedigrees but their status (and titles) rose by the accumulation of money and land. As the Duchess of Westminster so succinctly put it: 'English people are accustomed to be snobbish over money and titles but not to care a damn about pedigree.'[14] Her husband's family owned land in Mayfair, Kensington, and Chelsea—areas that became increasingly important. As a result, they received a baronetcy in 1761, which was elevated to an earldom twenty years later, and a marquessate in 1831, finally culminating in a dukedom in 1874.[15]

Yet in other European countries, noble families often have nothing left but the name. You find nobles everywhere in Italy,

[13] David A. Bell, 'Twilight Approaches'. Review of Benedetta Craveri, *The Age of Conversation*, in *London Review of Books*, 11 May 2006, 17.

[14] Loelia, Duchess of Westminster, *Grace and Favour: The Memoirs of Loelia, Duchess of Westminster* (London 1961), 140. Early modernists would not agree with this though. See Ronald G. Asch's section on the invention of pedigrees at the 2004 *Historikertag* in Kiel.

[15] Andreas Fahrmeier, 'Zwischen Leistungselite und ständischen Strukturen: Das britische Wirtschaftsbürgertum', in Franz Bosbach, Keith Robbins, and Karina Urbach (eds.), *Geburt oder Leistung? Birth or Talent? The Formation of Elites in a British–German Comparison* (Munich, 2003), 182.

bemoaned Luigi Barzini in 1956, in palaces, and even among the indigent on the street.[16] Were these families who had lost all noble insignia still noble, or had they become simply an 'imagined community'? The latter would prove Heinrich Heine's verdict that the aristocracy, like the devil, exists only because people believe in it.[17] Marcel Proust, however, would not have agreed: 'the power of such people is seen to reside not so much in their wealth or inherited position, much less in their talent or personality. Rather it lies in the power of names themselves, the imaginative recognition ascribed to them by others and the authority that the name appears to inscribe in them as people.'[18]

Apart from writers, sociologists such as Pierre Bourdieu have tried to explain the longevity of elite power by highlighting their symbolic capital (titles), their cultural capital (knowledge, taste), and their social capital (networks).[19] Whereas some historians resent the influx of such theories ('Parlez-vous Bordieu?' is a typical joke among historians of aristocracy) others have adopted them and find useful the work of Max Weber and Niklas Luhmann on the concept of 'habitus'—a distinctive definition of aristocratic behaviour. In Germany Heinz Reif developed the concept of 'Adeligkeit' to explain aristocratic identity (including déclassé nobles), based upon, among various other criteria, importance of blood, family, honour, and the ability to rule.[20] In

---

[16] Luigi Barzini, 'Die italienische Aristokratie: Europäischer Adel III', *Der Monat*, 9/99 (1956), 39.

[17] Oscar Wilde was of a similar opinion: 'You should study the peerage . . . It is the best thing in Fiction the English have ever done.' Oscar Wilde, *A Woman of No Importance* (London, 1893).

[18] For this see Simon Gunn, 'Ascription as Inscription: Occupations and the Transformative Powers of Names', paper given at the University of Greenwich, 22 Nov. 2002.

[19] Pierre Bourdieu, 'Der Habitus als Vermittlung zwischen Struktur und Praxis (1970)', in id., *Zur Soziologie der symbolischen Formen* (4th edn.; Frankfurt am Main, 1991); id., 'Ökonomisches Kapital, kulturelles Kapital, soziales Kapital', in Reinhard Kreckel (ed.), *Soziale Ungleichheiten* (Göttingen, 1983). See also Hans-Ulrich Wehler, 'Pierre Bourdieu: Das Zentrum seines Werks', in id., *Die Herausforderung der Kulturgeschichte* (Munich, 1998), 27–8; Monique de Saint Martin, *Der Adel: Soziologie eines Standes*, trans. Jörg Ohnacker (Constance, 2003).

[20] Heinz Reif, ' "Adeligkeit"—historische und elitentheoretische Überlegungen zum Adelshabitus in Deutschland um 1800', speech delivered at the Institute for European History in Mainz, 18 June 1997. This concept is questioned by Silke Marburg and Joseph Matzerath who describe the nobility as an 'Erinnerungsgruppe', an elite of memory. Silke Marburg and Josef Matzerath (eds.), *Der Schritt in die Moderne: Sächsischer Adel zwischen 1763 und 1918* (Cologne, 2001).

the essays that follow, the reader will see that some authors have been influenced by these theories and tried to be not too elitist with their elite. They therefore cover various sorts of nobles: rich landowners, those who had served traditionally in military or administrative capacities, and the déclassé nobility.

Arno Mayer's thesis that the power of the old regime lasted well into the twentieth century was, of course, an exaggeration and none of the authors in this volume agree.[21] Yet Mayer offered a much-needed provocation that gave a new impetus to studies of the aristocracy. Before Mayer one had been fed from the other extreme: endless master narratives of aristocratic decline which seemed to turn the history of the aristocracy into continual doom. Taken together, these decline stories would have meant that the nobility had lost all its power in the eighteenth, nineteenth, and twentieth century respectively.[22]

This line was supported by numerous contemporary aristocratic autobiographers who specialized in swan songs, as well as novelists. Countless Penguin classics describe the decline of the European aristocracies in the twentieth century. Evelyn Waugh showed sympathy for 'his' disorientated Catholic aristocrats (and their country houses) in *Brideshead Revisited*. Hugo von Hofmannsthal ceremoniously staged the late summer of the Austrian nobility and Tomasi di Lampedusa's *Leopard* buried the Italian nobility. Indeed, economic, political, and social transformation processes had been a constant companion of the aristocracy over centuries; and many aristocratic groups lost out.

European aristocracies certainly share a long tradition of experiencing crises, but they themselves were not permanently in 'search of lost time', or in a continuous Camelot. Instead, they constantly tried to restabilize and readjust themselves. The torturous journey tracing the rise, fall, and occasional rebirth of aristocracies is therefore at the centre of these essays. All authors used the challenge and response model to understand how their nobles coped. The particular challenge at the centre of this volume is, of course, the fall-out from the First World War, which was naturally much easier to handle for the winners than

---

[21] Arno Mayer, *The Persistence of the Old Regime: Europe to the Great War* (New York, 1981).

[22] Cannadine's *Decline and Fall of the British Aristocracy* therefore stands in a long historical tradition. His theories were questioned by Peter Mandler's work. Peter Mandler, *The Fall and Rise of the Stately Home* (New Haven, 1997).

the losers. However, nobles were suddenly confronted with republics, revolutions, and an influx of 'Bolshevist' ideas. The Red threat varied from country to country, of course; but the international network of the European aristocracy tried to turn it into a common experience—a class war seemed to be imminent. How, if at all, did they as a result become a focus for anti-democratic tendencies? Or, to quote Dominic Lieven's last sentences in *The Aristocracy in Europe 1815–1914*: 'In extremis, would aristocrats be sufficiently reactionary or civilised to remain constrained by traditional conceptions of religion and honour, or would insecurity, resentment of lost status and agnosticism lead them down the path towards totalitarian nationalism and its inevitable companion, barbaric anti-Semitism?'[23] Debates about a new order (preferably based on the old one) in which aristocrats would play a leading role took place in all countries after 1918.

The interwar years seem to have given some nobles brief political opportunities—in Germany for those surrounding Hindenburg, in Hungary those following Horthy, in Spain those collaborating with Franco. This would indicate that in countries in which fascist or authoritarian regimes were successful the aristocracy experienced a last hurrah. Yet what part did they really play in such movements? Are we perhaps falling for a left-wing conspiracy theory by overestimating the nobility's political prowess and underestimating the degree to which they often stood as a conservative bulwark against the radical right?

What, though, is meant by the 'radical right'? As with fascism, agreement on a common definition is difficult to find and this book will not claim any false precision. What is *not* meant is the concept of a 'conservative revolution', a phrase particularly popular in the German historiography. Generally speaking, the radical right was composed of groups that existed in small numbers on the political margins of Europe before the First World War, but became increasingly powerful in the interwar years. There were affinities and coalitions between conservatives and the radical right. Disgruntled former Tories in Britain, for example, were as much fascinated by authoritarian and later fascist regimes as Prussian conservatives who eventually turned to Hitler.[24] Yet

---

[23] Lieven, *Aristocracy in Europe*, 242.

[24] Martin Blinkhorn (ed.), *Fascists and Conservatives: The Radical Right and the Establishment in Twentieth-Century Europe* (London, 1990).

there were also conservatives in the old sense, who found the 'modernistic' and anti-religious side of these new movements alienating. Usually the 'classic' countries of research on fascist and radical right-wing regimes are Germany, Italy, Spain, Romania, Hungary, and Austria. These countries are to be found in this volume, but other case studies, of so-called 'stable democracies' such as Great Britain, France, Belgium, and the Netherlands, have to be analysed as well to understand whether and why aristocrats reacted differently here.[25] In the essays that follow, authors include under the term 'radical right' fascist, National Socialist, and authoritarian regimes, though Ignác Romsics does not see the Horthy government in this context.

Generally speaking, the social profiles of members of radical right-wing movements have in the past shown a high proportion from the lower middle classes. Yet the higher echelons of society were by no means absent, as the following essays show. In this, the generational issue seems to have played a part. For Germany it has been shown that it was often younger aristocrats who persuaded their parents to join. Whether this was also the case in other countries is still unknown. Yet nobles who joined had a great impact, especially in the early stages of these movements. Aristocratic members, or 'Drawing Room Nazis' as Diana Mitford called them, were not only a great public relations catch, they were also door-openers to other important circles. Because of their illustrious names, they were particularly 'visible' and gave the radical right a new social respectability.

What was it that attracted the nobility to these movements? Anti-parliamentarism? The mixture of modern and traditional elements? Anti-Semitism and racist concepts? The pomp, the symbols, the militarism, the 'masculinity' of the movement? Or was it the charisma of leaders that attracted them as in the case of Romania, where a fusion between the old Romanian aristocracy and the new 'charismatic aristocracy' of the Iron Guards was forged? (Constantin Iordachi shows in his essay that this led to them advocating 'cultural purification' and 'national regeneration' coupled with a virulent anti-Semitism.)

Each essay will give its own particular combination of answers to these questions. The authors also try to show what kept

[25] See e.g. Philip Morgan, *Fascism in Europe 1919–1945* (London, 2002).

aristocrats away from these movements.[26] Apart from differing
political traditions and value systems, the role that religion still
played in the aristocracy could be decisive. This is the focus of
Jan de Maeyer's essay on the Belgian aristocracy. Though
Belgian aristocrats were at first very much impressed by Degrelle,
his subsequent alienation of the Catholic Church turned them
away. In Germany and Hungary, as Conze and Romsics show,
the religious dividing lines between Catholicism, Calvinism, and
Protestantism could also play a part when it came to the question
of 'to join or not to join'. The Calvinist petty noble Horthy did
not particularly appeal to Catholic Hungarian *grand seigneurs*, and
the Catholic Bavarian noble could not sympathize with the
paganism of the Nazi movement.

    However, right-wing movements could not have been
prompted to resist the attractions of fascism merely for religion
(after all Catholicism did not prevent the Westphalian nobility
from falling for Hitler). One reason why Bavarian aristocrats
were comparatively immune might have been the dignified
example of Crown Prince Rupprecht.[27] Could it have been a
sense of monarchism that kept these Bavarian nobles relatively
suspicious of Nazism? Monarchist movements could work as a
bulwark against the radical right, but they could also become its
bedfellow as the Italian case shows. In his essay Jens Petersen
demonstrates that it was the monarch's willing cooperation and
lack of charisma that made it possible for Mussolini to step into
the regal vacuum.[28] This had an enormous impact on nobles
elsewhere. For many aristocrats all over Europe the Italian
model seemed an ideal solution. As Conze, Malinowski, and
Urbach indicate in their essays, the Italian example played a
great part in winning over nobles to the fascist idea. (For
example, the contacts of the Hitler supporter Philip von Hessen
with the Italian monarchy were instrumental here.)[29]

[26] 'Red' aristocrats were such a minor occurrence that they get only an occasional
mention.

[27] For this see Dieter J. Weiß, *Kronprinz Rupprecht von Bayern (1869–1955): Eine politische
Biographie* (Regensburg, 2007).

[28] For a general overview see Alexander de Grand, *Fascist Italy and Nazi Germany: The
'Fascist' Style of Rule* (London, 1995); Wolfgang Schieder, 'Faschismus', in Richard von
Dülmen (ed.), *Fischer-Lexikon Geschichte* (Frankfurt am Main, 2003), 199–221.

[29] Institut für Zeitgeschichte (IFZ), ZS 918, Befragung des Prinzen von Hessen, 6 May
1947. Jonathan Petropoulos, *Royals and the Reich: The Princes von Hessen in Nazi Germany*
(Oxford, 2006).

Ideological cross-currents flowing between European nobles are an important and so far neglected reason why many fell for the radical right. This brings us back to Wittgenstein's idea about criss-crossing. Noble families, particularly on the Continent, were interrelated or had befriended each other. That these links had an effect on their geographical as well as 'mental' map is obvious. Nobles still emulated and stimulated each other and suprana-tional ideological transfers were therefore not uncommon in a group which had such cosmopolitan roots. The higher aristoc-racy, in particular, did not exist in a national vacuum. Despite the First World War, which tore international families apart, contacts were re-established very quickly. It is, however, particu-larly difficult to untangle this complex international network.

How can one imagine such an abstract concept of networks? A good way of visualizing it is to look at the network paintings of the New York artist Mark Lombardi. His pictures are narra-tive structures, unveiling the secret entanglements of a small elite of politicians with multinational companies. Lombardi is obsessed with conspiracy theories, but if one wants to under-stand the links that European aristocracies tried to sustain amongst each other and with various power centres over a long period of time, one could draw a similar picture: in the early nineteenth century still with strong brush strokes, later on with increasingly shaky ones. Yet despite growing shakiness, these contacts also made them ideal 'transmitters' or intermediaries for the radical right. Prince Max Hohenlohe, who is mentioned in Urbach's essay, was such a transmitter who, for a while, regained some political influence. He lived in Czechoslovakia and Spain (where he had married into an influential family) and worked for Hitler, Franco, and the British Foreign Office, spreading the gospel of National Socialism. The common link was the fear of Bolshevism. The influence the Russian nobility had on their scared European cousins has so far been neglected. It was not possible to find a Russian contributor for this book.[30] However, in his recent monograph on white émigrés after 1917, Michael Kellogg mentions aristocrats and their political dealings with fascist regimes. He comes to the conclusion that they

---

[30] Julia Hildt has just started a dissertation at the University of Bonn on autobiogra-phies of the exiled Russian aristocracy after 1917.

'contributed extensively to the making of German National Socialism'.[31]

To understand the aristocracy in the twentieth century one has to use political, economic, and social history in combination. However, in this volume economic aspects play only a secondary part. This is because of the lack of research by economic historians on noble families and the problem of getting exact figures from the archives (in Germany, for example, wills are to this day not available).

Of course, cultural approaches are important too. The enormous power of country houses, for example, has been proved by Peter Mandler's study and in Germany historians have tried to explain the aristocratic mindset, for example, by studying their hunting patterns. This is a very specialized angle, though, and for countries such as Spain or Hungary, where the study of aristocracy is in its early stages, it seems more important to write a political and economic history of the aristocracy. When this base is achieved, a story of aristocratic Spanish hunting patterns would not seem frivolous anymore.

Furthermore, cultural interpretations can be deceiving in pressing the sources too far. Cannadine, for example, interprets John Sargent's famous 1905 painting of the Marlborough family as an example of the new dominance of an American heiress.[32] Indeed, like so many of his compatriots, the 9th Duke of Marlborough married a rich American to save his estates. In Sargent's painting Consuelo Vanderbilt stands two steps above her husband, towering over her children. Cannadine sees this as a sign of her power, but if one reads Vanderbilt's memoirs, the reason for this arrangement was quite banal: 'I was placed on a step higher than Marlborough [her husband] so that the difference in our height—for I was taller than he—should be accounted for.'[33] The 9th Duke of Marlborough, who commissioned the portrait, was, like many aristocrats, too much of an expert in careful stage setting to have given away any possible inequalities within the family.

---

[31] Michael Kellogg, *The Russian Roots of Nazism: White Émigrés and the Making of National Socialism 1917–1945* (Cambridge, 2005), 1.

[32] David Cannadine, Preface to *Decline and Fall*, p. xiii.

[33] Consuelo Vanderbilt Balsan, *The Glitter and the Gold* (Maidstone, 1973), 146.

PART I

Western Europe

2

A Counter-Revolution *d'outre-tombe*: Notes on the French Aristocracy and the Extreme Right during the Third Republic and the Vichy Regime

STEPHAN MALINOWSKI

Few will doubt that aristocracy and modernity have ever had an easy time with one another. Sooner or later—at least when viewed from a non-British standpoint—political and economic modernity exerts a deadly effect on the aristocracy, although this does not prevent the aristocracy from making an occasional comeback. Radical and early experience with political death and resurrection in the guise of modernity is the first way in which the French aristocracy can be described as an avant-garde by its European peers.

In 1957 Nancy Mitford summed up the difficulties of continued existence after such a political death in a malicious image: 'An aristocracy in a republic is like a chicken whose head has been cut off: it may run about in a lively way, but in fact it is dead.'[1] Mitford's chicken metaphor seems convincing if we look at the interest the historiography of the French aristocracy in the twentieth century has generated. While it is easy to get lost in the literary forest of analyses of the extreme right,[2] there is very little to be found on the political history of the aristocracy after 1914. Despite recent work on the French aristocracy in the twentieth century,[3] mostly inspired by Pierre Bourdieu, it would be true to say that literally nothing has been published on the topic under

[1] Nancy Mitford, 'The English Aristocracy', in Alan S. C. Ross et al., *Noblesse Oblige: An Enquiry into the Identifiable Characteristics of the English Aristocracy* (London, 1956), 39–61, at 39.
[2] Probably the best and most comprehensive overview is to be found in Jean-François Sirinelli (ed.), *Histoire des Droites en France*, 3 vols. (Paris, 1992).
[3] Monique de Saint Martin, *L'Espace de la Noblesse* (Paris, 1993); Eric Mension-Rigan, *L'enfance au château: Aristocrates et Grands Bourgeois. Education, Traditions, Valeurs* (Paris, 1994).

discussion here for the period after the First World War—not a single monograph and apparently not even a relevant essay. An examination of the work of French historians of aristocracy and specialists on the radical right produces a meagre result. The *Dictionnaire historique de la vie politique française au XXe siècle* has never heard of the aristocracy,[4] and the *Histoire des Droites en France*, edited by Jean-François Sirinelli, over approximately 2,500 pages, offers no more than a few scattered facts about individual aristocrats and does not take a systematic approach to the aristocracy as a social group.[5] And even Pierre Nora's celebrated work on *lieux de mémoire* does not remember the aristocracy, even though it runs to seven volumes.[6]

If Mitford's metaphor is correct, and the French aristocracy has really long been 'dead', then the explanation for its absence from historiography about the twentieth century is easy to find. Historians have never felt much need to write about dead chickens. Given the state of research outlined here, this essay can do no more than provide a few observations and hypotheses. In it, I cannot provide any answers; rather, my aim is to formulate questions about a gap in the historiography of twentieth-century France.

Even a brief look at the astonishing comebacks staged by the French aristocracy in the nineteenth century shows that Mitford's chicken metaphor has its limits. While the other chickens in the coop usually pay their slaughtered colleagues little attention, the *Terreur* phase of the French Revolution was not only the beginning of the aristocratic end, but also the beginning of the intellectual and political counter-revolution. The first observation upon which any history of the French aristocracy has to build is that the emergence of the counter-revolution in France is linked with the aristocracy—earlier, more directly, and more inevitably than in the rest of Europe. Following the abolition of its privileges, the execution of the king, emigration, and return, the French aristocracy had to find its way in a society without an aristocracy. But it is also true that earlier, more directly, and more inevitably than in the rest of Europe, the French

---

[4] Jean-François Sirinelli (ed.), *Dictionnaire historique de la vie politique française au XXe siècle* (Paris, 1995).

[5] Sirinelli (ed.), *Histoire des Droites en France*.

[6] Pierre Nora (ed.), *Les Lieux de mémoire*, 7 vols. (Paris, 1984–92).

aristocracy had time, in exile,[7] to adjust to the revolutionary principles of egalitarianism and meritocracy in a newly shaped society. If we pinpoint its political death to the years between 1790 and 1793, then—with apologies to Chateaubriand—we can speak of a *contre-révolution d'outre tombe*, a counter-revolution from beyond the grave.[8] For more than a hundred years, and thus much longer than a chicken can run around without its head, the aristocracy diplayed considerable energy and regenerative powers in this counter-revolution.

This essay will begin by discussing five structural peculiarities of the French aristocracy. In three further sections, it will comment on the relationship between the aristocracy and the radical right. In general, it should be pointed out that the relevant political touchstones date not to the period after 1918, but rather to the time of the Dreyfus affair, that is, between 1880 and 1900. A large part of the *mésalliance* which, during the interwar period, the European aristocracy entered into with radical right-wing movements clearly distinguishable from traditional conservatism, had its origins long before the war in France, and the same is true of the dynamic which drove this *mésalliance*. The avant-garde role which the French 'new right'[9] assumed before its equivalents in Italy and France was noticed early, and from various perspectives.[10]

I *The Fragmentation and Reinvention of the Aristocracy*

The new aristocracy created by Napoleon was a competitive elite established on meritocratic principles. It also represented an invitation to integrate the old and new aristocracy in a newly created

[7] Karine Rance, 'L'Émigration nobiliaire française en Allemagne: une "migration de maintien" (1789–1815)', *Genèses*, 30 (1998), 4–28; ead., 'Mémoires de nobles français émigrés en Allemagne pendant la Révolution Française: la vision rétrospective d'une expérience', *Revue d'histoire moderne et contemporaine*, 64/2 (1999), 245–62.

[8] François René vicomte de Chateaubriand (1768–1848) arranged for his famous *mémoires d'outre tombe* to be published posthumously.

[9] Stefan Breuer, *Nationalismus und Faschismus: Frankreich, Italien und Deutschland im Vergleich* (Darmstadt, 2005); id., *Ordnungen der Ungleichheit: Die deutsche Rechte im Widerstreit ihrer Ideen 1871–1945* (Darmstadt, 2001).

[10] Hannah Arendt, *Elemente und Ursprünge totalitärer Herrschaft* (1st publ. 1951; Munich, 1986); Ernst Nolte, *Der Faschismus in seiner Epoche: Action française, Italienischer Faschismus, Nationalsozialismus* (Munich, 1963).

'granite block', as the programme was called, designed to stabilize a disintegrating society.[11] The Bourbon restoration did
nothing to change this. The *Charte* of 1814 recognized old and
new titles equally. In addition, there were the *orléaniste* creations
of the period 1830 to 1848, the *bonapartiste* aristocrats of the years
1852 to 1870, and, especially, the claims that created a pseudo-
aristocracy—remarkable at least in numerical terms—and that
no state institution resisted effectively.[12] In political and social
terms, the interaction between revolution and counter-revolution
resulted in an early and radical fragmentation of the aristocracy.
This was not cushioned by a gravitational centre, and the process
of fragmentation accelerated relentlessly in the nineteenth
century. Thus Isabelle Brelot, leading historian of the French
aristocracy in the nineteenth century, speaks of a *nébuleuse nobiliaire*, a configuration without clear external contours. Brelot sums
up her analysis of the radical reformations and successful adapta-
tions to a transformed world in the phrase *noblesse réinventée* (reinvented aristocracy).[13]

Undoubtedly, individual families retained considerable influence regionally, and in specific sectors such as the civil service,
the military, and diplomacy, the aristocracy as such continued to
be strongly over-represented. Yet the revolution whose end, with
François Furet, we can date to the years around 1880,[14] permanently broke the aristocracy as a political force. The failure of the
monarchical reaction between 1873 and 1877 and the republican
purges created deep divisions. There is good reason for the fact
that the social and political historiography of the early Third
Republic speaks of elites rather than the aristocracy.[15]

---

[11] Natalie Petiteau, *Élites et mobilités: La noblesse d'Empire au XIXe siècle (1808–1914)* (Paris,
1997).

[12] This in sharp contrast to the titles of the German aristocracy, effectively protected
until 1918. Harald von Kalm, *Das preußische Heroldsamt (1855–1920): Adelsbehörde und
Adelsrecht in der preußischen Verfassungsentwicklung* (Berlin, 1994).

[13] Claude-Isabel Brelot, *La Noblesse réinventée: Nobles de Franche-Comté de 1814 à 1870*, 2
vols. (Paris, 1992).

[14] François Furet, *Revolutionary France, 1770–1880* (London, 1995).

[15] Christophe Charle, *Les Élites de la République* (Paris, 1987), 379–405; id., 'Noblesse et
élites en France au début du XXe siècle', in *Actes du colloques de l'École française de Rome: Les
Noblesses européennes aux XIX et XXe siècles* (Rome, 1988), 407–33; id., *La Crise des sociétés
impériales: Allemagne, France, Grande-Bretagne. Essai d'histoire sociale comparée* (Paris, 2001),
112–21.

II *Successful Adaptations*

As in most European countries, in France the aristocracy remained profoundly over-represented in three professional areas: the military, the civil service, and large landownership. There is some question as to how many aristocrats encroached on the bourgeois professions, in particular, trade, finance, and industry. However, there is no doubt that the dual competition the old aristocracy experienced from the bourgeoisie on the one hand and the newly ennobled aristocracy on the other forced the old aristocracy to become socially more adaptable and flexible. In a 'de-aristocratized society' (*entadelte Gesellschaft*),[16] the aristocracy had to develop different strategies from those used in societies that continued to be led by the aristocracy. In France far more than in other countries, confrontation with the principles of meritocracy and egalitarianism had been among the aristocracy's formative experiences since the French Revolution. Aristocratic attempts to achieve stability within this society in France were more noticeable than attempts to organize an uprising against a society dominated by the bourgeoisie. These included modernization strategies, taking in the Grandes Écoles as well as careers in the Bonapartist and republican state. The slow and relatively successful adaptation to egalitarian and meritocratic principles during the long nineteenth century may well mark the most important social and historical distinction between France and Germany, where a large part of the Prussian aristocracy reacted to similar demands with great hostility. Until 1918, any form of social, political, and cultural opening towards the bourgeoisie could be blocked[17] much more successfully in Prussia than in France, where the pressure towards convergence with the bourgeoisie and its core professional fields was much stronger. In France, since the 1890s at the latest, a fundamental willingness and ability to compromise had been established in the aristocracy—not among

---

[16] Heinz-Gerhard Haupt, 'Der Adel in einer entadelten Gesellschaft: Frankreich seit 1830', in Hans-Ulrich Wehler (ed.), *Europäischer Adel 1750–1950* (Göttingen, 1990), 286–305.

[17] Heinz Reif, 'Adelserneuerung und Adelsreform in Deutschland 1815–1874', in Elisabeth Fehrenbach (ed.), *Adel und Bürgertum in Deutschland 1770–1848* (Munich, 1994), 203–30; Heinz Reif, 'Adelspolitik in Preußen zwischen Reformzeit und Revolution 1848', in Hans-Peter Ullmann and Clemens Zimmermann (eds.), *Restaurationssystem und Reformpolitik: Süddeutschland und Preußen im Vergleich* (Munich, 1996), 199–224.

all of them, but in a significant proportion. It was this ability that was sought, largely in vain, among the German aristocracy as late as 1930.

III *Catholicism*

The ability to achieve a compromise with the outcome of the French Revolution was encouraged not only by economic and social pressures, but also by Catholic social teaching. Here mention should be made of the nobility's remarkable and successful attempts to come to terms with the Republic, including the Cercles catholiques d'ouvrier (Catholic workers' circles). There is no question that their founders, Albert de Mun and the Marquis de la Tour du Pin de la Charce were, like their institution, legitimist, anti-democratic, and anti-socialist. In the case of the Marquis de la Tour du Pin's hierarchical, anti-industrial, and anti-bourgeois social model, the concept was also clearly reactionary.[18] But if historical and political terms are to retain their meaning, then there is one thing that it was not: radical right wing, pre-fascist, or fascist. Rather, what is remarkable is that the aristocratic attempt to reach out politically and build bridges to the lower classes was expressed in the language not of pre-fascism but of Catholic conservatism. The moderating impact of this exercise, which lasted over several generations, was still noticeable within the French aristocracy of the interwar years. Even more significant was the encyclical *Rerum novarum* and, in 1892, Pope Leo XIII's *ralliement*, which had been demanded by all French Catholics, that is to say, the rapprochement with the Republic. Albert de Mun and many of the loyal Catholic aristocrats rallied to this call, although in different ways.[19] At this point the aristocrats' intransigent and combative stance against the Republic was weakened.

---

[18] Robert Talmy, *Aux sources du catholicisme social: L'École de la Tour du Pin* (Paris, 1963).

[19] Philippe Levillain, *Albert de Mun: Catholicisme français et catholicisme romain du Syllabus au Ralliement* (Rome, 1983); Jean-Marie Mayeur, *Catholicisme social et démocratie chrétienne: principes romains, expériences françaises* (Paris, 1986).

IV *The First World War*

Within the officer corps of the French Republic, the aristocracy represented as much of an avant-garde of killing and being killed as was the case in the armies of its opponents.[20] However, France's victory in the First World War was interpreted as a republican victory, which shored up the Third Republic. Overall, the victory brought the aristocracy and the Republic closer together. France in general did not suffer the immense losses sustained by the German aristocracy as a result of its defeat in the war, whose significance cannot be overestimated.[21] The French victory of 1918 was a republican victory with aristocratic contributions. Jean Renoir's magnificent war film of 1937, *La Grande Illusion*,[22] which tells the story of an encounter between two enemy air force officers in the First World War, expresses this succinctly. The German Captain von Rauffenstein shoots down the plane of his enemy, Captain de Boeldieu. But as social equals, with a common culture, world-view, and *habitus*, friendship between them is possible. De Boeldieu accepts Rauffenstein's offer of friendship, but at the end, while strictly observing aristocratic manners, he dies a patriotic hero's death in solidarity with his Jewish and proletarian comrades. Although this film, which contains much wishful thinking and many political errors, does not convey the reality of the French officer corps,[23] these famous scenes may be read as a powerful illustration of the accelerated process by which sections of the French aristocracy were reconciled with the Republic and its principles. This process of reconciliation, which was potentially possible for all the warring armies with a significant proportion of aristocratic officers, was able to

---

[20] Marcus Funck, 'The Meaning of Dying: East Elbian Noble Families as Warrior-Tribes in the Nineteenth and Twentieth Centuries', in Greg Eghigian and Matthew Paul Berg (eds.), *Sacrifice and National Belonging in Twentieth-Century Germany* (College Station, Tex., 2002), 26–63.

[21] Marcus Funck, *Feudales Kriegertum und militärische Professionalität: Der Adel im preußisch-deutschen Offizierkorps 1860–1935* (forthcoming); Stephan Malinowski, *Vom König zum Führer: Deutscher Adel und Nationalsozialismus* (Berlin, 2003), 198–293.

[22] Jean Renoir, *La Grande Illusion* (1937), with Pierre Fresnay and Erich von Stroheim in the leading roles.

[23] William Serman, *Les Officiers français dans la nation, 1848–1914* (Paris 1982); id. and Jean-Paul Bertaud, *Nouvelle histoire militaire de la France, 1789–1919* (Paris, 1998); Robert O. Paxton, *L'Armée de Vichy: Le corps des officiers français, 1940–1945* (Paris, 2004).

take place only in the victorious powers. Here, too, the contrast with Germany, where the stab-in-the-back myth blamed the Weimar republic for defeat, could not be greater.

V *Right-Wing Aristocratic Fantasies*

The German example demonstrates—and perhaps the same could be said of most European countries—that the lingering significance of the aristocracy in the twentieth century must always be examined at two levels. First, the genuine elite positions and the areas of influence retained by the aristocracy must be examined. And secondly, attention must be paid to the aristocratic dreams and neo-aristocratic conceptions of other groups, especially those of the educated middle classes who would dearly have loved to have been 'aristocrats' themselves, and who thus increased the significance of the aristocracy. It is this second aspect which seems to have been largely missing in France. Charles Maurras, the founder of the neo-monarchist movement, may well have dreamed of an alliance between the right-wing intelligentsia and the old aristocracy in his early works, but his later concepts became progressively more pragmatic. His king appeared more like a *Führer* and the elite he longed for had already been realized in the meritocratic principles of the Republic.[24] A further master thinker of the radical right, Maurice Barrès, and, following him, much of the Bonapartist right, no longer tried to deny that the revolution had happened in their thinking. A French 'Monck' was always dreamt of,[25] but never a possibility. Since the Boulanger crisis at the latest, the most successful movements of the radical right had functioned more as parts of the Republic than as agents of the *ancien régime*, and the participation of prominent aristocrats did not change this.[26] Even as an ideal and a dream, the aristocracy no longer represented a guiding principle among the radical right. This, too, represents a marked contrast with Germany, where the aristocracy, or at least

[24] On Maurras's ideas about king and elite cf. Nolte, *Der Faschismus in seiner Epoche*, 61–190; Pierre Boutang, *Maurras: La destinée et l'Œuvre* (Paris, 1984); and Victor Nguyen, *Aux origines de l'Action française* (Paris, 1991).

[25] This is a reference to Oliver Cromwell's general, George Monck (1608–70), who played a key role in the restoration of Charles II.

[26] Zeev Sternhell, *Maurice Barrès et le nationalisme français* (Paris, 1972).

specific aristocratic imaginings from the *völkisch* movement to the SS, remained a constant and significant point of reference.[27]

The five aspects outlined so far were clearly not sufficient to make the aristocracy a bastion of democratic republicanism. But the following three points concerning the relationship between the aristocracy and the radical right suggest that the French aristocracy's political orientation was much less clear-cut than might at first appear.

VI *Anti-Semitism*

In his *Recherche du temps perdu*, Marcel Proust describes how the anti-Semitism in the Dreyfus affair brought the prince closer to his coachman. Indeed, the aristocracy in France—and probably everywhere in Europe as well—used anti-Semitism as an early and radical weapon against the Republic, but also as a bridge to facilitate communication with the petty bourgeoisie and the lower classes. In the 1890s, Edouard Drumont and Jules Guérin, as publicists, agitators, and politicians, presented one of the most brutal forms of anti-Semitism in Western Europe. Alongside a crude hate campaign, we already see the emergence of armed bands of thugs and terrorists recruited among butcher boys. Their financiers included no less a personage than the duc d'Orléans, pretender to the French throne.[28] In the Boulanger affair, in which an anti-Semitic Bonapartist *coup* attempted to sweep away the Republic, many prominent names from France's richest aristocratic families featured among Boulanger's supporters. The eccentric marquis de Morès and the duchess d'Uzès, whose impressive château near Avignon also served as a counter-revolutionary communication centre, are merely the most prominent of many such examples.[29] Before and after the Dreyfus affair, and

---

[27] Eckart Conze describes the SS's (imaginary) closeness to the aristocracy in his 'Adel unter dem Totenkopf: Die Idee eines Neuadels in den Gesellschaftsvorstellungen der SS', in Eckart Conze and Monika Wienfort (eds.), *Adelsgeschichte als Gesellschaftsgeschichte: Deutschland im europäischen Vergleich im 19. und 20. Jahrhundert* (Cologne, 2004), 151–80; Alexandra Gerstner, *Rassenadel und Sozialaristokratie: Adelsvorstellungen in der völkischen Bewegung (1890–1914)* (Berlin, 2003); Breuer, *Nationalismus und Faschismus*, 178–94.

[28] Michel Winock, *Édouard Drumont et Cie: antisémitisme et fascisme en France* (Paris, 1982); Stephen Wilson, *Ideology and Experience: Antisemitism in France at the Time of the Dreyfus Affair* (New Jersey, 1982).

[29] William D. Irvine, *The Boulanger Affair Reconsidered: Royalism, Boulangism and the Origins*

until her death in 1932, a woman with the *nom de guerre* 'Gyp' was one of the most influential anti-Semites in France. When asked about her profession in a court in 1899, she replied: 'anti-Semite'. Her real name was longer: Sibylle-Gabrielle Marie-Antoinette de Riqueti de Mirabeau, comtesse de Martel de Janville.[30] The Dreyfus affair generated an immense paper trail documenting the close link between the aristocracy and radical anti-Semitism. To cite just one example: after the suicide of Colonel Henry, the perpetrator of the forgeries which were intended to prove Dreyfus's guilt, the radical anti-Semitic *Libre Parole* began a signature and fund-raising drive in honour of the dead forger. The 14,000 signatories included 1,097 aristocrats. Aristocrats themselves made up 0.14 per cent of the population. In the anti-Semitic fund-raising drive the aristocracy provided 8 per cent of the signatories and 16 per cent of the money contributed.[31] In *Recherche du temps perdu*, the duc de Guermantes calls out : 'Quand on s'appelle le marquis de Saint-Loup, on n'est pas dreyfusard, que voulez-vous que je vous dise!' (When your name is the marquis de Saint-Loup then you aren't likely to be a Dreyfusard, what do you expect me to say!) And, in fact, Isabelle Brelot's detailed study[32] turns up a broad majority of aristocrats precisely where one would expect to find them: in the anti-Dreyfus camp. However, as Brelot shows, these findings are less clear-cut than would appear at first glance. From a strictly French perspective, the aristocracy appears as one of the most important proponents of a radical, biologically conceived anti-Semitism. But from a comparative European perspective, what is more striking is the significant group of aristocrats who stood out within the Dreyfusard camp as defenders of the Republic. It is precisely the existence of this camp—which continued to grow in the interwar period—which is remarkable and surprising. There was no comparable group

of the Radical Right in France (New York, 1989), 73–124; Philippe Levillain, *Boulanger: Fossoyeur de la monarchie* (Paris, 1982), 139–63.

[30] Willa Z. Silverman, 'Profession, Antisemite: Ideology and Gender in the Life and Works of Gyp', *Nineteenth-Century French Studies*, 23/1–3 (Winter 1994–5), 222–43; ead., *The Notorious Life of Gyp: Right-Wing Anarchist in Fin-de-Siècle France* (New York, 1995).

[31] Stephen Wilson, 'Le Monument Henry: la structure de l'antisémitisme en France, 1898–1899', *Annales Économies, Sociétés, Civilisations*, 32/2 (1977), 265–91.

[32] Claude-Isabelle Brelot, 'Entre nationalisme et cosmopolitisme: les engagements multiples de la noblesse', in Pierre Birnbaum (ed.), *La France de l'Affaire Dreyfus* (Paris, 1994), 339–61. For the quotation from Proust see ibid. 339.

within the German aristocracy during the Kaiserreich around 1895; nor would there be two or three decades later.[33]

VII *The Fragmentation of the Political Right and the Fascist Invitation*

Two lines of argument from the acrid debates surrounding France's radical right should be mentioned here: first, the question of a French fascism. One interpretation maintains that there was never a powerful fascist movement in France. Proponents of this view point out the country's long republican tradition, which supposedly inoculated a sufficient majority of Frenchmen against fascism. Non-French historians may note that this interpretation is largely promoted by Frenchmen: René Rémond, Serge Berstein, Philippe Burrin, and Pierre Milza are some of the best-known names.[34] The second interpretation claims the opposite, going so far as to identify the origins of fascism in the pre-1914 Third Republic. In this view, France is the land of the Revolution. But even more, it is the land of the counter-revolution which had aready donned the garb of fascism before the Dreyfus affair. France, it is maintained, did not have to wait until the Vichy regime in order to bring forth a fully developed and powerful fascist movement. At this point, non-French historians notice that the chief proponents of this interpretation are non-French: Hannah Arendt, Ernst Nolte, William Irvine, Robert Soucy, and above all, Zeev Sternhell.[35] This debate is significant in our context because fascism was only able to establish itself where its dynamic encountered weakness and inconsistency on the part of the conservative elites.[36]

---

[33] Malinowski, *Vom König zum Führer*, 594–609.

[34] René Rémond, *La Droite en France de 1815 à nos jours: Continuité et diversité d'une tradition politique* (Paris, 1954); Serge Berstein, 'La France des années trente allergique au fascisme: à propos d'un livre de Zeev Sternhell', *XXe siècle*, 2 (Apr. 1984), 87; Pierre Milza, *Fascisme français: Passé et Présent* (Paris, 1987); Philippe Burrin, *La Dérive fasciste* (Paris, 1986); Jacques Juillard, 'Sur un fascisme imaginaire: à propos d'un livre de Zeev Sternhell', *Annales ESC*, 39 (1984), 849–61; Leonardo Rapone, 'Fascismo: né destra né sinistra?', *Studi storici*, 25 (1984), 799–820.

[35] Arendt, *Elemente und Ursprünge*; Nolte, *Der Faschismus in seiner Epoche*; William Irvine, 'Fascism in France and the Strange Case of the Croix de Feu', *Journal of Modern History*, 63 (June 1991), 294; Robert Soucy, *French Fascism: The First Wave 1924–1933* (New Haven, 1986); id., *French Fascism: The Second Wave 1933–1939* (New Haven, 1995). On this debate cf. Michel Dobry (ed.), *Le Mythe de l'allergie française au fascisme* (Paris, 2003).

[36] As Stanley G. Payne has recently shown most convincingly in his comparative study, *A History of Fascism, 1914–1945* (Madison, 1995).

A second line of argument revolves around the ideological classification of the radical right and its origins. Zeev Sternhell raised hackles when he emphasized the radical left-wing origins of the *droite révolutionnaire*, the allegedly French origins of fascism,[37] and maintained that the radical right-wing groups in the period in between were 'neither right nor left'.[38] Regarding Italian fascism, Emilio Gentile has emphasized how much the notion of a fascism from the left represents a mirage which has lured—or been generated by—many intellectual historians.[39] Following Gentile here, it seems appropriate to leave French right-wing extremism where it belongs in functional terms: on the far right. From the perspective of aristocratic history, the leftist roots of some radical right-wing groups in France are nevertheless significant. It can be assumed that Jacobin elements in thought, language, and style, along with party leaders who had been socialists or Communists in their youth,[40] must have had a deterrent effect on a large part of the aristocracy.

There was, indeed, a concentration of aristocrats in the two organizations which were entirely free of leftist roots. First, Action française, a product of the Dreyfus affair founded by Charles Maurras—a mixture of monarchism, anti-Semitism, bands of thugs, and exalted intellectualism—penetrated deep into aristocratic circles and continued to exert an immense intellectual appeal well beyond the Second World War.[41] Secondly, there was the Croix de feu, a mass movement founded in 1927 under the leadership of the colonel and war hero Count François de la Rocque. It represented not only the largest group but also a comprehensive, militarily organized, radical right-wing movement in the Third Republic. Some specialists play down the

---

[37] Zeev Sternhell, *La Droite révolutionnaire 1885–1914: Les origines françaises du fascisme* (Paris, 1978).

[38] Id., *Ni Droite, ni gauche: L'idéologie fasciste en France* (Paris, 1983).

[39] Emilio Gentile, *Qu'est-ce que le fascisme?* (Paris, 2004); id., *Storia del Partito Fascista* (Rome, 1989). For criticism of a definition of fascism drawn from the history of ideas cf. Michel Winock, 'Fascisme à la française ou fascisme introuvable?', *Le Débat*, 25 (May 1983), 41.

[40] Sternhell, *Ni droite, ni gauche* and, on two of the most important exponents of this type, Marcel Déat, *Perspectives socialistes* (Paris, 1930); Reinhold Brender, *Kollaboration in Frankreich im Zweiten Weltkrieg: Marcel Déat und das Rassemblement national populaire* (Munich, 1992); Jean-Paul Brunet, *Jacques Doriot: du communisme au fascisme* (Paris, 1986).

[41] Eugen Weber, *Action française: Royalism and Reaction in Twentieth-Century France* (Stanford, Calif., 1962).

Croix de feu as 'political boy-scouting for adults' (René Rémond),[42] while others, such as Robert Soucy, speak of a fully developed fascist movement with 700,000 members. The organization's vice-president was Duke Pozzo di Borgo. In their Belgian exile, Count de la Rocque's two brothers belonged to the advisory staff of the pretender to the throne, who was among those who financed the Croix de feu.[43]

The radical right-wing organization Action française, too, displayed clear connections with the aristocracy. The prevalence of aristocratic names among the financiers, members, and leaders of both organizations is greater than in all other radical right-wing groups.[44] To be sure, any finding of a different nature would be astonishing for a neo-monarchist and anti-democratic group of any size. However, the notion of a fascist invitation to the aristocracy seems untenable on account of the fragmentation of the radical right. Unlike the Italian and German aristocracy, the French aristocracy was never tempted by the existence of a closed fascist fighting movement.

In a highly influential interpretation, René Rémond has shown that the three monarchies of the nineteenth century corresponded to three political families of the right (*légitimistes, orléanistes, bonapartistes*) which frequently reshaped themselves but never entirely disappeared in the twentieth century.[45] The legitimist heir to the throne, the comte de Chambord, alias Henri V, died without a successor in 1883.[46] The Bonapartist *prince imperial,* Eugène Louis, the only son of Napoleon III, had died in the ranks of the British colonial troops in the struggle against the Zulus in 1879. What remained were the Orléanist pretenders, the duc d'Orléans, later the comte de Paris, who financed various radical right-wing groups without ever developing stable relationships with the radical right or being able to prevent conflicts with the Action française. The fragmentation of the right into

[42] For criticism of René Rémond's position, see the discussion in Kevin Passmore, 'Boy-Scouting for Grown-Ups? Paramilitarism in the Croix de Feu and PSF', *French Historical Studies*, 19/2 (Fall, 1995), 527–57.

[43] Soucy, *French Fascism: The Second Wave*, 104–203, esp. 135; Weber, *Action française*, 312; Kevin Passmore, 'The Croix de Feu: Bonapartism, National Populism or Fascism', *French History*, 9/1 (1995), 67–92.

[44] Weber, *Action française*, 124–36, 257–76.

[45] Rémond, *La Droite*, 15–45.

[46] Marvin L. Brown, *The Comte de Chambord: The Third Republic's Uncompromising King* (Durham, NC, 1967).

three irreconcilable families, the instability of the constantly shifting organizations—Action française, Jeunesse patriotes, Croix de
feu, Parti social français, La Cagoule, La Solidarité française, Le
Faisceau, Parti populaire français, and the Rassemblement
national populaire—to name just the most important among
them, prevented the formation of a homogeneous fascist bloc on
the Italian or German model. As a powerful bloc able to seize
power and form a new state, fascism in Italy and Germany issued
both a challenge and an invitation to the old aristocracy. In all
European countries with a strong fascist movement, the aristocracy was effectively faced with the choice of becoming part of
a conservative alternative, or else climbing aboard the fascist
juggernaut. The Prussian nobility, at least, largely chose the
latter option, while the Italian aristocracy found a different
answer in October of 1922, marching on Rome, from that of
June of 1943, when Mussolini was overthrown. In France, this
constellation and challenge, it could be argued, never existed.
Without the charisma, the individual radical right-wing associations and leagues were unable to make the old elites an offer, or
to challenge them in a bloc.[47] For this reason, in France we find
merely individual aristocrats in individual radical right-wing
organizations whom professional historians have yet to classify in
any coherent fashion. There is no evidence to support the existence of a general tendency. After all, for a group like the aristocracy which had international networks, pre-existing models were
important. Renzo De Felice, the doyen of Italian fascism
research, stated in a frequently cited interview that in at least one
respect the responsibility of the conservative elites in Germany in
1933 was considerably larger than that of the Italian elites before
1922, because by 1933 the Germans already knew what they were
getting into.[48]

This notion, and the idea of European aristocracies learning
transnationally in dealings with the fascist movements of Europe,
can also be applied to France. It is obvious that for the French
aristocracy the fascist March on Rome was also a constant reference point for a *coup d'état*, whereas for the monarchists it was a
model demonstrating the compatibility of dictatorship and

---

[47] Breuer, *Nationalismus und Faschismus*, 197.
[48] Renzo De Felice, *Der Faschismus: Ein Interview von Michael A. Ledeen* (Stuttgart, 1977), 48.

monarchy. However, in Germany more than in Italy, where this notion developed later among an aristocracy that was increasingly losing political power and whose hopes for restoration had been radically disappointed, it just as clearly represented a negative point of reference. Count de la Rocque, the leader of the largest right-wing organization, who rejected the *coup* attempt of 1934, retained certain barriers against anti-Semitism and, during the war, kept both the Gestapo and de Gaulle at arm's length, is just one of many examples.[49]

VIII *Vichy*

In addition to the better-known *Travail, Famille, Patrie*, one of the Vichy regime's watchwords was *La terre, elle ne ment pas* (the soil does not lie). At least in ideological terms, Vichy was attractive to right-wing intellectuals and aristocrats alike.[50] As in the Dreyfus affair, it is hardly surprising that the authoritarian, anti-Semitic Vichy regime with its emphasis on the family, decentralization, soil, and discipline found considerable sympathy among the aristocracy. As part of the French upper classes, and a small part of the functional elites in the state and officer corps, the aristocracy made its own contribution to bringing about what Marc Bloch has analysed, in masterly fashion, as *étrange défaite*,[51] which went far beyond the military disaster. The attraction that Vichy and its ideology-mixing anti-democratic, reactionary, and radical right-wing elements must have exerted on large sections of the aristocracy seems too obvious to need further explanation. But in view of the opposition facing Vichy, things were more complex here too. The highly complicated situation France had found itself in since the summer of 1940, involving defeat, division, and occupation of the country, as well as the fact that sections of the political right took the path of resistance, prevented collective

[49] Jacques Nobecourt, *Le Colonel de La Rocque 1885–1946, ou les Pièges du Nationalisme Chrétien* (Paris, 1996).

[50] On the 'mythical' connection with 'the soil', see Pierre Barral, 'La terre', in Sirinelli (ed.), *Histoire des Droites*, iii. 49–69. The saying famously attributed to Pétain, incidentally, was coined by Emmanuel Berl, an urban intellectual. It stands for the connection between aristocratic tradition and the thinking of radical right-wing intellectuals, which can be found in many European countries.

[51] Marc Bloch, *Strange Defeat: A Statement of Evidence Written in 1940* (New York, 1968); French edn.: *L'Étrange Défaite* (Paris, 1940).

collaboration between the aristocracy and radical right-wing groups in wartime. Reference to some prominent examples must suffice.

It is worth recalling the officer Pierre Dunoyer de Segonzac, director of the elite school founded in Uriage castle in 1940. The circle assembled there provides one of the best-known examples of an aristocratic humanism that despised both fascism and parliamentary democracy. After the school closed, Segonzac went underground and became a commander in the French *Résistance*.[52] Beginning in 1940, we can find aristocrats among collaborators, among those sitting on the fence, and within the internal and external resistance.[53] Patriotic and military traditions and the occupation of the country by the arch-enemy provoked a number of different reactions among the aristocracy, ranging from collaboration to withdrawal into private life to resistance. In Germany, predatory war and the idea of settling the East had captured the enthusiasm of considerable parts of the aristocracy. Similarly, the military struggle, organized from exile and from the colonies, against the German arch-enemy could appeal, largely with success, to aristocratic traditions and potentials. So far, no one has attempted to evaluate these groups systematically. No one has come up with an answer to the interesting questions of whether and to what extent aristocratic chateaux were used as conspiratorial meeting places, and of whether and to what extent aristocratic networks were used to build the resistance movement. In any case, there was no shortage of aristocratic names among the members and heroes of the Forces françaises de l'intérieur.

In the case of Charles de Gaulle, the name sounds more aristocratic than his family in fact was. His origins and original sympathy for Action française, however, indicate important fault lines within this milieu. Among the most prominent aristocrats, apart from de Gaulle, to denounce Vichy, continue the war in the colonies, and land in France in 1944 were Jean de Lattre de Tassigny, commander of the First Army and signatory of the German capitulation, and Philippe de Hauteclocque-Leclerc,

---

[52] Bernard Comte, *Une utopie combattante: L'École des cadres d'Uriage, 1940–1942* (Paris, 1991).

[53] Jean-Luc Pinol, '1919–1958: Le temps des droites?', in Sirinelli (ed.), *Histoire des Droites*, i. 291–389, at 327–36.

commander of the Second Tank Division, who was celebrated as the liberator of Paris in August 1944.[54]

Also impressive in this respect is the biography of Emmanuel d'Astier de la Vigerie (1900–69), naval officer and journalist. After the *étrange défaite* of 1940, this aristocrat founded the resistance group La Dernière Colonne, co-founded the resistance newspaper *Libération*, was de Gaulle's envoy to London, and was later a leading member of the Mouvements unis de la résistance and the Comité français de Libération nationale. D'Astier, who shared his commitment to the *Résistance* with two older brothers[55] and a niece, became a Gaullist interior minister. Awarded the Lenin Prize, he was a Communist deputy until 1958.[56]

I shall illustrate what has been outlined here about the adaptation and political differentiation within the French aristocracy by taking one prominent family as an example. A recent biography of Josée Laval, daughter of the head of the Vichy regime, Pierre Laval, who was executed in 1945,[57] reveals an astonishing proximity to collaborationist accounts of themselves, and provides next to no analysis, but is none the less interesting because of its subject. Josée Laval had married Count René de Chambrun in 1935. He belonged to an old family which could trace a direct line of descent from La Fayette. With this marriage to the daughter of the rich and powerful Laval, Count Chambrun secured a place in the country's power élite, thus pursuing a policy of modernization which had a long tradition in his family. In the mid-nineteenth century, the counts had, by marriage, inherited the world-famous Baccarat crystal glass factory and thus a considerable fortune. Around 1890, two Chambrun brothers further modernized the family by marrying the daughters of

54 Bernard Destremau, *Jean de Lattre de Tassigny* (Paris, 1999); Christine Levisse-Touzé, *Philippe Leclerc de Hauteclocque (1902–1947): La Légende d'un héros* (Paris, 2002).

55 François d'Astier de la Vigerie (1886–1956), *Saint-Cyrien*, cavalry officer, served as an officer at the front in the First World War, pilot, air commodore 1936, head of the French air force 1939, member of the Dernière Colonne, commander of French troops in Britain, ambassador to Brazil. Henri d'Astier de la Vigerie (1897–1952), *Polytechnicien*, artillery officer in the war, member of various resistance groups, chief of police in Algiers, 1942, organized the assassination of the collaborator Admiral François Darlan. The assassin, a young Royalist named Fernand Bonnier de la Chapelle, claimed to have acted in agreement with the comte de Paris, the successor to the throne.

56 Emmanuel d'Astier de la Vigerie, *Sept fois sept jours* (Paris, 1961); id., *Les Dieux et les hommes: 1943–1944* (Paris, 1952); Laurent Douzou, *La Désobéissance: Histoire d'un mouvement et d'un journal clandestin. Libération-Sud (1940–1944)* (Paris, 1995).

57 Yves Pourcher, *Pierre Laval vue par sa fille, d'après ses carnets intimes* (Paris, 2002).

American millionaires, thus ensuring the family close contacts to the ruling elite of the USA. While the international lawyer René Chambrun managed the family's wealth as director of Baccarat, the inner circle of relatives included generals, ambassadors, and deputies. One family member, a commanding general in the French army, even became director general of the National City Bank.

In 1931 the writer Jean Giraudoux had this to say about the counts of Chambrun: 'Oh, I know this family well. It is perfect. In it one finds a diplomat, whose ineptitude is preparing the war, a deputy who is voting for the war, and a general who will lose the war!'[58] The family provides an outstanding example of successful adaptation to the modern age while maintaining an unmistakably aristocratic and stylish lifestyle. It also provides an insight into the political fragmentation of individual families. The career path of Count Chambrun, son-in-law of the top collaborationist Laval, reads like the prototype for a collaborationist and, after 1945, for an incorrigible member of the extreme right. In Marcel Ophuls's pioneering film about collaboration and resistance during the Vichy period, *Le Chagrin et la pitié* (1971) Count Chambrun is portrayed as a *brutta figura*, who stands out in the whole film for his blasé attitude, arrogance, and political blindness, which persists through the decades. But this does not sum up the family history as a whole. Among the cousins we find a Chambrun who was one of the eighty representatives who refused to support Marshal Pétain on 10 July 1940—the only French senator to do so.[59] Among the nephews we also find a count who fought as a colonel of the Forces françaises de l'interieur in the *Résistance*.[60] In its feats of social conformity, its successful attempts to reinvent itself socially and culturally, and its political fragmentation, the family brings together the features that can be considered typical of the French aristocracy.

In conclusion, one might suggest two possible explanations for

---

[58] In the original version: 'Je connais bien la famille. Elle est complète: on y trouve un diplomate dont les maladresses mèneront, peut-être à la guerre, un parlementaire qui la votera, un général qui la perdra.' Jean Giraudoux, quoted in Pourcher, *Pierre Laval*, 65.

[59] Marquis Pierre de Chambrun (1865–1954), deputy and senator for Lozère, left-wing Republican, then independent deputy.

[60] Gilbert de Chambrun, colonel of the Forçes françaises de l'interieur, regional commander in the Languedoc. On this cf. Gilbert de Chambrun, *Journal d'un militaire d'occasion* (Montpellier, 2000).

the lack of interest historians have shown for the aristocracy. First, we might think that our French colleagues have simply not done their homework and have thereby missed an entire category of research. Anyone who has any knowledge at all of French historians will conclude that this is highly unlikely. The second possibility is that there has been a recognition that a collective history of the aristocracy in the twentieth century amounting to more than a history of separate individuals and families could perhaps hardly be written for France. At the beginning of the interwar period, on which the essays in this volume concentrate, the French aristocracy had already been waging a 130-year struggle against egalitarianism, and a large section of the aristocracy had increasingly adapted itself to its rules. Still important at local level to the present day, featuring individuals who stand out as positive or negative, and like the aristocracy everywhere a master of self-presentation and memory,[61] the highly fragmented French aristocracy was obviously no longer in a position to present itself as a political collective of national significance in the twentieth century. It had suffered far too many deep ruptures. Obviously, after more than a century of social and political fragmentation, after a long struggle between fighting and adapting to the Republic, the chicken without a head was politically dead at last.

[61] Marcus Funck and Stephan Malinowski, 'Masters of Memory: The Strategic Use of Memory in Autobiographies of the German Nobility', in Alon Confino and Peter Fritzsche (eds.), *The Work of Memory: New Directions in the Study of German Society and Culture* (Urbana, Ill., 2002), 86–103.

3

Between *défence social* and Anti-Communism: The Belgian Aristocracy

JAN DE MAEYER

The British historian Martin Conway astutely described Belgium as a country too divided—ideologically, socially, economically, and geographically—for the radical right to make a breakthrough.[1] The Leuven historian Louis Vos also rightly noted that another factor that is often underestimated, though it should not be, is the critical stance of the Roman Catholic Church and Catholic Action towards National Socialism and the radical right (as a divisive factor in the Catholic Unity Party).[2] However, this is not to suggest that the country was not confronted with the rise of the radical right in the interwar period, and therefore the question about the position or attitude of the aristocracy is particularly relevant in Belgium.

However, the relevance of this question is not fully recognized in the historiography. In fact, the literature is inadequate with respect to the nineteenth and twentieth centuries in Belgium. No systematic or concerted research has been done, although a good start has been made. Between 1960 and 1970 a series of licentiate (Master's) theses on the political and social position of the aristocracy in the nineteenth-century rural districts were supervised by Romain van Eenoo and Jos de Belder at the University of Ghent.[3] In recent years at the University of Leuven, also as part

---

[1] Martin Conway, 'Explications pour un échec', in Francis Balace, Gaston Braive, and Alain Colignon (eds.), *L'Extrême droite en Belgique francophone: De l'avant à l'après-guerre*, CREHSGM (Brussels, 1994), 79–104, at 100.

[2] Louis Vos, 'De politieke kleur van jonge generaties: Vlaams-nationalisme, Nieuwe Orde en extreem-rechts', in Rudi van Doorslaer (ed.), *Herfsttij van de 20ste eeuw: Extreem-rechts in Vlaanderen, 1920–1990* (Leuven, 1992), 15–47 at 32.

[3] Jos de Belder, 'Adel en burgerij, 1840–1914', *Nieuwe Algemene Geschiedenis der Nederlanden*, 12 (1977), 78–98; e.g. Ludwina Casier, 'De politieke aanwezigheid van de adel

of the policy, pursued by the Documentation and Research
Centre for Religion, Culture and Society (KADOC), of collecting the endangered records of aristocratic families, we have tried
to promote research on the ideological, social, and cultural
aspects (daily life, education, and travel) of the aristocracy in the
nineteenth and twentieth centuries.[4] Unfortunately, there are still
no studies of the property of aristocrats and the management of
their assets, their attitude to relationships and marriage, or their
presence in the world of finance and insurance. Because there is
so little interest in research on the aristocracy, there are no
surveys of the topic except those by the Brussels historian Paul
Janssens (sometimes in collaboration with Luc Duerloo), and
even here the nineteenth and twentieth centuries are more of an
epilogue.[5] In this context reference should be made to the work
of Marie-Pierre d'Udekem d'Acoz (née Verhaegen), who in 2003

op het platteland rond Brugge in de 19de en 20ste eeuw' (Master's thesis, University of
Ghent, 1983); K. Depoorter, 'Mentaliteitsstudie van de 19e eeuwse adel in België
(1789–1914): peiling aan de hand van gedrukte bronnen' (Master's thesis, University of
Ghent, 1977); L. de Ruyck, 'De adel in het kanton Zomergem en het IV e kanton van
Gent gedurende de XIXe eeuw' (Master's thesis, University of Ghent, 1979); Frieda
Dierickx-Visschers, 'De liberale adel in de provincie West-Vlaanderen, 1830–1914'
(Master's thesis, University of Ghent, 1981); R. Janssen, 'Mentaliteitstrekken van adellijke
families in de XIXe eeuw: probleemstelling en benadering via familiearchieven' (Master's
thesis, University of Ghent, 1973); Patrick van Damme, 'De adel in het kanton Oosterzele
in de 19de eeuw: Mentaliteitstrekken van adellijke families' (Master's thesis, University of
Ghent, 1979); M. van Gestel, 'De adel in België 1830–1893' (Master's thesis, University of
Ghent, 1970).

    [4] Jan de Maeyer, 'KADOC: Documentatie- en Onderzoekscentrum voor Religie,
Cultuur en Samenleving', *Driemaandelijks Bulletin van de Vereniging van de adel van het Koninkrijk
België/Bulletin trimestriel de l'association de la noblesse du royaume de Belgique*, 242 (2005), 41–9;
Emiel Lamberts (ed.), *The Black International/L'Internationale noire: 1870–1878. The Holy See
and Militant Catholicism in Europe/Le Saint-Siège et le Catholicisme militant en Europe*, KADOC-
Studies, 29 (Leuven, 2002); e.g. Rebecca Gysen, 'Een onderzoek naar de mentaliteit en
het dagelijks leven van de adel in de negentiende eeuw: twee casestudy's' (Master's thesis,
University of Leuven, 1999); Katrien Philippen, 'De Traditie van de elite: Analyse van de
stellingnamen en het discours van de adel in de Senaat tussen 1870 en 1894' (Master's
thesis, University of Leuven, 1999); Anne Vanthienen, 'Gaston van de Werve et de
Schilde: Aristocraat in een overgangstijd naar meer democratie' (Master's thesis,
University of Leuven, 2000); Erwin Verbeken, 'Adel en Oorlog: Bijdrage tot de studie van
de Belgische adel: casestudy. De mentale en materiële weerslag van de Eerste
Wereldoorlog (1914–1918)' (Master's thesis, University of Leuven, 2002); See also some
Master's theses supervised by my colleagues Henk de Smaele and Vincent Viaene, e.g.
Nathalie Delaere, 'Graaf Félix-Amand de Mûelenaere (1793–1862)' (Master's thesis,
University of Leuven, 2005).

    [5] Luc Duerloo and Paul Janssens, *Wapenboek van de Belgische adel van de 15de tot de 20ste
eeuw* (Brussels, 1992); Paul Janssens, *L'Évolution de la noblesse belge depuis la fin du Moyen Age*
(Brussels, 1998).

published a detailed study in both French and Dutch on the Belgian nobility and their role in the resistance during the Second World War.[6]

I *The Political and Social Position of the Aristocracy in Belgium:*
A Story of Revival and Loss

It is at the very least a noteworthy paradox that, although the Belgian constitution of 1831 was one of the most modern and liberal in Europe, it allowed the king to bestow aristocratic status on deserving families and/or individuals, or to raise them to the nobility. By specifically denying associated privileges, the constitution was in keeping with the French Revolution; on the other hand, it also followed in the wake of the restoration of Napoleon I (1800/1804–14) and William I of the United Kingdom of the Low Countries/Netherlands (1815–30) by allowing for the possibility of a new aristocracy, giving them a status guaranteed by the constitution.[7]

The Belgian kings still use the right to confer title. On the eve of the Second World War they had raised 829 families and/or individuals to aristocratic rank (see Table 3.1).

TABLE 3.1 *The aristocracy in Belgium, 1830–1940*

[Recognition of] old nobility	401
Elevation by Napoleon I and William I	24
Elevation by Leopold I, Leopold II, Albert I, and Leopold III	404
TOTAL	829

Source: Marie-Pierre d'Udekem d'Acoz, *Voor Koning en Vaderland: De Belgische adel in het verzet* (Tielt, 2003), 19. By permission of Uitgeverij Lannoo.

Leopold II (with 127 titles) and Albert I (with 153), in particular, awarded many titles. In the case of Leopold, the awards were part of an effort to gain supporters for his modernizing and colonial policies; in the case of his successor, it was more a question of

[6] Marie-Pierre d'Udekem d'Acoz (née Verhaegen), *Voor Koning en Vaderland: De Belgische adel in het verzet* (Tielt, 2003).

[7] Jan C. H. Blom and Emiel Lamberts, *History of the Low Countries* (1st edn.; New York, 1999), 313–32 and *passim*.

recognizing those who had contributed to national politics (including economic and cultural affairs) and to the defence of the country during the First World War.[8] In total, on the eve of the Second World War, the Belgian aristocracy numbered about 11,420 members, or 0.13 per cent of the Belgian population, representing quite a limited elite. As a consequence of the Belgian kings' policies towards nominations, the aristocracy expanded with an influx from the ranks of the *haute bourgeoisie*: bankers, financial and insurance experts, industrialists, architects, academics, and politicians. Thus this elite gradually lost its old, feudal character and acquired a more contemporary character of its own. The rapprochement between the old and the new aristocracy and/or the *haute bourgeoisie* also resulted in an increasing number of exogenous marriages.[9]

Nevertheless, having experienced a revival up to about 1900, the nobility in Belgium then disappeared ever more quickly from the social scene. A number of indicators illustrate the gradual surrender of their influence in society. The National Congress that drew up the constitution in 1830–1 consisted of 200 members, 70 of whom were aristocrats. This was the opposite of the ratio in the Chamber of Representatives and the Senate (see Tables 3.2 and 3.3).

TABLE 3.2 *Chamber of Representatives: percentage of aristocratic members*

1846	30.0
1886	15.9
1912	11.4
1939	2.4

Source: Alfred van der Essen, 'La part de la noblesse dans les charges publiques', in a special issue of the quarterly bulletin of the Association of the Belgian Nobility (ANRB-VAKB) (Sept. 1987), 100–11.

[8] Jan de Maeyer, *De rode baron: Arthur Verhaegen 1847–1917*, KADOC-Studies, 18 (Leuven, 1994), 204–5.

[9] d'Udekem d'Acoz, *Voor Koning en Vaderland*, 19–20; Luc Duerloo, 'Adelserkenning en - rehabilitatie', in *Le Droit nobiliaire et le Conseil Héraldique (1884–1994)/ Het adelsrecht en de Raad van Adel (1884–1994)* (Brussels, 1994), 217–20; Jos de Belder, 'Veranderingen in de sociaal-economische positie van de Belgische adel in de 19de eeuw: Een terreinverkenning', *Tijdschrift voor Geschiedenis*, 92 (1980), 483–501.

TABLE 3.3 *Senate: percentage of aristocratic members*

1831	82.3
1846	70.0
1912	32.0
1939	7.0

Source: van der Essen, 'La part de la noblesse dans les charges publiques', 100–11.

It is important to note here that the number of aristocratic members in the liberal party in particular declined. By contrast, of the eighty-eight members of parliament belonging to the conservative or Catholic party between 1870 and 1878, there were forty-nine aristocrats, or 56 per cent of the total. By 1914 the conservative party had thirty-four aristocratic members, or 38 per cent of the total, indicating that the nobility had gradually concentrated its position of power in the Catholic party, and this would remain the same in the interwar period. In contrast to the Chamber of Representatives, the Senate developed into a de facto aristocratic chamber. This was partly intentional, but also partly the result of a number of other factors: the high fee that would-be senators were required to pay to put themselves up for election (2,000 gold franks); the minimum age requirement (40 years); and the fact that until 1921 senators did not receive any remuneration. The gradual disappearance of the nobility from the Chamber of Representatives had much to do with the introduction of the general plural vote in 1893, and of proportional representation in 1899, which had a democratizing effect on the legislative chambers. The Senate continued to be elitist more or less until 1919, when universal male suffrage was introduced. This was followed in 1921 by a revision of the constitution which abolished the high fees required and granted senators remuneration. However, the democratization of the Senate proceeded slowly, partly because the age requirement of 40 years was retained. The main impact of the reform was to be seen in the entry of the socialist party into this august assembly.[10]

[10] Stefaan Fiers and Eliane Gubin, 'De fysionomie van de Kamer van Volks-vertegenwoordigers', in Emmanuel Gerard, Eliane Gubin, and Jean-Pierre Nandrin (eds.), *Geschiedenis van de Belgische Kamer van Volksvertegenwoordigers 1830–2002* (Brussels, 2003), 89–128, at 115–16; Emmanuel Gerard, 'De Senaat 1918–1970', in Veronique Laureys and Marc van den Wijngaert (eds.), *De geschiedenis van de Belgische Senaat 1831–1995* (Tielt, 1999), 140–212, at 163; d'Udekem d'Acoz, *Voor Koning en Vaderland*, 34–6.

Developments at government level were comparable to those in the Senate (see Table 3.4).

TABLE 3.4 *Composition of Belgian governments: percentage of aristocratic members*

1846	62.0
1886	28.5
1912	30.0
1939	7.0

Source: van der Essen, 'La part de la noblesse dans les charges publiques', 100–11.

Changes in the provincial councils can be compared with those in the Chamber of Representatives. I take here the example of the province of Antwerp, which is the subject of a thorough study being conducted at the present time (see Table 3.5).

TABLE 3.5 *Provincial council of Antwerp: position of the aristocracy*

Year	Aristocracy	Total	%
1836	11	46	23.9
1848	13	46	28.0
1872	14	58	24.1
1898	7	73	9.6
1914	6	75	8.0
1921	2	80	3.0

Source: Steve Heylen, Bart De Nil, and Bart D'hont (eds.), *Geschiedenis van de provincie Antwerpen: Een politieke biografie* (Antwerp, 2006). I wish to thank Steve Heylen for his collaboration in this research.

The position of the nobility in the corps of provincial governors (what in France are called the *prefects de la République*), developed comparably to the Senate (see Table 3.6).

However, at the level of the district commissioners, the aristocracy largely retained their position: in 1846 they constituted 37 per cent of the total, while in 1939 they accounted for 21 per cent. The fact that their power increasingly came to be based at local rather than national level is also made clear in a study of the evolution of the mayoralty of the districts. Until 1938 Belgium

TABLE 3.6 *Corps of provincial governors: number of aristocrats*

1886	7 out of 9
1912	5 out of 9
1939	3 out of 9

Source: van der Essen, 'La part de la noblesse dans les charges publiques', 100–11.

still had 166 aristocratic mayors, or 14 per cent—a relatively high percentage by comparison with the position of the aristocracy in the population as a whole (0.13 per cent).[11] A similar downward trend can be discerned in the composition of the army, while, unsurprisingly, the number of aristocrats in the cavalry increased (see Tables 3.7, 3.8, and 3.9).

TABLE 3.7 *Belgian army—general staff: percentage of aristocrats*

Year	Civic Guard	Lieutenant General	Major General
1846	83.0	54.0	22.0
1886	16.5	22.2	6.25
1912	20.0	20.0	11.0
1939	–	20.0	3.0

Source: van der Essen, 'La part de la noblesse dans les charges publiques', 100–11.

TABLE 3.8 *Belgian army—infantry: percentage of aristocrats*

Year	Higher officers	Officers
1846	7.0	0.7
1886	5.2	3.0
1912	1.6	1.0
1939	0.2	0.7

Source: van der Essen, 'La part de la noblesse dans les charges publiques', 100–11.

The upper magistracy presents a similar picture. But in an opposing trend, we see that gradually more and more Belgian aristocrats moved into the world of high finance, mortgage

[11] d'Udekem d'Acoz, *Voor Koning en Vaderland*, 37.

TABLE 3.9 *Belgian army—cavalry: percentage of aristocrats*

Year	Higher officers	Officers
1846	10.0	3.3
1886	31.0	17.0
1912	21.0	12.0
1939	26.6	20.7

Source: van der Essen, 'La part de la noblesse dans les charges publiques', 100–11.

companies, specialized insurance, and major industry. The situation was not so bad in the interwar period (see Table 3.10).

We gain the impression that the situation was very favourable in the 1920s, but that the aristocracy lost influence in the 1930s, except in some companies such as Vieille Montagne and Sofina. However, a lack of research means that no exact figures are available for this—the examples here are mere indications.[12]

On the whole, then, we gain a picture of an aristocracy that, after the First World War, had to give up its political and social position and, in particular, forfeit the revival it had experienced in the nineteenth century (evident in the Senate and in local politics). The changing figures mirror the negative self-image that dominated in aristocratic circles in the interwar period (more in politics than economics).

II *From 'défense social' to Anti-Communism:*
The Aristocracy and the Radical Right

Sections of the aristocracy in Belgium were indeed attracted to the radical right during the interwar period. These included more members of the old nobility than of the new aristocracy, and more men than women. However, a distinction must be made between sympathizers, who were merely attracted to the radical right (the majority), and active militants (a minority).[13]

---

[12] Ginette Kurgan-van Hentenryck (ed.), *Dictionnaire des Patrons* (Brussels, 1996), *passim*.
[13] d'Udekem d'Acoz, *Voor Koning en Vaderland*, 361 and *passim*; Blom and Lamberts, *History of the Low Countries*, 348–65.

TABLE 3.10 *High finance and industry: ratio of aristocrats to total number of board members*

Company	1893–4	1900–1	1912	1921	1928	1936	1948
Anciens Établissements D'Ieteren Frères					0:7		0:7
Ateliers metallurgiques	1:12				1:10	1:12	0:9
Banque de Paris et des Pays-Bas		3:20	5:27				
Banque Nationale de Belgique	1:13	1:14	2:18	1:17	1:28	1:23	0:28
Charbonnages Helchteren et Zolder			4:18	6:24	5:25	3:22	2:21
Charbonnages Limbourg-Meuse			2:31	0:19	1:21	4:24	5:24
Charbonnages Winterslag				3:14		4:14	
Compagnie des Mines et Fonderies de Zinc de la Vieille Montagne	5:17	5:17	5:17	5:18	5:16	5:15	4:15
Compagnie du chemin de fer du Congo	5:22			5:23			
Compagnie Financière belge des Pétroles (Petrofina)					3:26		2:18
Compagnie internationale des Wagons Lits et des Grands Express européens		6:15	6:10	6:26	3:25		
Forges de Clabecq			2:16	1:10	0:9	0:10	0:10
L'Immobilière Bruxelloise	9:13	9:13	6:9	5:8			1:6
L'Immobilière d'Anvers	2:5	1:6	2:8				
Produits chimiques Tessenderloo					0:8	0:6	0:13
S.A. de la Nouvelle Montagne	1:9	1:9	1:17	2:10	3:15	2:14	
Société belge des Tramways de Moscou (2e réseau)	0:9	0:9	0:8	0:4			
Société financière de Transports et d'Entreprises industrielles (Sofina)					1:20	6:44	5:35
Société Générale	5:16	6:17	9:17	8:18	5:26	5:30	7:33
Société John Cockerill	1:11	1:10	2:12	0:12	0:12	1:12	4:29
Union minière du Haut-Katanga			3:13	1:14	1:16	1:23	0:16

Source: Compiled by the author from *Le Recueil financier: Annuaire des valeurs cotées aux bourses de Belgique*, 1 (1893–4), 8 (1900–1), 19 (1912), 28 (1921), 43 (1936), 55 (1948).

1. *The Impact of the First World War*

What was the source of the great attraction that the radical right
exerted on the nobility? After the First World War the aristocracy felt that it was living in a disenchanted world. Everything
had apparently changed. The aristocracy was not alone in feeling
this way; it was also a perception that dominated among intellectuals and artists, both on the French-speaking side and among
Flemish speakers, though it was more common among Catholics
than non-Catholics (liberal or left). A feeling of abandonment
pervaded society as a whole.[14]

A number of elements or factors can explain this sense of
collapse. Perhaps the most difficult to deal with psychologically
was the confrontation with devastation after the war. There
were the images of the ruined city of Ypres, but there were
dozens of such cities (including Dinant, Namur, Leuven, and
Dendermonde). The inventory of war damage in Belgium was
frightening: about 50,000 dead; 70,000 wounded; 200,000 badly
damaged houses; 120,000 hectares of agricultural land laid waste;
a bisected railway network; and livestock decimated. A rough
estimate indicates that within four years Belgium had lost 16–20
per cent of its national assets. Not only towns and villages, but
also dozens of castles were either completely run down, having
been used for years to billet soldiers, plundered, or blown to bits.
In 1918–19 many aristocratic families faced the question of
whether to rebuild—in other words whether they should resume
their pre-war lifestyle. One factor that should not be underestimated here was the slowness of paying out war damages, and
families felt that they were ruined more often than was actually
the case.[15]

Moreover, they felt unjustly treated by the nation. Had not the
aristocracy volunteered on a large scale during the war? For the
first time since 1830, the Belgian aristocracy had been able to
display its loyalty to king and fatherland. One fifth of its members
had been recruited or had volunteered, and had thus experienced the horror of war at first hand. But after the war, they saw

[14] d'Udekem d'Acoz, *Voor Koning en Vaderland*, 25–6.
[15] Sophie de Schaepdrijver, *De Groote Oorlog: Het koninkrijk België tijdens de Eerste
Wereldoorlog* (7th edn.; Amsterdam, 2002), 289–314; Leen van Molle, *Chacun pour Tous: Le
Boerenbond Belge, 1890–1990*, KADOC Studies, 9 (Leuven, 1990), 137–40; d'Udekem
d'Acoz, *Voor Koning en Vaderland*, 25–6; Verbeken, *Adel en Oorlog*, 107–31.

themselves as browbeaten by the abrupt introduction of mass democracy (universal suffrage), which they felt went hand in hand with a climate of loathing, even contempt, for the aristocracy on the part of the working classes. The spectre of a new French revolution or of a repetition of the October revolution of 1917 haunted the salons. People talked about 'le coup de Lophem', the agreement that was reached in November 1918 between King Albert I and the ministers of the existing political parties. This laid down that, in anticipation of constitutional reform, the next legislative elections would be conducted on the basis of universal male suffrage.[16]

Then there were other factors: the uncertain international post-war climate (with tensions concerning German war reparations, the occupation of the Ruhr in 1923–5, and the Locarno Pact of 1925); the difficult socio-economic situation with the crisis in the Belgian frank in 1925–6; the grip on society that the labour movement, both socialist and Christian, appeared to have (with the introduction of social legislation concerning servants); the rise in taxation (inheritance taxes increased by a ratio of 1 to 5); and not least the consequences of the Agricultural Lease Act of 1929.[17] If, as already noted, the conservative wing of the Catholic party was to be the refuge of the Belgian nobility, then it could no longer ignore the call for a democratizing, radical reform of the party which would break the power of the elites in favour of social groups such as the farmers, workers, small businessmen, and tradesmen. In effect, in 1921 the old Catholic party transformed itself into a class party. The policy of *défense social*—that is, socializing the working classes to resist the temptation of revolution by moral education and training, reducing unemployment, remedying the problem of alcoholism, educating the working classes in the ways of bourgeois society, and channelling the demand for social and political emancipation through the general plural vote—seemed to have failed. The investment of aristocratic grandparents and parents in the *œuvres sociales*, the

---

[16] d'Udekem d'Acoz, *Voor Koning en Vaderland*, 21; Blom and Lamberts, *History of the Low Countries*, 348–63; Emmanuel Gerard, *De Katholieke Partij in Crisis: Partijpolitiek leven in België, 1918–1940* (Leuven, 1985), 62–115.

[17] Ibid. 171–243; I have gained the impression that some of the aristocratic families we focused on in this study made good money out of agricultural leasing during the First World War. This means that the government made adjustments. See Verbeken, *Adel en Oorlog*, 107–31; van Molle, *Chacun pour Tous*, 194–201.

anti-socialist committees, and so on seemed to have been a waste of time. The Belgian aristocrat felt unthanked and, in short, the dupe of history: the consequence was frustration, a feeling of defeatism, and a sense that it would be better to be a commoner than an aristocrat.[18]

2. Action Française and Belgian Nationalism

I agree with Martin Conway that two generations in particular opted for a radical reaction.[19] One was the generation of war veterans who felt personally ignored. Their frame of mind is illustrated by the protest and occupation of the forecourt of the Palace of Nations in July 1920. The other was the generation of young people which, in the context of the post-war climate of Catholic Action, opted for the regeneration of an organic, corporatized society, an idealized image of the new Middle Ages (Berdjajev). It was precisely these two generations that felt attracted to Action française at the beginning of the 1920s. The works of Charles Maurras were widely read and discussed in Catholic, intellectual, and aristocratic circles. Their involvement was not so much for the benefit of Action française itself. Rather, they were motivated by sympathy and especially by a desire to borrow the arguments of Action française as the basis for an unprecedented, completely new form of radical Belgian nationalism. This was to be based on reinforcing the executive power (the king), the introduction of corporatism, and the unrealistic dream of extending the country as far as its natural boundaries—that is, annexing Maritime Flanders as far as the Schelde, the Dutch province of Limburg (Maastricht) as far as the Maas, and the Grand Duchy of Luxembourg. All of this was considered compensation for the efforts they had made in the war. Active nationalist circles existed in the 1920s in, for example, Liège, Brussels, and Ghent. In February 1921 the *Revue latine* (1920–2)

---

[18] Marie-Sylvette Dupont-Bouchart, 'Stratégies du maintien de l'ordre en Belgique et en France au XIXe siècle: la doctrine de la défense sociale', in E. V. Heyen (ed.), *Historische Soziologie der Rechtswissenschaft*, Jus commune. Veröffentlichungen der Max-Planck-Instituts für Europäische Rechtsgeschichte. Sonderhefte. Texte und Monographien, 26 (Frankfurt am Main, 1986), 79–105; Gerard, *De Katholieke Partij in Crisis*, 171–243; Emmanuel Gerard, 'L'épanouissement du mouvement ouvrier chrétien (1904–1921)' and 'Adaptation en temps de crise (1921–1944)', in id. and Paul Wynants, *Histoire du mouvement ouvrier chrétien en Belgique*, KADOC Studies, 16, 2 vols. (Leuven, 1994), i. 115–73, 175–245; d'Udekem d'Acoz, *Voor Koning en Vaderland*, 24–7.

[19] Conway, 'Explications pour un échec', 81–3.

announced the founding of the Ligue politique anti-révolution-naire and the Ligue de la jeunesse nouvelle (1923) based around the review *La Jeunesse nouvelle*, which was succeeded by the Ligue pour la restauration de l'ordre et de l'autorité dans l'état (1925), whose organ was the new bulletin *Pour l'autorité*. It is important to note that a number of aristocrats were on the editorial board. At the beginning of the 1930s the Légion nationale had about 5,000 members and maintained connections with the movement Pour l'autorité, an authoritarian, nationalist action group of Catholic alumni of Leuven University. A dozen aristocrats were among its core of activists. Given its ideological origin, this form of Belgian nationalism was, above all, a threat to the changing Catholic party.[20]

3. Anti-Communism

If Belgian nationalism (for king and fatherland) was an important ideology among the aristocracy, its anti-left-wing and pronounced anti-Communist stance was equally important. As mentioned above, the Russian revolution of 1917 had had a deep psycho-logical effect. The aristocracy's opposition to Communism was in keeping with its nineteenth-century anti-socialist attitudes. Influential aristocrats financed or became active members of anti-socialist committees with the goal of challenging the Third International. In a certain sense history seemed to be repeating itself during the interwar period. The most important anti-Communist organization was, of course, Action et civilisation (1932). The Spanish Civil War brought matters to a head when the Belgian aristocracy also came out in support of General Franco. Their support was not only verbal: money was collected for the victims of the Popular Front, and Action et civilisation sponsored two ambulances which were sent to Spain with the necessary volunteer crew. The two members of the Belgian aris-tocracy who died in the nationalist cause were publicly acclaimed. Numerous publications presented the Popular Front as the Antichrist to be resisted. Examples were Viscount Charles

[20] Ibid.; Gerard, *De Katholieke Partij in Crisis*, 245–59 and 360–8; Eric Defoort, *Charles Maurras en de Action Française in België* (Nijmegen, 1978), 91–195; Gaston Braive, 'Tentations droitières dans la jeunesse étudiante catholique', in Balace, Braive, and Colignon (eds.), *L'Extrême droite*, 17–40; Jacques Prévotat, *Les Catholiques et l'Action française: histoire d'une condamnation, 1899–1939* (Paris, 2001), 236–9, 241–2; d'Udekem d'Acoz, *Voor Koning en Vaderland*, 74–6.

Terlinden's book *L'Espagne martyre* (1937) and Count Alexandre van der Burch's *Le Calvaire ibérique* (1938).[21]

4. Rexism and Léon Degrelle

The sympathy for Franco was small beer, however, in comparison with the attraction that the ultra-right, populist organization Rex, and its fanatical leader Léon Degrelle, exercised on the mainly Catholic aristocracy from about 1930 until about 1937. Coming out of Catholic Action, Degrelle advocated an authoritarian model for society which was based on anti-liberalism, anti-socialism, and anti-Communism, initially with a patriotic and royalist slant. Its original plea for moral values, integrity, and opposition to corruption magnetized young aristocrats. They felt attracted to Rexism's 'social' programme, that is, its criticism of capitalism (which quickly slid into anti-Semitism) and its advocacy of social solidarity, a corporatist system, and of legislative protection for the family, both nuclear and extended (the abolition of inheritance taxes for heirs in the direct line, and the reintroduction of the general plural vote for male heads of families).[22] From being a dissident right-wing movement within the Catholic world, Rexism went on to become a successful party during the socio-economic crisis of the 1930s. The election results demonstrate this (see Table 3.11).

Rexism was successful in aristocratic circles not only because of its policies: Degrelle was also an adept manipulator who, even in his student days at Leuven, had made contact with dozens of aristocratic figures from the best families. Indeed, he deliberately cultivated his aristocratic contacts in order to give his movement the necessary *gravitas* and status. It is not surprising, then, that between 1936 and 1939 Rex's twenty-one members of parliament included two aristocrats; and that of its twelve senators, two were aristocrats. In addition, there were five other aristocrats in the party organization. Marie-Pierre d'Udekem d'Acoz discovered that in total there were eleven aristocrats in the upper echelons of

[21] Ibid. 76–8; Gerard, *De Katholieke Partij in Crisis*, 464–5; Francis Balace, 'La droite belge et l'aide à Franco', *Belgisch Tijdschrift voor Nieuwste Geschiedenis/ Revue belge d'histoire contemporaine*, 18/3–4 (1987), 505–689.

[22] d' Udekem d'Acoz, *Voor Koning en Vaderland*, 49–67; Gerard, *De Katholieke Partij in Crisis*, 378–83 and 394–7; Emmanuel Gerard, 'La responsabilité du monde catholique dans la naissance et l'essor du rexisme', *La Revue nouvelle* (Jan. 1987), 67–77; Conway, 'Explications pour un échec', 83–5; Alain Colignon, 'Le Rexisme, un pré-Poujadisme?', in Balace, Braive, and Colignon (eds.), *L'Extrême droite*, 41–77.

TABLE 3.11 *Results of the elections to the Chamber of Representatives and Senate, 1936 and 1939*

| | 1936 votes | | 1939 votes | |
	No.	%	No.	%
Antwerp	19,213	5.86	6,414	1.95
Brabant	68,685	14.22	30,501	6.32
West Flanders	24,891	9.59	7,757	2.99
East Flanders	22,288	6.49	4,870	1.42
Hainaut	33,961	8.72	14,830	3.95
Liège	55,582	19.36	21,796	7.58
Limburg	5,738	5.89	3,015	3.14
Luxemburg	19,146	29.06	8,026	12.74
Namur	21,987	20.35	6,612	6.38

Source: Colignon, 'Le Rexisme, un pré-poujadisme?', 75. By permission of Edition De Boeck Université.

the Rexist organization, ten of whom belonged to the old nobility, and that all those who had met the necessary requirements had been war volunteers.[23]

5. *The Verdinaso and Joris van Severen*

The Verdinaso organization exercised a similar attraction on the aristocracy. This was the Association of National Solidarity Supporters of a Greater Netherlands (het Verbond van Dietsche Nationaal Solidaristen) founded by Joris van Severen in 1931. The Leuven historian and expert in research on nationalism, Lode Wils, described van Severen as an aristocrat who had strayed into politics. Unlike the populist and crude demagogue Léon Degrelle, van Severen was well-groomed, well-mannered, and cultivated—and not unpopular with aristocratic women. Verdinaso also addressed aristocratic interests, was committed to an authoritarian, nationalist, and fascist Greater Netherlands state, and sponsored a corporatist professional organization, a youth organization, and a militia. Above all the fact that Verdinaso also put loyalty to the king first was important for its aristocratic followers.[24]

[23] d'Udekem d'Acoz, *Voor Koning en Vaderland*, 49–67.
[24] Ibid. 46–9; Antoon van Severen, *Joris van Severen: Het verhaal van een leven*, 2 vols. (Torhout, 1998), ii. 165–247; Lieven Saerens, 'Het "Wendepunkt" (1933–1940)', in Peter

6. *The Years 1936–7: A Turnaround?*

At first sight it seemed that the aristocracy in Belgium would indeed be swallowed up by the radical right. Nothing, however, was further from the truth. Around 1936–7 the aristocracy made an important turnaround that resulted in their adopting a greater distance. An important factor here was the discussion group that, from 1936, gathered around the Benedictine Antoine de Meester (himself of noble background) in the abbey of Zevenkerken in Loppem near Bruges. The group's goal was to bring about a re-evaluation of the aristocracy, to break through the dominant negative and defeatist attitudes, and to move the nobility towards a renewed involvement in society on modern lines. Like the Association of Belgian Aristocrats (Vereniging van de Adel van België), founded in 1935, the group in Zevenkerken also reflected on the identity and role or mission of the aristocracy. Admittedly, they did this from a Catholic point of view but, surprisingly, non-Catholics were also invited to give lectures—such people as the socialist Max Lamberty. The result was a series of publications including that by de Meester himself, *Aristocratie* (1936), and Jean-Charles Snoy et d'Oppuers's *L'Aristocratie de demain* (1936), but also *Aristocratie et fierté* (1937) by the dissident Rexist Eugène de Hemricourt de Grunne (about which more below). These publications had one thing in common: they wanted to give the aristocracy some backbone.[25]

Against the background of this internal re-evaluation, the aristocracy in Belgium began to distance itself from the radical right by 1936–7. This was revealed most clearly in their attitude towards Rexism. The fact that in 1936 Degrelle had come to a political agreement with the federalist, separatist, and radical Flemish National Association (Vlaams-Nationaal Verbond) went too far for many members of the aristocracy—they considered loyalty to king and nation to be of paramount importance. The

Anthonissen et al. (eds.), *Ast Fonteyne 1906–1991: Een kwestie van stijl*, KADOC Artes, 4 (Leuven, 1999), 99–125, at 118–19; Conway, 'Explications pour un échec', 85–6; see the biography of van Severen by Lode Wils, *Joris van Severen: Een aristocraat verdwaald in de politiek* (Leuven, 1994), *passim*.

[25] d'Udekem d'Acoz, *Voor Koning en Vaderland*, 28–32; for the significance of the abbey see Christian Papeians de Morchoven, *L'Abbaye de Saint-André Zevenkerken* (Zevenkerken, 2002), *passim*.

fact that Degrelle also came into conflict with Cardinal van Roey and the whole establishment in 1936–7, resulting in his condemnation by the cardinal in 1937, made him a figure to be avoided. When Degrelle responded by making approaches to Nazi Germany, he completely alienated many aristocrats (and Catholics). Earlier, a number had raised their eyebrows when the news had leaked of Mussolini's dubious financial support for Rexism. In June 1937, therefore, Hubert d'Ydewalle, the chief editor of *Le Pays réel*, resigned from Rex; then in November 1937, Senator Xavier de Hemricourt de Grunne (a brother of the rabid anti-Rexist Eugène de Hemricourt de Grunne) decided to become an independent senator. Various dissidents subsequently evolved into vehement opponents of Rexism which from that time on they challenged in word and deed. An example is Robert du Bois de Vroylande's biting satire of 1936 entitled *Quand Rex était petit*, in which Léon Degrelle was presented as Léon Bluff. Another is his *Fables* (with illustrations by the well-known cartoonist Hergé), a remarkable book published in 1942 which was full of veiled attacks on the New Order. Its publication cost the chief editor of the first issue of *Rex* magazine his life: he was betrayed and arrested by the Nazis in February 1944. A similar development can be observed with regard to Verdinaso. When the organization succumbed to the lure of the Nazis following the execution of its leader in May 1940, it was supported by only a small group of aristocratic sympathizers.[26]

This brings us to the question of what attitude the aristocracy in Belgium finally adopted to the Nazi occupation during the Second World War. According to the study by Marie-Pierre d'Udekem d'Acoz, the result of all this was that a relatively large number of Belgian nobles (904) participated in the resistance to Nazi Germany in the Second World War, while a proportionately small number of aristocrats (33) were convicted of collaboration. Loyalty to king and fatherland finally gained the upper hand; tradition proved stronger than the lure of power. It is not surprising, then, that it was those young people who had played an active role in changing the nobility's public profile, such as Jean-Charles Baron Snoy et d'Oppuers, who came to the fore in

---

[26] Gerard, *De Katholieke Partij in Crisis*, 431–6, 468–83; d'Udekem d'Acoz, *Voor Koning en Vaderland*, 53–63, 68, 78–9, and 176; Braive, 'Tentations droitières dans la jeunesse étudiante catholique', 36; Conway, 'Explications pour un échec', 84–5.

the 1950s in the movements for Christian Democracy and European integration.[27]

III *Conclusion*

The story of the relationship between the Belgian aristocracy and the radical right might sound like a love story, a tale of attraction and rejection. However, this aspect of the plot, moving from sympathy to actual involvement, from sceptical distance to open antagonism, is not the essence of the Belgian story. More important, it seems, is the psychological aspect: out of frustration, misdirected self-interest, and the feeling of being unappreciated, a social elite for a time deliberately devoted itself to the legitimation of the radical right and the New Order—which cleverly took advantage of this, it must also be said. Whether intentionally or not, the frustrated aristocrats achieved the desired model. Is this a dramatic love story with a moving and happy ending relating the aristocracy's great contributions during the resistance in the Second World War? Or did the relationship end in bitterness?

[27] d'Udekem d'Acoz, *Voor Koning en Vaderland*, 361–87; Philippe Chenaux, 'Les démocrates-chrétiens au niveau de l'Union Européenne', in Emiel Lamberts (ed.), *Christian Democracy in the European Union (1945/1995): Proceedings of the Leuven Colloquium, 15–18 November 1995*, KADOC Studies, 21 (Leuven, 1997), 449–58.

4

Age of No Extremes?
The British Aristocracy Torn between
the House of Lords and the
Mosley Movement

KARINA URBACH

At the height of the Nuremberg trials the British ambassador to Washington, Lord Halifax, wrote to the Duchess of Portland: 'My dearest Ivy, I am amused with you saying that some of the peers are apprehensive of being summoned to give evidence at Nuremberg.'[1] At a time when his fellow aristocrats were still living in fear, Halifax had already received a summons: 'Goering has requested me and Alex Cadogan to go and testify to how earnest a seeker of the peace he was up to the war.'[2] Of course Halifax, the foreign secretary closely associated with appeasement, was used to being showered by invitations from Nazis;[3] yet why did other peers seriously fear that they might also be summoned to a war crimes tribunal?

To this day it is difficult to estimate the number of British nobles with leanings to the radical right. This is mainly because access to private archives is restricted. But even when such access is granted private collections often turn out to have been

[1] Lord Halifax to Ivy, 7th Duchess of Portland, 2 Dec. 1945, Welbeck Private Archives. I would like to thank Lady Anne Bentinck and Welbeck's Curator, Derek Adlam, for giving me access to the papers of the 6th and 7th Dukes of Portland (uncatalogued).

[2] In the end Halifax was saved such public embarrassment. Sir Alexander Cadogan (1884–1968) had been permanent under-secretary since 1938. His father, the 5th Earl of Cadogan, brought up his seven sons in aristocratic grandeur. Alexander later attended Eton and Balliol College, Oxford. See David Dilks (ed.), *The Diaries of Sir Alexander Cadogan 1938–45* (London, 1971).

[3] The Nazis courted Halifax relentlessly, via the embassy in London and, of course, during his visits to Berlin. See from 1935 onwards the papers of the German ambassador von Hoesch. Nachlass Dr Leopold von Hoesch, 1881–1936, Personalien Staatsmänner, Pol. II R 77121, Politisches Archiv des Auswärtigen Amtes Berlin and the papers of the Dienststelle Ribbentrop, Pol. 2 R 102792.

sanitized. Descendants have understandably developed a selective memory—connections with authoritarian regimes or radical
right-wing groups were not seen as laudable after 1945 and were
thereafter erased from the family archives. Even in cases of well-
known British Nazi supporters such as Viscount Lymington
(later 9th Earl of Portsmouth), whose papers are deposited in a
public archive, letters from his German, Austrian, and Italian
friends are missing.[4]

Nor are works of reference illuminating. Burke's *Peerage*, which
lists affiliations, does not mention, under the entry for the
Marquis of Graham (later 7th Duke of Montrose) and his brother
Lord Ronald, the affiliation: 'member of the Right Club'.
However, they had been ardent supporters of various fascist
groups and eagerly contacted the German embassy to arrange an
'educational' trip to Berlin: 'We would also like to see if possible a
Labour Service Camp and a Concentration Camp—in fact
anything which might help to throw a true light on the situation
as opposed to what we read in the Press.'[5] This bizarre enquiry
was not unusual. Files of the German foreign ministry are full of
applications from members of the British upper class to meet
Hitler. The infamous 'Gestapo Müller' was busy checking their
pedigrees to make sure that the *Führer* would not be embar-
rassed—after all, some members of the British nobility seemed to
have Jewish blood.[6]

In general, British aristocrats have been perceived as setting an
example for their European cousins, who were not as charismatic, urban, wealthy, or adaptable to the modern world. This
image extended to the twentieth century, when the British aristocracy was considered to have been politically reliable—a
Horthy regime or Prussian camarilla would never have been

---

[4] Lymington himself gave a bowdlerized version of his activities in the 1930s and 1940s:
Earl of Portsmouth, *A Knot of Roots* (London, 1965). However, the German foreign
ministry has kept his enthusiastic letters which started in 1933. Politisches Archiv des
Auswärtiges Amtes, Berlin. Nachlass Dr Leopold von Hoesch, 1881–1936, no. 14
Privatdienstschreiben Auswärtiges Amt 1932–4.

[5] Their 'impeccable' credentials included a letter of introduction from Hitler's court
jester, Putzi Hanfstaengel. Lord Ronald Graham to Attaché H. Fritz Randolph, 2 Nov.
1934, Archiv des Auswärtigen Amts Berlin, Politische und kulturelle Propaganda in
England Pol. 26, R 77171. The address of Graham's letter, 28 Sumner Place, Onslow
Square, SW7, is interesting. Onslow Square is only a few hundred yards from 83 Onslow
Gardens, which is where William Joyce lived by 1937. At the time South Kensington was
a semi-run-down area and Onslow Square seemed to attract budding fascists.

[6] 24 Feb. 1937, Archiv des Auswärtigen Amts Berlin, Pol. 36 R 102827 Judenfrage.

possible in England. Aristocrats who are known to have supported radical right-wing groups have often been portrayed as eccentric figures, or marginalized as disgruntled, 'declining landowners'.[7] A recent panegyric for the aristocracy came to the conclusion that 'Class war, socialism, fascism were un-English ideas, only suitable, if suitable at all, for foreign countries.' This was because of the British aristocracy, which 'for three centuries guaranteed the rights and liberties of all the British people so effectively as to make a written constitution unnecessary'.[8]

So, all is well on the Western Front of the European aristocracies? In Kazuo Ishiguro's *Remains of the Day*, fictional Nazi sympathizer Lord Darlington is in close contact with Oswald Mosley and dabbles in appeasement. He is suspicious of democracy: 'The world's far too complicated a place now for endless members of parliament debating things to a standstill . . . Germany and Italy have set their houses in order by acting.'[9] The character of Darlington could have been based on various contemporary aristocrats who were disillusioned with democracy: the Marquis of Tavistock, a Nazi sympathizer who wanted to strike a peace deal with Hitler, or Lord Londonderry, former secretary of state for air, who defended Nazi Germany and not just for political purposes.[10] But, to put it in literary terms, is Ishiguro's Lord Darlington as representative of the twentieth century as Anthony Trollope's Duke of Omnium was for the nineteenth?[11]

The contemporary left would have answered in the affirmative. They suspected an aristocratic conspiracy: Mosley has 'wealthy, aristocratic, influential friends; men who have powerful controlling influence in industry; in parliament, and in particular the

[7] Cannadine thinks that they were mainly 'déclassé and marginal aristocrats'. David Cannadine, *The Decline and Fall of the British Aristocracy* (London, 1992), 547.

[8] Peregrine Worsthorne, *In Defence of Aristocracy* (London, 2004), 27–8.

[9] Kazuo Ishiguro, *Remains of the Day* (London, 1989), 155 ff.

[10] Londonderry wanted Britain to rearm or strike a deal with Germany. His and Lady Londonderry's autobiographies reveal that they also felt a true affinity with the Nazi regime. Marchioness of Londonderry, *Retrospect* (London, 1938) and Marquess of Londonderry, *Ourselves and Germany* (London, 1938). See also N. C. Fleming, *The Marquess of Londonderry: Aristocracy, Power and Politics in Britain and Ireland* (London, 2005) and Ian Kershaw, *Making Friends with Hitler: Lord Londonderry and Britain's Road to War* (London, 2004).

[11] It is possible that Ishiguro simply meant this as a literary joke, but the difference between the real Whig politician Bedford of the nineteenth century and his radicalized relative in the twentieth century could not be greater. For Tavistock, see the autobiography by his son, Duke of Bedford, *A Silver Plated Spoon* (London, 1959).

Tory party machine. Mosley is a millionaire and has wide family ties with sections of the ruling circles . . . The fact that these families were personally friendly with Hitler arose from their common bond of hatred of the working class.'[12] The Earl of Kinnoull supported this line of argument when in 1934, during a House of Lords debate on the British Union of Fascists, he accused fellow peers of supporting and financing fascist movements in Britain.[13]

Today we know that upper-class support for Mosley was short-lived.[14] We are also aware of the political, economic, and military reasons for appeasing Hitler; and this essay will not repeat the extensive research that has been done on the subject. Yet 'there was a body of conservative opinion which took a serious interest in Fascism, both for its qualities of leadership and for its corporatist theories'.[15] In the 1920s and 1930s this body was in constant flux, its make-up and doctrines changed quickly, and one has to distinguish between many shades of grey. The question therefore is: who thought what, when, and why?

This essay will concentrate on only one group and ask how representative radical right-wing ideas were of the aristocracy. Why were British aristocrats attracted to such ideas? And were only declining landowners and eccentrics affected by them, as Cannadine argues? If so, why are the richest and most illustrious aristocratic names to be found among supporters of the radical right?[16]

The aristocrats under scrutiny in this essay mainly belonged to the peerage. Compared with the long pedigrees of German aristocrats, theirs were relatively 'young', yet they were much richer

---

[12] HO 45/24893 National Archives, Kew. Home Office reports quoting the paper *Socialist Appeal*, Supplement, Headline: Class influence released Mosley.

[13] 'Fascist Organisation in this country', in Parliamentary Debates, Fifth Ser. xc, House of Lords, Session 1933–4, pp. 1008 ff. The BUF had been founded in Oct. 1932. Before that there were minor parties such as the British Fascists, the Imperial Fascist League, and the British People's Party, a creation of the Marquis of Tavistock. See T. Linehan, *British Fascism 1918–39: Parties, Ideology and Culture* (Manchester, 2000).

[14] To feel affinity for authoritarian regimes, Nazi Germany, or British fascist groups did not necessarily mean that one had to become a Mosley supporter. See for this Arnd Bauerkämper, *Die 'radikale Rechte' in Großbritannien* (Göttingen, 1991), 180 ff.; Martin Pugh, *'Hurrah for the Blackshirts': Fascists and Fascism in Britain Between the Wars* (London, 2005); Richard Thurlow, *Fascism in Britain: A History 1918/1985* (London, 1987); and Kenneth Lunn, *British Fascism* (London, 1980).

[15] Richard Griffiths, *Fellow Travellers of the Right: British Enthusiasts for Nazi Germany 1933–39* (London, 1980), 15.

[16] See n. 7 above.

than their Continental counterparts. Still, since the 1880s the British aristocracy had increasingly suffered from economic problems and a growing fear of social upheaval. In this respect the Parliament Act of 1911 marked a turning point.[17] In 1999 the Earl of Romney was still bemoaning this loss of leadership and favoured a benevolent dictatorship of the well informed.[18] Born in 1910, Romney was the last link in a chain of reactionary British aristocrats, the 'diehards'. Before the First World War this group had advocated a national and military awakening, criticized the decadent and plutocratic influences at Edward VII's court (there are parallels here with the German nobility's criticism of William II), favoured the programmes of eugenicists, opposed reform of the House of Lords, and tried to prevent the introduction of Home Rule for Ireland.[19]

The diehards remained a minority that symbolized the strongly nationalist aspect of the higher-ranking nobility. What they feared most was the rising power of socialism: 'a poisonous weed of huge proportions, destroying our national defences and warping the strength of the nation . . . Socialism narcotic-like has drugged the spirits of patriotism into a forced slumber.'[20] After the war surviving diehards continued to sympathize with radical right-wing organizations,[21] and the sons of diehards would, for cultural and political reasons, be more receptive to fascist ideas in the 1920s and 1930s.

The enormous loss of aristocratic officers during the First World War has often been seen as one reason for the subsequent

[17] 'From that moment attendance fell to smaller figures than ever known before, and has never recovered.' Remark by Lord Selborne in 1932, quoted in Rhodri Walters, 'The House of Lords', in Vernon Bogdanor (ed.), *The British Constitution in the Twentieth Century* (Oxford, 2003), 200. The role of the House of Lords has recently received more attention: Andrew Adonis, *Making Aristocracy Work: The Peerage and the Political System in Britain 1884–1914* (Oxford, 1993) and Emma Crewe, *Lords of Parliament: Manners, Rituals and Politics* (Manchester, 2005).

[18] Obituary, *Daily Telegraph*, 10 June 2004.

[19] See Gregory D. Phillips, *The Diehards: Aristocratic Society and Politics in Edwardian England* (Cambridge, Mass., 1979). Their ideology was a strange amalgam of anti-modern and modern elements. Paul Kennedy calls them also 'in certain respects, forward-looking, dissatisfied with negative Conservatism and optimistic about forging a link with the "common man" '. Paul Kennedy, 'The Pre-war Right in Britain and Germany', in id. and Anthony Nichols, *Nationalist and Racialist Movements in Britain and Germany before 1914* (Oxford, 1981), 10.

[20] Phillips, *Diehards*, 90.

[21] For this see W. D. Rubinstein, 'Henry Page Croft and the National Party, 1917–22', *Journal of Contemporary History*, 9 (1974), 129–48.

erratic behaviour of the aristocracy. In many families the sense of personal identity with country properties seemed to decrease with the death of the direct heir. Furthermore 'le grand moan'— complaints about economic downfall, resonated across the land and the 'suffering' of British aristocrats impressed even a German visitor. Indeed, the Bavarian Crown Prince Rupprecht, who visited London in 1932, noted in his diary: 'a butler seems to have become a mythical person'.[22]

It has consequently been argued that aristocrats became more disgruntled as commodity prices fell sharply and rents dwindled after 1918. The *Estate Gazette* reported in 1921 that one-quarter of England had changed hands, which led F. M. L. Thompson to conclude that a social revolution in landownership had taken place, the greatest transfer of land since the sixteenth century (although later he himself described this claim as an over-dramatization). This theory has recently been challenged by John Beckett and Michael Turner.[23] Beckett argues that to this day the figures are difficult to verify and articles such as those in the *Estate Gazette* or *The Times* must be seen in the political context of the time. Headlines such as 'Duke of Portland is selling his estates' were misleading because only small portions of such estates were sold off and not, as the newspapers assumed, to war profiteers, but to tenant farmers who had worked on them for generations.

Reports about 'aristocratic estates dying' had surfaced as early as 1912. After the war the fear that land might be nationalized played a part in creating further hysteria. In fact, by 1921 the land market had settled back to normal. Sales, in terms of acreage sold and prices achieved, peaked in 1919; by 1921 they had sunk back by one-third.[24] Beckett argues that for a short

[22] I would like to thank Dieter J. Weiß for his generous help in providing me access to Crown Prince Rupprecht's comments on Great Britain. Dieter J. Weiß, *Kronprinz Rupprecht von Bayern (1869–1955): Eine politische Biographie* (Regensburg, 2007).

[23] F. M. L. Thompson, *English Landed Society in the Nineteenth Century* (London, 1963). Later he amended his verdict: id., *English Landed Society in the Twentieth Century*, i. *Property: Collapse and Survival*, Transactions of the Royal Historical Society, 5th ser. 40 (1990), 1–24. British Agricultural History organized a conference to reassess these theories: British Agricultural History Winter Conference 10 Dec. 2005, Institute of Historical Research, Senate House. English Landed Society in the Nineteenth and Twentieth Centuries: A Celebration of the Work of F. M. L. Thompson. Beckett and Turner presented their findings here.

[24] In the discussion that followed this paper F. M. L Thompson and other speakers pointed out that sales of gentry land were not included in Beckett's research. It was

period many aristocratic families solved economic problems accumulated in the nineteenth century by selling land, and that this should not be seen as a sign of their imminent bankruptcy. It was not the catastrophe for the aristocracy that they themselves and the press claimed.

This essay will therefore argue that economic fears were not as great as political ones—otherwise rich aristocrats would not have been as infected by the radical right as their poor counterparts. Instead, three points of political fear will be identified: Ireland, the Empire as a whole, and repercussions on the homeland. All three were linked with the biggest of all fears: that of Communism. As a result of the Russian revolution of 1917, '[t]here had not been such a wholesale threat to the integrity and customs of the European states system—commonly proclaimed as Western civilization—since the revolution in France of 1789.'[25]

The problems of the aristocracy had started in Ireland. The Troubles had a psychological impact even on English aristocrats who only followed the reports from a distance in the *Morning Post*. In 1919 the same sort of stories of resistance by brave noblemen emerged from Ulster as had come from Pomerania or Mecklenburg in 1918.[26] There German landowners had fought off unruly peasants; in Ireland country houses were raided for arms by the IRA: 'masked men marched in on the undefended house of Lady Una Ross [dragged her into the garden and made her watch as her house was] burnt to the ground'.[27] Lady Londonderry reported that someone of her class reacted to such stories with aristocratic fighting spirit. She took pleasure in a certain cult of violence, and always carried a loaded pistol. (She actually fired it when her house was attacked—an action that frightened her own security staff more than any threat from Sinn Fein.) Less influential names were not spared either: 'Coolmore was raided by twelve masked men one night. One of the intruders held a pistol at the stomach of the old butler and ordered him to

agreed that it was difficult to get exact numbers for them because most were done via solicitors and not made public.

[25] Jonathan Haslam, *Chill Shadow: A History of the Cold War* (forthcoming).

[26] For this see Stephan Malinowski, *Vom König zum Führer: Sozialer Niedergang und politische Radikalisierung im deutschen Adel zwischen Kaiserreich und NS-Staat* (Berlin, 2003), 198 ff.

[27] Marchioness of Londonderry, *Retrospect*, 214.

hand over his master's service revolver. "I would sooner be shot than let one of you touch my Captain's things".'[28] Not all staff remained so deferential; strikes (including a chauffeurs' strike) seemed to be a foreboding of a socialist future.[29] Altogether 200 country houses were burnt down between 1920 and 1923,[30] which led people like Lady Londonderry to conclude that Ireland was not yet ready for 'democracy as the British know it . . . It is not for southern Ireland. They are of a different race. They want firm, wise but powerful control, to prevent them from trying to eat each other up.'[31]

But even in England things seemed to get out of hand. In September 1918 Lord Cecil wrote: 'It looks as if we shall be precious near a Revolution before long.'[32] The end of the war prevented this, but for many aristocrats the 1920s were dominated by fear of Bolshevism. There were two catalysts that had an impact on aristocratic thinking: first, the fears transmitted via the communication channels of international aristocratic networks; and, second, the national fears created by indigenous scaremongers. The fear of the new evil, Communism, began on the Continent, where aristocratic Baltic and Russian refugees brought tales of persecution to their countries of refuge: 'Some surviving Romanovs did feel that they possessed a certain expertise on revolutions, an expertise that they were all too ready to share . . . Romanov exiles took a wry pleasure in nodding knowingly at the sight of a strike or procession of unemployed workers,

---

[28] Mark Bence-Jones, *Twilight of the Ascendancy* (London, 1987), 188.

[29] Ibid. 190.

[30] Before the Troubles started there were about 2,000 country houses in Ireland. Ibid. 195.

[31] Marchioness of Londonderry, *Retrospect*, 189.

[32] Lord Cecil to his wife, 4 Sept. 1918, Lord Cecil of Chelwood Papers CHE 6/1–164. Hatfield House Archives. See also his papers in the British Library: 'It may well be that when the war is over, we shall only be at the beginning of our troubles.' Memo by Lord Robert Cecil, confidential, Oct. 1916. British Library (henceforth BL), Add. 51102. Also Kenneth Rose, *The Later Cecils* (London, 1975), 127 ff. According to the Duchess of Westminster the aristocracy led rather a schizophrenic life: 'The dark shadows were caused by labour problems, strikes and unemployment. From time to time I wrote cheerfully in my diary that we seemed to be on the brink of a bloody revolution, but it was a possibility which had been at the back of the minds of the upper classes since the days of Marie Antoinette and which they had got quite used to, so in the next sentence I went on to describe how I was trimming a hat or arranging a dinner party.' Loelia, Duchess of Westminster, *Grace and Favour: The Memoirs of Loelia, Duchess of Westminster* (London, 1961), 123.

as if to say: "Ah yes, I've seen this before. Your turn, affectionate cousins, is only a matter of time".'[33]

Even amongst the British aristocracy, which had not been directly affected by revolutionary movements, horror stories circulated via networks of old friends. The Earl of Portsmouth, who had no relations on the Continent, still empathized deeply with the plight of his friends in the Austro-Hungarian aristocracy. In Hungary he stayed at a 'semi-ruined castle. The gutting of the castle was Bela Kun's work . . . Bela Kun had been worse than the war in many ways, and ranked with the peace treaties in the Hungarian Soul.'[34]

Marriage networks had an even stronger impact. The letters of Maria Alexandrova exemplify this. Daughter of Tsar Alexander II, and a member of the English royal family by marriage, she had been a German duchess since the 1890s. She had spent the war in Germany and in 1919 warned her English nephew, King George V, most urgently of the dangers of Bolshevism: 'What pursues me like a nightmare is the probability that the great mass of the [German] population, losing all hope for their future existence, might be driven by despair into extreme bolshevism . . . I warn you of what might become a danger to the rest of Europe. You may be sure that I am not prompted by any anti-English or pro-German feeling, but by the intense pain I have suffered through the horrible fate of my own family.'[35]

Apart from warning of imminent danger, Maria Alexandrova was also appealing indirectly in her letter to the aristocracy's long memory, their common European roots—the 'international chain of the aristocracy'. Prince Rohan, later a National Socialist, even believed that the aristocracy 'beyond all national passion [was united by] a common heritage, blood that has often

[33] John J. Stephan, *The Russian Fascists: Tragedy and Farce in Exile, 1925–1945* (London, 1978), 4. Cannadine underestimates their impact when he uses the old cliché that Russian émigrés just 'drove taxis and worked as waiters in Paris'. Cannadine, *Decline and Fall*, 699. Taylor reduces them to the level of the catwalk. S. J. Taylor, *The Great Outsiders: Northcliffe, Rothermere and the Daily Mail* (London, 1992), 257.

[34] Earl of Portsmouth, *A Knot of Roots*, 140. In Mar. 1919 Béla Kun (1886–1939) formed a Hungarian government dominated by the Communists and ruled by force. Admiral Horthy overthrew this regime in August 1919 and Kun had to flee to Austria. In 1939 he was murdered during the Stalinist purges.

[35] Co-author of this letter was her son-in-law, Prince Ernst II Hohenlohe-Langenburg. See Nachlass Fürst Ernst II Hohenlohe Langenburg (uncatalogued), Zentralarchiv Neuenstein, Neuenstein.

been mixed, a common social niveau and attitude to life's problems'.[36] Consequently they had to stand together now against the wave of Communism. Lord Cecil tried to turn this into policy when he wrote in early August 1919 to Balfour: 'It is the interest of the associated governments to stop the westward advance of Bolshevism before it has penetrated Germany and Austria.'[37]

Nonetheless, appeals to the aristocracy as a whole at times of need created secondary fears that would not have been so effective if they had not been mixed with specifically national problems. For the British aristocracy two perceived threats played a role, to varying degrees: a pan-European one and, more importantly, a national one. The Soviet Union threatened the Empire. Its first target had been China, though officially not part of the Empire, still Britain's second biggest trading partner. The 8th Duke of Northumberland was obviously not alone in waging his war against Communism.[38] The Duke represents a link between the pre-war diehards and post-war fascism. In the 1920s he used the House of Lords for his anti-Bolshevist speeches and acquired ownership of the *Morning Post*, which was widely read in aristocratic circles.[39] The *Morning Post* reported Bolshevist attacks on the Empire and came to the conclusion that 'Moscow . . . is making war on England.'[40]

Serious aristocratic politicians agreed. When in 1920, for instance, the Lloyd George coalition negotiated the first trade agreement with the Soviet Union, the foreign secretary, Lord Curzon, did not want to communicate with the Russian emissary: 'As things are at present, [the Foreign Office] sees itself

[36] The Earl of Portsmouth saw it similarly in the 1950s: 'What was, and still is, interesting is that there is a sort of international aristocratic family freemasonry which permeates Europe even now in a one-adult, one vote world.' Earl of Portsmouth, *Knot of Roots*, 146.

[37] 8 Jan. 1919, Robert Cecil to Arthur Balfour, BL Add. 51104.

[38] Ruotsila Markku is currently preparing a political and religious biography of the Duke.

[39] In 1924 Northumberland talked at length in the House of Lords about the Labour and Socialist International. See Parliamentary Debates, House of Lords, vol. 56, cols. 169–80 and 316–19; Lord Sydenham of Combe was at the side of Northumberland. See Sydenham's speeches in 1921: Bolshevist Propaganda—Legal Position to Cope With (vol. 45, cols. 547–54; 559); 1922: Bolshevist Propaganda—Position of Organized Associations (vol. 51, cols. 258–68); 1923: Russia—Persecution of Church Dignitaries (vol. 53, cols. 459–60); 1924–5: Russia—Soviet Missions; Centres of Disturbances Throughout the World; Hostile Propaganda; Centres of Attack on British Empire (vol. 60, cols. 121–4).

[40] *Morning Post*, 13 Jan. 1927.

expected to enter relations with a State which makes no secret of its intention to overthrow our institutions everywhere and to destroy our prestige and authority particularly in Asia.'[41] Here Curzon was defending his nation's interests as much as his class interests, as he was unable to distinguish between the two.

It was, therefore, no surprise that many aristocrats looked for alternatives. Italian fascism was the first form of fascism the British encountered. To be attracted to Italy was a British tradition, yet this admiration now went beyond adoring paintings and the countryside. In the 1920s the right wing of the Tory party was very much pro-Mussolini, who had suppressed the Communists after his March on Rome, and it supported the Anglo-Italian Axis politically.[42] Though fascism was not an 'organic' English idea, it seemed expedient to support it as a bulwark against Communism on the Continent. Churchill's famous Rome speech of January 1927 was typical of his class and his times: 'I will . . . say a word on an international aspect of Fascism. Externally your [Mussolini's] movement has rendered service to the whole world. The great fear which has always beset every democratic leader or a working class leader has been that of being undermined or overbid by someone more extreme than he. Italy has shown that there is a way of fighting the subversive forces . . . She has provided the necessary antidote to the Russian poison. Hereafter no great nation will be unprovided with an ultimate means against the cancerous growth of Bolshevism.'[43]

Churchill was restrained from speaking for Franco during the Spanish Civil War, yet he stayed in contact with a relative, the Duke of Alba, a supporter of Franco. Jacob Stuart Fitz-James y Falcó, Duke of Berwick and Duke of Alba was a descendant of Arabella Churchill, who had produced an illegitimate son with James II.[44] Although this connection may seem remote, for the

---

[41] Cabinet Meeting 14 Nov. 1920, quoted in Richard H. Ullman, *Anglo-Soviet Relations, 1917–1921*, iii. *The Anglo-Soviet Accord* (London, 1972), 412.

[42] The *Morning Post* saw in him the answer to their prayers: 'When Mussolini took hold of Italy, democracy, delirious with Communism, was swiftly and bloodily ruining the country. And because every other nation is menaced by the same disaster the example of Italy is peculiarly illuminating, as "a contribution to civilisation".' 'The Fascist Ideal', *Morning Post*, 29 Jan. 1927.

[43] Speech made on 20 Jan. 1927 in Rome. Quoted in HO 45/24893, National Archives, Kew.

[44] This son, James Fritz-James, was created a Spanish Grande and Duke of Liria by Philip V.

ancestor-conscious Churchill it was not. In all European aristocracies ancestors, current and future members of the family are one;
they exist outside the conventions of space and time. The family
and its glory has to be at the centre of the thinking of every
member. In the eyes of the prime minister, therefore, the Duke of
Alba was a relative. During his wilderness years as well as when
he was prime minister Churchill stayed in touch with Alba.[45] In
the Second World War Churchill used this international aristocratic network for political purposes. By then, Alba had become
the Spanish ambassador to the Court of St James's and received
intimate dinner invitations from Churchill—even though this was
seen as a security risk.[46] The prime minister, however, thought of
him as a 'cousin' who made a reliable go-between. [47] Though
Churchill kept quiet about Spain in public, many aristocrats
would have agreed with the verdict of a German–British aristocrat: 'I am so pleased that Franco succeeded in getting top [sic].'[48]

In the 1930s the interest had shifted from Italy to Germany.
After the war countless autobiographies by English aristocrats
made fun of the social disaster that the German ambassador to
London, the self-ennobled champagne salesman, Joachim von
Ribbentrop, had been and implied that no one had ever really
enjoyed having tea with those proletarian Nazis. Yet many
British aristocrats were attracted to National Socialism because
they had been treated to more than tea.[49]

Hitler's obsession with the British upper class and his hope of
influencing it have often been seen as delusions of grandeur.[50]
Unlike the more radical revolutionaries in the party, Hitler took

[45] Letter of 29 Nov. 1934, CHAR 2/210, Churchill Archives, Churchill College
Cambridge.

[46] For this see Kim Philby, quoted in Denis Smyth, *Diplomacy and Strategy of Survival*
(Cambridge, 1986), 265.

[47] Personal and Secret from Prime Minister: 'We must not put any slight upon the
Duke of Alba, who is a good friend to this country.' 26 Apr. 1943, CHAR 20/138B 227,
Churchill Archives, Churchill College Cambridge.

[48] Duke of Coburg, 2 Mar. 1939, to his sister, the Countess of Athlone.
AV/FF3/ACA/10, Royal Archives, Windsor.

[49] Lady Eleanor Cecil could not bear such talk when she stayed at the country houses
of her aristocratic friends: 'Nearly all my relatives are diehards and tender to Mussolini
(not so much lately) and to the Nazis, and idiotic about "Communism".' Quoted in
Cannadine, *Decline and Fall*, 550.

[50] The Germans were, of course, Anglophile even before Hitler came to power and
their picture of Britain was as outdated as his. For this see e.g. Gerwin Strobl, *The Germanic
Isle: Nazi Perceptions of Britain* (Cambridge, 2000).

ample time to entertain British visitors. Goebbels was not completely averse either. Apart from his friendship with Diana Mosley, he carefully monitored House of Lords debates.[51] Albrecht Haushofer therefore claimed that the Nazi regime was looking for 'a settlement with the British upper classes'.[52] If one considers how successfully the Nazis had targeted the German nobility, this was not such a far-fetched plan.

One concept of British society outlined in a paper by the German foreign ministry was that of a pyramid in which the upper class played a vital political role and consequently seemed to be a much more important player than its dethroned German counterpart.[53] These German aristocrats were, however, useful in doing the proselytizing. Aristocrats preferred talking to aristocrats, and access to each other was easily gained, even if there was no family connection.[54] The aforementioned international communication within the aristocracy worked again: German aristocrats passed on their positive experiences with the new regime to their English cousins in order to give Hitler more credibility abroad. British aristocrats and the royal family were bombarded with glowing reports about the Third Reich.

Some of the delivery boys were well chosen. By recruiting the Duke of Coburg, for example, the Nazis gained a direct channel to the British peerage and monarchy. For Coburg, the Nazis offered the chance to play a political role once again: 'but what pleases me most is that they still need our help. In spite of their saying nowadays that the young must rule.'[55] Coburg had strong personal reasons to hate the Communists. His sister-in-law Victoria was married to Grand Duke Cyril and used Coburg as a base to further her husband's candidature as the only legitimate

---

[51] How carefully the Nazis monitored the upper classes is shown by Goebbels's diaries. Elke Fröhlich (ed.), *Goebbels Tagebücher*, pt. 1: *Aufzeichnungen*, iii. 1 Apr. 1934 to Feb. 1936, 101, 241, 376, 405, 414 ff.

[52] Albrecht Haushofer was a professor of political geography at the University of Berlin and an adviser to Rudolf Hess. Quoted in Lynn Picknett, Clive Prince, and Stephan Prior, *Double Standards: The Rudolf Hess Cover Up* (London, 2001), 152–3.

[53] Report by Herr von Korostovetz, a former Russian diplomat who worked for the Nazi regime. Auswärtiges Amt Archiv Berlin, Pol. 29 77175.

[54] For this see Walter Demel, 'Der Europäische Adel vor der Revolution: Sieben Thesen', in Ronald G. Asch (ed.), *Der europäische Adel im Ancien Régime: Von der Krise der ständischen Monarchien bis zur Revolution (1600–1789)* (Cologne, 2001), 420.

[55] Duke of Coburg to his sister, Alice, Countess of Athlone, 2 Mar. 1939, AV/FF 3/ACA/10, Royal Archives, Windsor.

tsar in exile. This brought her into contact with the German extreme right, first Ludendorff, then Hitler, who in 1922 celebrated the infamous German Day in Coburg.[56] 'Charlie' Coburg wholeheartedly supported his Russian relatives and their new German friends, and tried to export this crusade to England. His correspondence with his sister, the Countess of Athlone, extracts of which have been made available by the Royal Archives in Windsor, indicates that in the 1930s he used her house as a base for propaganda talks, and later reported to Berlin on their outcome.[57]

British country houses must have been busy places in the 1930s, the last heyday of country house politics. Coburg was only one of many go-betweens. Jonathan Petropolous has recently shown how useful the Hesse family was to the Nazis in forging ties with the Italian and the British elite.[58] Goering even cultivated a ménage of aristocrats with international contacts, including Max Hohenlohe and the Wieds, for similar purposes.[59] The aristocratic grandeur of Goering, a self-styled renaissance man, who invited his British guests to hunting parties and entertained like Louis XIV, as Chips Channon noted, seemed familiar and appealing to international members of the aristocracy.[60] British aristocrats, true 'choreographers' themselves, were full of admiration for the pomp of fascist movements. Nor was the idea of

[56] For this Russian connection see Stephan, *The Russian Fascists*, 13. Stalin was paranoid about the émigrés. The Cheka even invented a front group, the Trust, which fooled monarchists. It became a source of misinformation for monarchist groups about events in Russia and aristocrats also invested in it financially. See Andrew Barros, 'A Window on the "Trust": The Case of Ado Birk', *Intelligence and National Security*, 10/2 (April 1995), 275.

[57] Thank you letter from Charles, Duke of Saxe Coburg, to Alice, Countess of Athlone, 15 Apr. 1936, AV/FF 3/ACA /10, Royal Archives, Windsor.

[58] Jonathan Petropoulos, *Royals and the Reich: The Princes von Hessen in Nazi Germany* (Oxford, 2006).

[59] MI5 papers released by the National Archives, Kew in 2005 show what an interesting propaganda crusade was pursued by two members of the Hohenlohe family. Stephanie Hohenlohe, who had married into the aristocracy, cultivated influential circles in Britain, first to lobby the cause of Hungary (a revision of the treaty of Trianon), later in the services of Hitler. Max Hohenlohe had excellent contacts to the FO and worked for Goering in Czechoslovakia, Spain, and Switzerland. By 1944 he had changed sides and offered his services to Allen Dulles. For this, see Karina Urbach, 'Nobilitäten und Netzwerke' (*Habilitationsschrift* in progress, 2008–9).

[60] Lymington was attracted to Goering's military side: 'I was introduced to Göring whom I say unashamedly I liked and got on with . . . He was jolly and full of fun, and had that sort of ace ex-airman's attitude to life which I so often found endearing among his British and American counterparts.' Earl of Portsmouth, *Knot of Roots*, 49.

charismatic leadership remotely alien to the British aristocracy—
they regarded themselves as the bearers of 'inherited glory'. 'The
cinema star had not yet eclipsed the duchess', as the Duchess of
Westminster put it.[61] To the British aristocracy, such people as
Horthy,[62] Mussolini, and Hitler seemed to be charismatic types
one could relate to—after all, were they not just observing a
benevolent paternalism?

Furthermore the Nazi policy of anti-Semitism did not prove to
be an obstacle to liking the regime. In England there had always
been a discourse about race. Lord Redesdale and Churchill had
admired Houston Stewart Chamberlain's *Foundations of the
Nineteenth Century*,[63] and the aristocratic discourse about racially
pure elites was as strong in Britain as in Germany (although in
Britain this was mainly connected with the Empire). After the
First World War anti-Semitic conspiracy theories thrived among
all classes and aristocrats were in the lead. Their anti-Semitism
ranged from the 'mild' forms used within the Cecil family to
obsessive outbursts such as those of the Duke of Northumberland
at the far end of the spectrum, who believed in a Jewish–
Bolshevik conspiracy. Richard A. Grosvenor, 2nd Duke of
Westminster, even consulted a book entitled *Jews Who's Who*,
which gave an exact breakdown of how much Jewish blood was
flowing in English aristocratic veins.[64] Such issues also worried
the organo-fascists who have recently been analysed by Dan
Stone. This group, in some ways similar to the German *Blut und
Boden* ideologues, were known as the English Mistery, and

---

[61] Loelia, Duchess of Westminster, *Grace and Favour*. This might refer to the Duchess of
Malfi: 'I am the Duchess of Malfi still.'

[62] 'As a dictator he was the nearest thing in my recollection to a larger English land-
lord . . . One felt instantly at home with a type of man one had always known.' To
Lymington, Horthy was a man of the gentry: 'Horthy was the country squire, fundamentally filling in the old regime for a king who never returned.' Earl of Portsmouth, *Knot of
Roots*, 160.

[63] Karina Urbach and Bernd Buchner, 'Der Briefwechsel zwischen Houston Stewart
Chamberlain und Prinz Max von Baden (1909–1919)', *Vierteljahrshefte für Zeitgeschichte*, 52/1
(January 2004), 121–77.

[64] 'Benny (the Duke of Westminster) was usually excessively careless about his belong-
ings and left his valuables lying about anywhere, but he used to lock up one book with
elaborate secrecy. This was called the Jews Who's Who, and it purported to tell the exact
quantity of Jewish blood coursing through the veins of the aristocratic families of
England. According to Benny, the Jews themselves, not liking to be revealed in their true
colours, had tried to suppress this interesting publication and his copy was the only one
that had escaped some great holocaust.' Loelia, Duchess of Westminster, *Grace and Favour*,
189.

believed in an 'organic society, . . . a holistic, unitary, racially pure body . . . in the sense of being rooted in the soil, and led by a hereditary landed aristocracy that instinctively performed its leadership role'.[65] Its members included anti-Semites as well as reactionary conservatives such as Anthony Ludovici and Viscount Lymington. The latter eventually left the Mistery and founded the English Array, which was pro-German.[66]

The papers of the German foreign ministry show that the Nazi regime placed great hopes in this movement. One reason was that lesser British royals had connections with the Mistery; another was that it held out the promise of becoming an opposition movement: 'this group is extremely anti-parliamentarian. It includes people from the politically interested upper classes, among them numerous members of the House of Lords.'[67]

The above points show that during the interwar period aristocrats were for a number of reasons attracted to fascist ideas. But ultimately the British aristocracy had more to gain by conformity. In the House of Lords debate of 1934 on the British Union of Fascists, the higher ranks of the nobility fought amongst themselves as to which interpretation was correct. After the aforementioned Earl of Kinnoull had accused his fellow peers of helping to finance fascist movements in Britain, Viscount Esher responded that if the choice had to be made between Stafford Cripps and Oswald Mosley, it would have to be Mosley: 'There are innumerable quiet people in this country, who hating both those gentlemen, will, if they are forced to choose between them, I am glad to say, choose Sir Oswald Mosley.'[68]

Viscount Cecil of Chelwood, who was later to become Londonderry's formidable opponent, considered this response

[65] Dan Stone, *Responses to Nazism in Britain, 1933–1939: Before War and Holocaust* (London, 2003), 164.

[66] See for this Richard Moore-Colyer, 'Towards "Mother Earth": Jorian Jenks, Organicism, the Right and the British Union of Fascists', *Journal of Contemporary History*, 39/3 (July 2004), 354; Jorian E. F. Jenks was the agricultural expert for the radical right. He fought for the impoverished landed aristocracy that had been ousted by an 'alien plutocracy'. According to Jenks the aristocracy should stay in charge: 'The aristocratic principle of respect for the past, careful husbandry of the present and stewardship for the future was pivotal to the organicist credo and, by implication demanded a stable society susceptible to sympathetic, yet firm, authority.' Ibid. 366.

[67] Bericht über politische Erneuerungsbestrebungen im Sinne autoritärer Staatsführung, Pol. 29 77175. 2 May 1934, Auswärtiges Amt Archiv, Berlin.

[68] 'Fascist Organisation in this country', Parliamentary Debates, Fifth Ser. xc, House of Lords, Session 1933–4, p. 1013.

dangerously nonchalant. He reminded the House that radical parties which believed they could come to power by force were a danger to the constitution. This House of Lords debate, with its three aristocratic archetypes ranging from the far left to the far right, shows how important this institution, written off by many as irrelevant, was for upholding aristocratic decorum. It played a crucial role in enabling fellow peers to exert social control over radical aristocrats. Its traditional political language and social code did not allow aggressive confrontations.

In Germany after long overdue reform debates, the first chambers and the Prussian Upper House disappeared in 1918, and soon afterwards the radical Deutsche Adelsgenossenschaft (DAG) usurped their position, forcing conformity on the German aristocracy. Britain had more political pluralism within the aristocracy than did Germany. 'Red' aristocrats, the Duchess of Atholl being the most prominent example, had always caught the limelight. Others were fairly apolitical, such as Nancy Mitford, Mosley's sister-in-law, who enjoyed making fun of him and her Hitler-obsessed sister Unity in *Wigs on the Green*.[69] The Mitfords were the most famous, but not the only, aristocratic family divided by politics.

Institutional ties with the government are, ultimately, what prevented the British aristocracy from following the same path as their German cousins. Aristocrats often had younger sons or sons-in-law in the 'House of Pretence' (that is, the House of Commons), unpopular though it might be, and this meant that for the sake of their careers they had to give due consideration to political and social issues. Furthermore, solidarity with the losers, for example, the impoverished Anglo-Irish aristocracy, was over by the 1930s. They were eventually written off, many ending their lives in genteel Irish poverty or in lodging houses on the south coast.[70]

Another reason why radical ideas were held in check amongst the English aristocracy was that this group, unlike their German

[69] Nancy Mitford had a rather complex relationship with her complex family. To Unity, who had sent her a newspaper clipping from Germany she wrote in 1936: 'Darling Stonyheart, We were all very interested to see that you were the Queen of the May this year at Hesselberg. Call me early, Goering dear, For I'm to be Queen of the May! Good gracious, that interview you sent us, fantasia, fantasia.' Quoted in Harold Acton, *Nancy Mitford* (London, 1975; new edn. 2004), 81.

[70] Cannadine, *Decline and Fall*, 699.

counterparts, had various lines of retreat. After losing formal and institutional status in 1918 the German aristocracy continued to focus on the land, and did not try to find new career opportunities. The English aristocracy, on the other hand, had more than one iron in the fire. They had never been totally dependent on life in the country—indeed, it was precisely their investment in urban centres, industry, and the Empire that had made them strong. Their relationship with country life was characterized by a mixture of pragmatism and mysticism. But despite any sentimental attachments, they took less and less responsibility for countryside affairs, for instance, in church matters.[71]

Because the British aristocracy had always worked at many levels as a local, national, and imperial elite, the Empire was an ideal safe haven in a crisis. It enabled the English aristocracy to create a flourishing parallel universe, an aristocratic Disneyland full of replica country houses and urban palaces. Many aristocrats, such as the Marquis of Graham (later 7th Duke of Montrose) or Lord William Scott (son of the Duke of Buccleuch), moved to the White Highlands of Kenya and Rhodesia, and created a feudal lifestyle. Viscount Lymington was to join them in 1947, deeply disappointed by post-war England.[72]

He should have counted himself lucky not to have been interned under Regulation 18B. In this respect the left was correct in suspecting an upper-class cover-up. A recently published MI5 file shows that another ardent fascist, Viscountess Downe, was not interned because '[i]f too many titled people are arrested the public might get the wrong idea as to the importance of the Fifth Column in this country.'[73] Many illustrious Hitler admirers—among them Tavistock, Buccleuch, Westminster, Brocket, Mar, and Queenborough—escaped prison. It could hardly be seen as surprising that the establishment was covering up for its own people. Halifax, for example, forwarded pro-Nazi correspondence he received from the public to Special Branch,

---

[71] For this see Peter Mandler, *The Fall and Rise of the Stately Home* (London, 1997) and Alun Howkins, *The Death of Rural England: A Social History of the Countryside since 1900* (London, 2003), 21–2.

[72] Pugh, *'Hurrah for the Blackshirts'*, 82.

[73] PRO KV 2/2146, National Archives, Kew. However the viscountess wanted to go to prison. Her lawyer even planned a 'question being put to the Home Secretary as to why you have not been detained while certain working class members in your constituency have'. Ibid.

but held back letters from members of his own class, such as Tavistock's correspondence.[74]

On the outbreak of war every aristocrat did his duty. For some this meant a schizophrenic lifestyle. The Marquis of Graham served on destroyers in the Mediterranean, but whenever he and his brother had time they were involved in pro-peace activities and secret meetings with the Duke of Westminster.[75] This group did not give up its ideologies overnight. Goering's feared invitation to Nuremberg in 1945 therefore should not have surprised peers. For once, a German seemed to show an ironical sense of humour.

[74] For this see Pugh, *'Hurrah for the Blackshirts'*, 307.
[75] Ibid. 289.

5

Distance and Attraction: Dutch Aristocracy and the Political Right Wing

HANS DE VALK

To take as a topic the attitude of the Dutch nobility towards the extreme political right in the interwar period presupposes that this can be treated as a case in its own right. Some preliminary questions, therefore, have to be answered. What was the status of the Dutch nobility in the early twentieth century? Did it possess any special social and political influence? Can it be treated as a separate part of the country's upper class? Thereafter, a brief survey of the confusing political landscape of the Dutch extreme right will be necessary to provide the background against which to place aristocratic commitment. Aristocratic political engagement with the extreme right wing will then be looked at from a political and social point of view, in general and in three individual cases.

As a result of the anomalous pattern of Dutch history, in 1900 the Dutch nobility differed from the nobilities of neighbouring countries with regard to its history, composition, and status.[1] In the sixteenth century, after a revolt against the King of Spain, the country had constituted itself as a republic. This has been described as a 'conservative revolution': ties with the past were not completely severed. In the Republic of the United Provinces, members of the princely House of Orange-Nassau acted as *Stadholder* (governor), thus keeping alive the notion of a 'virtual' king. The concept of nobility continued to exist and noble families had certain political privileges. No new ennoblements,

---

[1] For the history of the Dutch nobility see J. Aalbers and M. Prak (eds.), *De bloem der natie: Adel en patriciaat in de Noordelijke Nederlanden* (Amsterdam, 1987); Y. Kuiper, 'Adel in Nederland', in E. A. Ketelaar-de Vries Reilingh and Y. Kuiper (eds.), *Edel voor Adel* (The Hague, 2000), 77–98. A study group on the history of Dutch nobility has been publishing the yearbook *Virtus* since 1993. Most publications focus on the period before 1800.

however, could take place because of the lack of a sovereign to grant them. This situation came to an end with the Batavian revolution of 1796. After almost two decades of indirect and direct French rule, in 1814 a monarchy was set up under the House of Orange. The nobility was now given constitutional status, while the king received the power to ennoble. In 1815, when the present Netherlands and Belgium temporarily merged into one kingdom, King William I felt that the number of high-ranking nobles in the southern (ex-Austrian) Netherlands needed to be balanced. He therefore promoted to hereditary noble status many of the families whose members had served as magistrates in the former influential northern city governments, granting them knighthoods or baronetcies. The existing noble families were raised to the peerage. In practice, there was little social difference between these two ranks. During the nineteenth century, other Dutch and foreign families were incorporated into the nobility. The political privileges exercised by the Provincial Nobility Councils (*Ridderschappen*) lasted until the middle of the century. In 1848, a new liberal constitution abolished these councils, but the special status of the nobility was maintained. From the beginning of the twentieth century, appointments to the nobility took place very rarely, thus raising the social value of existing titles. Just before the Second World War, in a population of 8 million, there were about 250 noble families totalling some 7,000 members.

In the nineteenth century, a noble title was a sure sign of social distinction. With the *Patriciaat* of non-noble, distinguished families,[2] they made up the Dutch upper class. Since the early years of the twentieth century, their names could be found in the *Red Book* (for nobles) or the *Blue Book* (for the gentry).[3] Taken together, the political influence of these two groups was considerable. Up to 1913 they provided more than half the members of parliament and an even greater proportion of cabinet ministers. Nobles were well represented in the liberal and Protestant parties, and especially in the Catholic party, among army and navy officers, and in the upper echelons of the civil service, in particular, the diplomatic service. In the period between the wars, however, the aris-

---

[2] The Dutch *Patriciaat* is not identical to the English 'patriciate', which implies noble status; 'gentry' is the nearest equivalent.

[3] Thus called after the colour of their bindings; *Nederland's Adelsboek* (the *Red Book*) has been published since 1903, *Nederland's Patriciaat* (the *Blue Book*) since 1910. To be mentioned in the *Blue Book* a family had to meet certain conditions of social standing.

tocracy suffered a marked decline in political power. Of one hundred members of the lower house of parliament in 1917, thirteen were nobles and twenty-two members of the *Patriciaat*; by 1937 these figures had been reduced to six in each case.[4] This can be linked to a change in the electoral law in 1917, when the constituency system was replaced by proportional representation. Since then, party allegiance counted for more than status or networks of local and regional notables.

It is tempting to think that the social status and influence of the Dutch nobility declined correspondingly. This is certainly what the government thought in 1947. After the Second World War, special tribunals were set up in the Netherlands to 'cleanse' institutions and professional groups of those who had collaborated with the Germans during the occupation. A committee for the nobility, however, was regarded as unnecessary because of its lack of social significance.[5] This may well be the case as far as members of the *Patriciaat* were concerned, but recent publications by Jaap Dronkers have shown that, surprisingly, the aristocracy has maintained a privileged position in Dutch society right up to the present day.[6] It has succeeded in doing so by using what he calls its socio-cultural capital and networks, and by cleverly adapting to changing circumstances. It reminds us of the advice given by the Prince of Salina's nephew Tancredi in Lampedusa's famous novel *Il Gattopardo*: everything has to change, so that everything can remain the same.

When changes in the voting system reduced the effectiveness of existing political networks, members of the aristocracy shifted their attention to other fields, such as banking and industry. Distinguishing themselves in subtle ways from the bourgeoisie was one of the means used to keep themselves recognizable as a separate social group.[7] To be called 'middle class' is still one of

[4] J. T. J. van den Berg, *De toegang tot het Binnenhof: De maatschappelijke herkomst van de Tweede Kamerleden tussen 1849 en 1970* (Weesp, 1983), ch. 2, esp. 48–9.

[5] L. de Jong, *Het Koninkrijk der Nederlanden in de Tweede Wereldoorlog*, 14 vols. (The Hague, 1969–91), xii. 464.

[6] J. Dronkers, 'Is Nederlandse adel gedurende de twintigste eeuw maatschappelijk relevant gebleven?', *Amsterdams sociologisch tijdschrift*, 27 (2000), 233–68. Cf. id. and Huibert Schijf, 'The Transmission of Elite Positions among the Dutch Nobility During the Twentieth Century', in Eckart Conze and Monika Wienfort (eds.), *Adel und Moderne: Deutschland im europäischen Vergleich im 19. und 20. Jahrhundert* (Vienna, 2004), 65–82.

[7] Many interesting details about aristocratic lifestyle in the first half of the twentieth century, presented from a personal point of view, can be found in two recent books:

the worst insults in noble circles. Intermarriage between noble families was another way of holding the titled elite together, and this included many foreign families. We may conclude that during the interwar years the Dutch aristocracy had more reason to be satisfied with its social status and influence than a superficial appraisal of its diminishing political power might suggest.

When we turn to the political background for a brief survey of the radical right in Dutch politics between the wars, we are reminded of a Dutch expression: two Dutchmen are enough to found a new denomination and three a political party. This applies to a large extent to the extreme right. It is impossible to outline here the history of all the different parties and movements, the many changing alliances between them, and the conflicts and schisms among them.[8] Following the example of one of the best and most detailed monographs on the history of right-wing politics in the Netherlands,[9] we can distinguish between two periods: before and after 1930.

The period of 'normal fascism' from 1920 could be called 'the small crisis of democracy'. Many parties and movements arose, whose programmes ranged from ultra-conservative to straight, Italian-style fascist. These movements came from several sources, primarily right-wing Protestant liberals and Catholics. The reasons why people joined these movements also varied, but can be summarized as a general feeling of unease and social resentment. The political system was perceived as an abstract, individualistic expression of mass society. In the end, it was felt, it would crush family values, devalue the historical foundations of the Dutch nation, smother the voice of the social and intellectual elite, and leave the nation unprotected against the onslaught of socialism and Communism. The remedies advocated were changes in the system: a restriction of the vote; the strengthening of executive power; and political representation to be reformed

Agnies Pauw van Wieldrecht, *Vin-je dat we een hoed op moeten? Persoonlijke herinneringen aan een bijna vervlogen levensstijl* (Amsterdam, 2003), and Ursula den Tex's portrait of her mother: *Anna baronesse Bentinck, 1902–1989: Een vrouw van stand* (Amsterdam, 2003).

[8] Details on most of these parties and movements can now be found in a database compiled by K. P. S. S. Vossen, *Repertorium Kleine politieke partijen 1918–1967* (2003), which can be consulted on the Institute of Netherlands History's website, <www.inghist.nl/Onderzoek/Projecten/KPP>, accessed 23 Jan. 2007.

[9] A. A. de Jonge, *Crisis en critiek der democratie: Anti-democratische stromingen en de daarin levende denkbeelden over de staat in Nederland tussen de wereldoorlogen* (Assen, 1968).

in a corporative sense. The ultra-conservative and 'normal fascist' movements and parties either disappeared or radicalized in the early 1930s. Their share of the electorate had never risen above 1–2 per cent.

In the next phase, that of the 'great crisis of democracy', radical fascism and National Socialism gave rise to a number of movements, the most important being the National Socialist Movement (NSB), founded in 1931. Its programme was inspired by the example of Germany. It advocated racism, dictatorship, the abolition of democratic institutions, and a one-party system. Bolstered by the effects of the economic depression, the National Socialists succeeded in attracting up to 8 per cent of the vote in 1935, and grew into a mass movement with more than 50,000 members. The democratic parties, however, defended themselves effectively. In the elections of 1937, no more than 3 per cent of the vote was for the radical right.

Did aristocrats have a specific role to play in the Dutch right-wing movements? It is difficult to find anything more than anecdotal evidence concerning the political stance and ideological affinities of the Dutch nobility as a whole. It may, however, safely be assumed that most Dutch nobles could be found at the (democratic) right-wing end of the political spectrum, along with the other members of the upper and upper-middle classes. There is nothing to suggest that when voting they had a particular preference for the extreme right. Many historical studies of the Dutch radical right provide statistical data on membership, grouped according to variables such as profession, geographical origin, religion, and social status. But no historian has yet categorized members of the radical right according to title of nobility. So, what sources are available?

The Dutch National Archives contain a veritable mountain of records produced by the special tribunals set up after the Second World War comprising some 100,000 files concerning the prosecution of those who collaborated with the Germans. The index cards could be examined to see how many were titled, but the result would not show whether they had supported the radical right *before* the war. This would have to be checked in the files themselves—a thorough but impractical method of research.[10] It

---

[10] Special permission is needed for every individual file.

therefore seemed advisable to approach the question in a different way. Existing literature could be consulted to find nobles
playing roles of some importance in the radical right, such as
leaders and prominent members of parties and movements,
writers on political subjects, people in high office, influential
bankers, and industrialists. A number of monographs have been
written which, taken together, more or less cover the historiography of the radical right. Many of these are very detailed.[11] In
addition, two internet databases are available and can be
searched electronically. First, there is the repertory of small political parties since 1918.[12] This lists by name the central figures
involved. Another database contains an analysis of the reports of
the Dutch Internal Security Service (1918–40).[13] Fortunately, it
proved possible electronically to search the 35,000 names it
contains for titles of nobility, as these were almost always
provided. In this way, a fairly representative sample could be
obtained. The result is not impressive. All the sources together
yielded a total of thirty-nine different names, some of them
occurring more than once.

When interpreting this result, we should bear in mind the
following factors. In 1940 there were about 7,000 titled men and
women in the Netherlands. At least two-thirds of them were
adults; most of the males had received a good education, and
many held a university degree. Up to 1918 the Dutch nobility had
had a strong tradition of active political participation. All things
considered, it may safely be concluded that the Dutch aristocracy
resisted the attractions of right-wing extremism fairly well, and

---

[11] De Jong, *Het Koninkrijk der Nederlanden in de Tweede Wereldoorlog*, i and ii (dealing with
the period 1918 to 1940); A. A. de Jonge, *Het nationaal-socialisme in Nederland: Voorgeschiedenis,
ontstaan en ontwikkeling* (The Hague, 1968); id., *Crisis en critiek der democratie*; L. M. H. Joosten,
Katholieken en fascisme in Nederland, 1920–1940 (Hilversum, 1964); Jan Meyers, *Mussert: Een
politiek leven* (Amsterdam, 1984); Hans Schippers, *Zwart en Nationaal Front: Latijns georiënteerd
rechts-radicalisme in Nederland, 1922–1946* (Amsterdam, 1986); I. Schöffer, *Het nationaal-social-
istische beeld van de geschiedenis der Nederlanden: Een historiografische en bibliografische studie*
(Amsterdam, 1956); S. Y. A. Vellenga, *Katholiek Zuid-Limburg en het fascisme* (Assen, 1975);
Sytze van der Zee, *Voor Führer, volk en vaderland: De S.S. in Nederland* (3rd edn.; Alphen aan
den Rijn, 1987); Wim Zaal, *De Herstellers: Lotgevallen van de Nederlandse fascisten* (Utrecht,
1966); G. R. Zondergeld, *Een kleine troep vervuld van haat: Arnold Meijer en het Nationaal Front*
(Houten, 1986).

[12] Vossen, *Repertorium van Kleine Politieke Partijen* (cf. n. 8).

[13] B. G. J. de Graaff et al., *Reconstructie van de rapportage van de Centrale Inlichtingendienst
(C.I.), 1919–1940* (2001), <www.inghist.nl/Onderzoek/Projecten/RapportenCentrale
Inlichtingendienst1919-1940>, accessed 23 Jan. 2007.

kept its distance. It is likely that any active engagement went against the code of conduct of the Dutch noble class, particularly in the case of the National Socialist movements. Aristocrats looked down on the radical right because of the middle-class character of its leadership, the plebeian vulgarity of most of its members, its racism and populism, the parading in cheap uniforms, the equally cheap rituals, and finally, because they despised the movements for overstepping class boundaries.

All these factors come together in a literary source which provides an inside view, the novel *Dolly van Arnhem*, written by Henriette Laman Trip-de Beaufort, herself a member of the nobility,[14] during the Second World War and published in 1949. Over more than 600 pages, she tells the story of a Dutch noble family and how its way of life changed between 1890 and 1940. Doubts can and should, of course, be raised about the value of a novel as a historical source. In this case, the author is far from being a literary genius; her style is detached and the family she describes does not strike us as particularly exciting. Precisely for these reasons, however, the book could be considered instructive.

The main characters in the novel are a baroness and her twin brother, members of an established, well-to-do family in a rural area. They symbolize two diametrically opposed ways of confronting the modern world. The baroness is an energetic woman who, against her father's will, marries a Jewish musician and persuades her family to accept him. She leads an active intellectual life. Her brother, by contrast, is a layabout without a proper education, living on the money of his rich German wife, a countess. His main occupation is a job in the National Socialist Movement and he likes to be out drinking with his party cronies. The baron is a cynic who has lost the aristocratic ideals of his youth; he is waiting for the coming Nazi society to restore the social status he has lost through his decadent lack of energy. His sister, on the other hand, retains aristocratic standards of behaviour and in this way fulfils the obligations of her noble birth in changed social circumstances. She and most of the members of her family show a pronounced distaste when the brother with fascist leanings tries to convert them to his new religion. Although the baron has married within his class, it is he who

---

[14] The author (1890–1982) is well known for historical biographies.

appears to have placed himself outside the aristocratic community. The vigour and vitality of his sister, contrasting sharply with
his parasitic ennui, send a clear message: a real nobleman should
be a positive asset to society under any circumstances. To seek
refuge in a movement as 'un-Dutch' as National Socialism in
order to salvage the privileges of his noble status reveals a despi-
cable weakness of character.

The baron could serve as a model for many of the thirty-nine
black- or brown-shirted nobles mentioned above. If we examine
their personal and social circumstances, it seems that failure,
resentment, and nostalgia played a part in attracting many of
them to the extreme right. The biographical data supporting this
claim are provided by the *Red Book* cited above. In many cases,
their level of education, profession, social status, or marriage in
comparison with other members of their families points in this
direction. Although this research is rather impressionistic, it
allows us to draw some preliminary conclusions. In most cases,
the data for the individuals singled out did not match the average
for their families: many did worse than their families in general.
Although this does not prove that resentment and frustration
were the main motives for their political choice, it at least suggests
that in many cases the nobles concerned—or the noble*men*,
because there is only one woman on the list—may have been
seeking recognition of their noble status in the movements they
considered would be the major political force in the near future.
When we examine three individual cases more closely in the next
part of this essay, the assumption appears to be substantiated. In
addition, these examples serve to illustrate the spectrum of right-
wing political commitment in Dutch noble circles and the diversity of aristocratic life in the Netherlands in the interwar period.
We shall start on the 'left side' of the right wing.

I *Robert Groeninx van Zoelen*

Jonkheer Robert Groeninx van Zoelen (1889–1979) was a classic
example of a gentleman of leisure.[15] Although he called himself a

[15] The nearest English equivalent to the title 'Jonkheer' is 'Esquire'. A recent and
amusing biography: I. Cornelissen, 'Jhr. R.F. Groeninx van Zoelen (1889–1979)', in H.
Foppe (ed.), *In Den Haag geschied: 750 jaar in verhalen en beschouwingen* (The Hague, 1998),
213–36. For the family background see *Nederland's Adelsboek*, 83 (1993), 496–512.

journalist, he was, in fact, a man of independent means. When means happened to be short, he would fall back on his family and friends. He also worked as a part-time antiques dealer. He was well known and accepted in the Dutch upper class, to which his family traditionally belonged. Its members had been wealthy and influential as city magistrates and governors of the East India Company since the days of the Dutch Republic. In the early twentieth century, most of its members were married to other Dutch aristocrats, held high office, or worked as bankers. Robert's father lived on his private means; his mother was one of the queen's *dames du palais*.

Groeninx was the odd one out in his family. Although he had enjoyed a good education, he had not finished his university studies, preferring to spend his days in the high society of his native city, The Hague, seat of the Dutch government. He knew and met everyone: politicians, cabinet ministers, members of the Royal Court, leading bankers, and industrial tycoons. At a personal level, he was charming and gentlemanly. His sociability paid off by giving him access to inside information, which provided him with an additional income as a freelance journalist. He was a bon viveur with a rather Bohemian lifestyle, which raised his entertainment value in the eyes of more respectable members of the ruling class. The fact that he was a practising homosexual seems to have done him little harm. He may have been very discreet, but it is equally possible that his upper-class friends did not care much about middle-class values.

Politically, Groeninx was a right-wing liberal, as were most of his friends. Their social views were highly outspoken and they shared a proud patriotism full of class prejudice. What they feared most was socialism and the possibility of a socialist or Communist revolution. When an uprising seemed imminent in November 1918, in the aftermath of the First World War, Groeninx's political instincts came to life. He joined an association formed to provide armed defence against a possible revolt, and walked around with a revolver. From this moment, his political ideas and those of many of his brothers-in-arms evolved in a reactionary, ultimately fascist, direction. In the 1920s and early 1930s we find *Jonker* Rob in a leading capacity in many of the parties and movements of the radical right which had been founded in the Netherlands since Mussolini had seized power in

Italy. Within these organizations, however, he never belonged to the extreme wing. In many cases he deployed his undeniable talents as a political pamphleteer.

Groeninx's ideas were partly based on those of Italian fascism, but he never went all the way. Returning to the distinction between the 'small' and the 'great' crisis of democracy mentioned above, we might say that he never crossed the thin line dividing them. His proposals for constitutional change were not drastic. He advocated a strengthening of executive power and a much smaller role for parliament, to be elected in a more judicious, corporative way. In order to achieve these goals, political alliances in the country would have to be reshuffled. Since the introduction of the new voting system, Dutch politics had been monopolized by a coalition of religious parties; liberals were out of business. Groeninx rejected the class-transcending character of these parties, which he considered dangerous, especially at a time of economic recession. The upper-class elements in these parties, he suggested, should be persuaded back into a coalition with conservatives and liberals. Together, he believed, this united force could hold socialism at bay and procure the constitutional majority necessary to keep it there. He placed his hopes in one influential politician in particular, the Protestant party leader and former director of Royal Dutch/Shell, Hendrik Colijn (1869–1944), five times a cabinet leader in the interwar years. It turned out, however, that, despite his authoritarian leanings and sympathy for Italian fascism, Colijn would not take the chosen path, and Groeninx turned against him with a vengeance in the early 1930s. He showed himself to be a formidable opponent and almost succeeded in bringing the minister down by blackmail and by whipping up political scandals. In doing so, he put together a most unlikely coalition of supporters: the fascist circles in which he was well known, Colijn's former Royal Dutch chief, Sir Henry Deterding, and several other industrialists and bankers of the first rank who wanted the government to leave the gold standard, which was choking Dutch industry. Only tactical mistakes by Groeninx's fascist friends helped the minister to survive.[16] Disillusioned, Groeninx left politics until 1940. Soon after the German occupation in 1940, however, he assisted the

---

[16] Cf. H. Langeveld, *Hendrikus Colijn 1869–1944*, 2 vols. (Amsterdam, 1998–2004), ii. ch. 7.

organizers of the Nederlandsche Unie (Dutch League) as a political adviser. This League was a slightly anti-German mass movement, in which many of his old ideas resurfaced. When it misfired in 1941, he was active in the resistance against the Germans.

Groeninx can be located in the shady area between reaction, authoritarianism, and fascism. For him fascism was a means rather than an end. He was not a man fit for the barricades or the *Führerprinzip*; he was motivated primarily by a patriotism defined by aristocratic standards. He wanted to defend the class society he had known in his youth, before the tide of mass democracy had risen. Although on several occasions he called himself a 'popular fascist', in fact he was more of a nostalgic reactionary. Despite his prejudices and superficial anti-Semitism, he is the most sympathetic of the three examples chosen to be examined in this essay, and certainly the most intelligent.

II *Maximilien de Marchant et d'Ansembourg*

Our next example takes us substantially further to the right. The background of Count Maximilien de Marchant et d'Ansembourg (1894–1975) is as confusing as can be expected in an international noble family.[17] French, Belgian, German, Austrian, Polish, Czech, and Hungarian families can be found in his ancestry. His close relatives lived in Belgium and Germany. His German wife, a *Freiin* von Fürstenberg, could claim a Turkish grandfather. It is understandable that Max d'Ansembourg had little use for the concept of race, the Jewish one excepted. His family held ample estates in the Netherlands and abroad, and had several castles in the Dutch province of Limburg, where the d'Ansembourgs were influential. They were devout Catholics. Max's father sat as a member of parliament for the Catholic party. Nevertheless, his son was educated by German Jesuits and studied law at the university of Münster. In 1912, his father had him naturalized as a German citizen. His university career, however, ground to a halt after one year. When, at the same time, the First World War broke out, he

---

[17] Biographical note and further references in *Biografisch Woordenboek van Nederland*, (The Hague, 1994), iv. 321–3. For the d'Ansembourg family, see *Nederland's Adelsboek*, 75 (1984), 287–300.

volunteered as an officer in the German army, where he remained
until the end of the war. Seeking a suitable job, he worked in
several Dutch banks and at the state-run coal mines in Limburg.
In 1925 he finally found a position fitting for an aristocrat. As his
uncle's heir, he was appointed mayor of the village in which the
castle he had inherited was located.

D'Ansembourg had political ambitions and was elected as a
Catholic party member of the Provincial Council in Limburg.
After some years, however, he must have realized that his political
career had stalled. His party seemed to have lost its predilection
for the nobility. The region in which he lived was industrializing
rapidly and his rather feudal ideas were no longer considered as
received wisdom. He would go no further. He was not re-elected
in 1931. Two years later, he defected to the National Socialist
Movement. In his view, Catholic politics had grown materialistic
and were doomed. The Church, he suggested, should rely on
fascism and National Socialism to save its position in modern
society and, ultimately, to reconquer the world for Christ. He
considered that to work towards this goal was a task worthy of a
nobleman.

For the National Socialist Movement the Count was a prize
catch: a well-connected upper-class Catholic. He had to leave the
office of mayor because civil servants were not permitted to be
members of extremist movements. He could thus be paraded as a
martyr for the good cause and devote most of his time to the
Movement. Its leader, Anton Mussert, appointed him his adviser
for German affairs because of his international contacts. At the
same time, Mussert hoped that d'Ansembourg could help to
remove a serious obstacle to the party's growth. The Dutch
bishops had taken up the defence of the Catholic party in order
to prevent the leakage of votes and membership to National
Socialism and fascism. If these movements were placed under a
religious ban, some 40 per cent of the Dutch electorate would be
out of reach. To prevent this was of paramount importance, and
the only authority capable of doing so was the Vatican.

D'Ansembourg mobilized his family networks. He was, for
instance, related to Count von Huyn, a former archbishop of
Prague now attached to the Roman Curia, and to Count
Ledóchowski, the Polish Superior-General of the Jesuits. Their
Dutch 'cousin' bombarded them with pleading letters in favour

of fascism and National Socialism as a necessary response to liberal materialism: were they not the natural defenders of the Church? Under the circumstances (in particular, the friction between Nazi Germany and the Vatican), it comes as no surprise that neither his letters nor his visits to Rome had any success. In 1936, the Dutch Episcopate forbade Catholics from joining the National Socialist Movement. In response, the Count left the Church.[18]

The National Socialists offered d'Ansembourg what the Catholic party had failed to do: the recognition he felt he deserved, and access to the national political arena. From 1935 to 1940 he sat successively in both houses of parliament. His electoral successes in his home region showed that he enjoyed a certain degree of popularity. D'Ansembourg belonged to the moderate wing of the National Socialist Movement. This made his position increasingly awkward towards the end of the 1930s, when radical tendencies became more prominent. After the German occupation his star rose again as he coordinated contacts between the Dutch Movement and the German authorities. At the beginning of 1941, however, he was promoted out of the way and made a provincial governor. After the war he was considered a minor case. Having spent ten years in prison he returned to his castle, where he died in 1975.

D'Ansembourg is a typical example of a nobleman associating with the extreme right out of social resentment. Although he clearly lacked the intellectual capacity to fill a prominent place in national politics, he claimed it because of his title and fortune. A notion of hereditary rights also played a part. When frustrated in his advancement, he looked for an alternative in a right-wing movement that was essentially lower middle class: a class, he hoped, looking for leadership from its traditional social superiors. Contrary to his expectations, after 1945 it turned out that the social position of the nobility was still very solid. Max d'Ansembourg's family can provide supporting evidence. Neither his children nor his close relatives suffered the consequences of his behaviour, judging by the fact that one of his brothers, one of his sons, and two of his nephews held high office after the war.[19] In the middle

---

[18] J. P. de Valk, *Roomser dan de paus? Studies over de betrekkingen tussen de Heilige Stoel en het Nederlandse katholicisme, 1815–1940* (Nijmegen, 1998), ch. 12.

[19] One of his nephews was the Dutch ambassador to the Court of St James's in 2004.

classes the experience could be quite different. Here, mere membership of the Dutch National Socialist Movement sometimes resulted in entire families remaining ostracized for decades.

III *Ernst van Rappard*

My last example is also the most extreme: a Dutch nobleman who fought in the German SS and advocated the abolition of the Netherlands as an independent nation. The family of Ernst van Rappard (1899–1953) came from Germany.[20] In the nineteenth century, it had been incorporated into the Dutch nobility with the title of *ridder* (knight). Members of the family had held high state office, but most were active as army officers, technicians, and entrepreneurs in the Dutch East Indies. However, they were not associated with the real upper class. They did not marry into other noble families and in some cases even 'went native' in the Indies. Ernst van Rappard's own grandmother and great-grandmother were of Javanese extraction. He spent his youth in the Indies where his father worked. From 1921, he studied law at the university of Leiden, but decided to continue his university career in Germany and Austria. He studied economics at the universities of Berlin, Munich, and finally Vienna, where he took his doctorate.

His stay in the Austrian capital (1928–30) was decisive for the development of his political ideas. He attended the lectures of the conservative economist and social philosopher Othmar Spann (1878–1950) who won him over to the idea of a corporative social order. Moreover, he frequently moved in German and Austrian National Socialist circles. Under the influence of his political friends, he adopted extremely radical right-wing and Germanophile ideas. Van Rappard decided to dedicate himself to politics in order to bring about a National Socialist revolution in the Netherlands and to favour the country's entry into a greater German Reich. This was made possible by his father, who gave him a liberal allowance that permitted him to refrain from any normal occupation. Both his father and a brother also had marked right-wing leanings.

---

[20] For a biographical note and further references (not yet published in print), see <www.inghist.nl/Onderzoek/Projecten/BWN>, accessed 23 Jan. 2007. Cf. *Nederland's Adelsboek*, 76 (1985), 220–51.

In late 1931, van Rappard founded a political party. Its programme and style were almost completely copied from Hitler's NSDAP and he accordingly called it the Dutch National Socialist Workers' Party (NSNAP). Dictatorship, a one-party system, anti-Semitism, and Pan-Germanism were the cornerstones of its programme, especially the last two. The Netherlands belonged to Germany, van Rappard stated, because man is not allowed to separate that which God has united. The new party was not a great success, being best known for its in-fighting. Even more than other right-wing movements, it attracted a crowd of political obsessives and streetfighters, and soon split up into three competing factions. Moreover, its pro-German stance was not exactly a recommendation in Dutch fascist circles, where a bombastic patriotism came first and a Greater Holland, not a Greater Germany, was the ultimate objective. On the other hand, after 1933 van Rappard's German contacts kept him at arm's length because they preferred the much bigger, better organized, and more influential National Socialist Movement.

The greatest obstacle to political success, however, was the leader himself. His racist ideas about the superiority of 'German blood' could only raise a laugh when confronted with his own ancestry. He was a typical armchair scholar, socially inept; a bad organizer, administrator, and tactician; an undisciplined writer; and an even worse speaker. In his private life, he did not impress people as a suitable *Führer*: he lived on his father's money and had married his father's German housekeeper, eight years his senior, who bullied him in public. When his father died, he disbanded his party and in 1939 moved to Germany, where he did odd jobs for the Nazi regime.

After the German occupation of the Netherlands, van Rappard returned to re-establish his party, which soon attracted more than 15,000 members. It was favoured by the Germans as a means of radicalizing the Dutch National Socialist Movement. As soon as this goal was achieved in 1941, van Rappard's party was abolished. Subsequently, he enlisted with the German SS and fought in Eastern Europe. After the war, he was tried for high treason and received a death sentence, commuted to life imprisonment. He died in gaol in 1953.

Van Rappard has been described as an unselfish idealist who sincerely believed in German National Socialism and his own

Dutch version of it. He demonstrated his faith by fighting for it. The concept of nobility (not, of course, of 'plutocratic' aristocracy) played a certain part in his ideological make-up, but he never boasted about his noble status. Moreover, accepting Walther Darré's concept of *Neuadel aus Blut und Boden* (a new aristocracy based on blood and soil), he was convinced that the German race as a whole was noble. For him, a title just meant one more obligation to behave like a proper German. All in all, we may consider Ernst van Rappard a textbook case of an aristocratic eccentric on a social journey downwards, but in contrast to the cases of Groeninx and d'Ansembourg, elements of nostalgia and resentment are less conspicuous in his political commitment.

We may conclude that aristocratic commitment to the extreme right in the Netherlands between 1918 and 1940 was rather limited. The reasons why Dutch nobles kept their distance from right-wing movements and ideology seem to be of a social rather than an ideological nature. Few aristocrats were actively engaged and the reasons for their attraction were also of a social nature: they give a strong impression of being the less successful members of their class and families. When applied to three individual cases of nobles with fascist sympathies (at the same time illustrating the spectrum of right-wing political engagement in aristocratic circles), this finding appears to be corroborated.

PART II

Southern Europe

6

The Italian Aristocracy, the Savoy Monarchy, and Fascism

JENS PETERSEN

What political role did the aristocracy play in the early decades of a unified Italy? Researchers are widely divided in their opinions on this question. They range from the rose-tinted view of Arno Mayer, who regarded the *ancien régime* nobility as still at the core of Italy's social and political system, to opinions that speak of a rapid and unstoppable decline.[1] Although aristocratic values continued to shape the path of upward mobility for the middle classes, nobility as such did *not* play an important role in the Italian nineteenth-century social structure, because it did not constitute a well-defined group in itself, due to its regional more than national status. Paolo Farneti has analysed the 1,321 positions of minister and secretary of state in the forty-five cabinets between 1861 and 1913. What emerges is a deep caesura—also perceived as such by contemporaries—between the governments of the *Destra Storica* (Historical Right) from 1861 to 1876, and the seizure of power by the left in the 'parliamentary revolution' of 1876. Up to 1876 there was a total of 237 ministers and secretaries of state. In these first fifteen years, the aristocracy accounted for 43 per cent of the total. They were found mainly in landowning (in absolute terms, forty-two people) and the military (thirty-eight), but also filled significant positions in the administration (seven), and culture (eight). Aristocratic prime ministers of these years include not only Cavour himself, but also Bettino, Baron Ricasoli, Alfonso La Marmora, and Federico Luigi, Count Menabrea. Farneti sums up: 'The ruling political class of the Historical Right displayed three elements of homogeneity. It

Translated by Angela Davies, GHIL.

[1] Jens Petersen, 'Der italienische Adel von 1861 bis 1946', in Hans-Ulrich Wehler (ed.), *Europäischer Adel 1750–1950* (Göttingen, 1990), 243–59. The present essay is based in part on this study.

consisted largely of landowners who were members of the middle-ranking aristocracy, and the majority of them had shared the experience of participating in the Risorgimento.'[2]

A completely different picture emerges for the decades after 1876. The share of the aristocracy sank from 43 to 16 per cent; that of landowners went down from 21 to 3 per cent. The percentage in the military was more stable, reducing from 23 to 15 per cent. Here, too, the reduction in the proportion of aristocrats was striking. Whereas before 1876, 70 per cent in this category had been aristocrats, by 1903 the percentage of aristocrats had fallen to 22. Looking at the statistics over thirty years actually reduces some of the highest values, as they include the aristocratically influenced reactionary cabinets of Antonio Starabba, Marchese di Rudini, and Luigi Pelloux, shortly before the turn of the century. The first cabinets of the left, after 1876, contained practically no aristocrats. In this year a new political elite came into power. It was highly bourgeois in character, consisting of lawyers, other professionals, journalists, and state officials.

Giovanni Giolitti's decade (1903–13) was a period of consolidation. The proportion of aristocrats rose slightly from 16 to 20 per cent. The military and landowners each regained 1 per cent (rising from 15 to 16 per cent and from 3 to 4 per cent respectively). On the whole, however, the predominance of lawyers, state officials, and professionals continued. The governments of that decade have gone down in memory as the Golden Age of the Italian bourgeoisie.

The composition of the Senate provides a further field for research. At Italy's unification, it comprised about 150 members. A compromise procedure had been worked out between the crown and the government for the recruitment of new members. The prime minister presented the monarch with a list of suggestions, from which the monarch then selected a certain number of candidates. 'Strong' prime ministers, such as Agostino Depretis, Francesco Crispi, and Giolitti, were able to use this procedure to increase the number of members and acquire a more tractable Senate. As the minimum age for membership was 40, the average age was far above 50 and soon passed 60. Thus it was that by the 1880s the Senate already comprised more than 300

---

[2] Paolo Farneti, *Sistema politico e società civile* (Turin, 1971), *passim*, quotation at 169.

members and, in 1913, its membership topped 450. As far as the proportion of aristocrats is concerned, two series of data are significant: first, the average composition of the body as a whole; and secondly, the origins of the new members. In his recently published investigation, *Lo stato fascista e la sua classe politica*, Didier Musiedlak traces the following developments. The average proportion of aristocrats as a percentage of all senators in the period 1861–75: 39.3 per cent (new recruits: 33.2 per cent); 1876–86: 31.6 per cent (19.9 per cent); 1887–96: 25.4 per cent (18.2 per cent); 1897–1902: 23.8 per cent (21.5 per cent); 1903–14: 20.1 per cent (14.5 per cent); 1915–22: 17.6 per cent (13.3 per cent).[3]

Thus during the first fifteen years, the aristocrats' share of senators was still almost 40 per cent, sinking to 20 per cent by the time of the First World War. The decline is even more striking when we look at the figures for new recruits. Here it falls from a third to less than a seventh. If the aristocracy had been the dominant element in the Senate at the start, then during the final phase of the liberal system it became marginal even in this body, the 'final refuge of the elite of liberal Italy'.[4]

According to Mayer, politics, administration, the army, and diplomacy were the crucial areas in defending traditional structures of privilege. The army did not enjoy high prestige in Italy, with the exception of Piedmont. The navy was largely a bourgeois affair. But even in the army's officer corps, the aristocracy had held only a few residual positions since the 1880s—depending on the arm of the service and the tradition of the unit, representing between 5 and 20 per cent. In 1872 the percentage of aristocrats in the officer corps was 8.3 per cent; in 1887 the figure was 3.1. Aristocrats still filled positions of power as generals. Among the generals, 39.7 per cent were aristocrats in 1863. By 1872 this figure had fallen to 35.4 per cent, and by 1887 to 33.6 per cent. However, almost all chiefs of the general staff in the twentieth century, from Alberto Pollio to Armando Diaz and Pietro Badoglio, were bourgeois when they were appointed to this top job, and were ennobled only afterwards. Among the administrative elite of the prefects, too, we gain the impression

---

[3] Didier Musiedlak, *Lo stato fascista e la sua classe politica 1922–1945* (Bologna, 2003), 76–91.

[4] Ibid. 74.

that by the turn of the century, the proportion of aristocrats had shrunk so much that they filled only residual positions.

According to Sergio Romano, diplomacy formed an 'aristocratic bastion'.[5] Of the 866 officials in the foreign ministry between 1861 and 1915, 43.2 per cent were aristocrats. However, the aristocracy clearly dominated in the core area of diplomacy, where it provided two-thirds of the 314 people employed. In the consular service it provided almost a third, and in the home service a good quarter. The big embassies in Vienna, London, Paris, Berlin, Petersburg, and Madrid were exceptions. Of the sixty-eight 'big' ambassadors, thirty-nine (that is, 57.4 per cent) were members of the aristocracy, and more than half of them came from the former Kingdom of Sardinia. The aristocracy, often still with direct access to the monarch, was best able to maintain its position of power in this core area. But the tendency towards bourgeoisification did not stop at the diplomatic service. From the beginning of the twentieth century, the proportion of aristocrats among new recruits decreased markedly, and before 1914, it hardly amounted to a third.

According to estimates, the aristocracy which came into being after 1860, drawing on the nobilities of individual states and the patriciates of individual cities, comprised between 6,000 and 7,000 families. One list, dating from 1878, which is full of gaps and was obviously compiled by an amateur, mentions 7,676 names,[6] one-third of whom came from Piedmont. An examination of the families listed in Vittori Spreti's book of the Italian peerage,[7] suggests that around the turn of the century, the entire closed circle can hardly have numbered more that 50,000. A book of the peerage of 1933 lists 7,750 families, comprising 41,853 individuals. As many institutional incentives were lacking, no powerful representation for the aristocracy emerged at national level. The first ever national aristocrats' conference did not take place until 1930. The lack of an influential newspaper organ was indicative. In the former Bourbon kingdom and in Sicily, legitimist aristocratic families continued to exist. And in Rome and the surrounding areas, the sharp distinction between the 'black'

---

[5] Sergio Romano, 'La nobiltà, lo Stato e le relazioni internazionali', in *Les Noblesses européennes au XIXe siècle* (2nd edn.; Rome, 1971), 536.

[6] L. Carpi, *L'Italia vivente* (Milan, 1878), 76–7, quoted from Farneti, *Sistema politico*, 172.

[7] Vittorio Spreti (ed.), *Enciclopedia storico-nobiliare italiana*, 8 vols. (1928–36; repr. Bologna, 1981).

aristocracy which was orientated towards the pope, and the 'white' aristocracy that looked to the Savoyards, was maintained. On the whole, the deep antagonism between the liberal state and the Catholic Church had a strong influence on the position of the aristocracy and limited its opportunities for action. Catholic aristocratic families loyal to the pope kept their distance from the state. Since the *Non expedit* of 1874, the pope had forbidden them to become actively involved in politics at national level. The important part that the Catholic aristocracy had played in building up Catholic associations, credit unions, and the Catholic cooperative movement demonstrates how much organizational and cultural energy was available and could have been used in a different historical situation. Nor did the monarchy attempt to create a new aristocracy loyal to itself by initiating a broad wave of ennoblement.

Between 1861 and 1922, about 330 ennoblements took place; between 1922 and 1946 the figure was around 300. During Italy's liberal period the king elevated about five people to the aristocracy each year; during the fascist period this figure tripled, to about fifteen. These figures do not include elevations in rank, of which there were about 170 in the period from 1861 to 1914. Silvio Lanaro speaks of a three-part plan followed by north Italian entrepreneurs in their quest for ennoblement: (1) acquiring a title; (2) adopting an aristocratic lifestyle; and (3) marrying into an aristocratic family.[8] To fit into the new way of life, they had to buy patrician palaces in the cities and aristocratic villas in the country. The list of names to be mentioned here is long, and includes Crespi, Borletti, Florio, Rossi, Mazzonis, Marzotto, Volpi, and Cini.

The ennoblement of Italian citizens by the pope, which the state was prepared to recognize after 1924, also gave this process a certain boost. Another 250 families or so were involved here. In some cases this was a recognition of considerably older claims, some dating back as far as the eighteenth or nineteenth centuries.[9] In addition to these ad hoc arrangements, the Lateran treaties of 1929 contained the following agreement (Concordat article 42): 'Italy agrees, by legal decree, also to recognize the aristocratic

---

[8] Silvio Lanaro, *L'Italia nuova: Identità e sviluppo 1861–1988* (Turin, 1988), 39 ff.
[9] F. Pericoli, *Titoli nobiliari riconosciuti in Italia* (Rome, 1963).

titles created by the Pope after 1870, including those which he will create in future.'[10] The cost of registering an aristocratic title was high, presumably to act as a deterrent. How attractive belonging to the aristocracy continued to be, however, is illustrated by numerous decrees and circulars—for example, those from the years 1870, 1884, 1898, 1899, 1901, 1903, 1905, 1923, and 1925— directed against the abuse of aristocratic titles. These circulars list a wide range of possible abuses, which suggest that the reality behind them was widespread: simple usurpation, the continuation of titles granted *ad personam*, inflation of titles, adoptions, the resurrection of defunct titles, and the use of foreign titles. During the fascist period, these abuses must have reached such levels that, in addition to legal sanctions, the government applied additional fines of 1,000 to 5,000 lire for the misuse of aristocratic titles. In case of recurrence, the fines were doubled.[11]

I

In Anthony L. Cardoza's view, Italy's participation in the First World War vastly accelerated the decline of the aristocracy. Many of the facts and processes which he establishes for Piedmont presumably also applied in other parts of Italy. If the late nineteenth-century agrarian crisis had already had a severe impact on the income of the aristocracy, most of which came from the land, then Italy's entry into the war in May of 1915 presented this elite with unprecedented challenges. 'The war proved to be a considerably more pivotal event than the agricultural depression of the 1880s and 1890s in the decline of Piedmont's nobility.'[12] Cardoza calls the First World War 'the great watershed in the history of Italy's traditional elites'.[13] Long-term leases, often running for periods of more than ten years, tax increases, and growing state regulation meant that incomes stagnated or even shrank, while increases in the cost of living and incipient inflation (by 1921 the lira had lost 75 per cent of its

---

[10] Pericoli, *Titoli nobiliari*, 11.

[11] Spreti (ed.), *Enciclopedia storico-nobiliare italiana*, i. 172.

[12] Anthony L. Cardoza, *Aristocrats in Bourgeois Italy: The Piedmontese Nobility, 1861–1930* (Cambridge, 1997), 212–13.

[13] Ibid. 11.

value) meant that expenditures rose enormously. The statistics presented by Cardoza show that the proportion of aristocrats worth less that 100,000 lire (1914 value) increased from 46 per cent on average for the years 1901 to 1912, to 70 per cent in 1922–3. The group of aristocrats worth more than 750,000 lire, which in the period 1901 to 1912 had accounted for 11 per cent of the whole, had disappeared completely by 1922–3. Cardoza speaks of a 'sharp decline in the nobility's share of large fortunes',[14] while at the same time, the huge boom in the armaments industries was creating enormous fortunes for entrepreneurs. Arrigo Serpieri has estimated that during the war and the immediate post-war years, large absentee landowners in the Po region suffered a loss of about one-third of their real income. At that time there was a massive 'shift of wealth from the landowner to the leaseholder'.[15] At the same time, the demand and the price of agricultural land was rising. Many leaseholders were able to make themselves independent by buying their lands. Large landowners, whether aristocratic or not, were under huge pressure to sell. Cardoza speaks of an 'aristocratic exodus from the land'. 'What had been a gradual and strategic withdrawal by aristocratic families from the countryside before 1914 became a full-scale exodus in the early 1920s.'[16] According to work done by Arrigo Serpieri, between 1914 and 1922 around 10 per cent of the land used for agriculture in the Po valley changed ownership. Many former leaseholders formed the core of a peasant class which owned small or middle-sized holdings. It proved to be a strong opponent of the socialist agricultural workers' movement which received fresh impetus after 1918, and was among the strongest supporters of the early fascist movement in rural areas.

II

With the First World War, the masses made their entrance onto the stage of Italian politics. The country had mobilized more than six million soldiers, drawing most of them from the illiterate rural

---

[14] Ibid. 215.
[15] Arrigo Serpieri, *La guerra e le classi rurali italiane* (Bari, 1930), 116–18; Cardoza, *Aristocrats in Bourgeois Italy*, 214.
[16] Ibid. 215.

populations of central and southern Italy. In May 1915 Italy had entered the war, against the wishes of the majority of the population whose attitude was neutralist, under pressure from 'interventionist' lobby groups, whose members included the ex-socialist Benito Mussolini. The socialists had rejected participation in the war from the start. However, instead of gaining the rapid victory over Austria–Hungary that the politicians expected, Italy became embroiled in a protracted war of attrition. After 1917 the myth of the Bolshevik revolution began to exert an increasing fascination for the Italian left. During the *biennio rosso*, the two 'red' years of 1919 and 1920 immediately after the war, Italy seemed to be on the brink of revolution. In 1919–20 the Nitti government tried to ward off these profound social changes by introducing proportional representation. The first elections in the history of unified Italy not to be directed and influenced by the government via the prefects in the provinces were held in November 1919 and resulted in a divided parliament. In northern and central Italy the new mass parties of the socialists and Catholics predominated, whereas in the south, the old liberal and democratic groups of notables continued in power. In this parliament, the aristocracy had shrunk to an insignificant minority of 5.3 per cent. Socialists, Catholics, and liberals, however, proved to be incapable of forming a coalition with each other. In this stalemate situation of mutual immobilization, which produced only short-lived and weak governments, the fascist movement founded by Mussolini began its rise.

This movement presented a populist mixture of right-wing and left-wing goals that initially seemed to have little chance of success. Fervently anti-Bolshevik and nationalist, even imperialist, it demanded that Italy must not be tricked out of the fruits of its 'gigantic' victory; at the same time, it was also republican and anticlerical, with anti-monarchical undertones, and was strongly critical of the traditional leadership elites. In its first election manifesto of 1919 it demanded, among other things, constitutional reform (eventual abolition of the monarchy and the Senate), expropriation of Church property, a strongly progressive income tax, and high inheritance taxes to pay for the aftermath of the war.

During the war, and then especially after it, there was a widespread longing in Italian society for a strong leader, going along with a desire for order and authority. The institution of the monarchy was unable to fulfil these wishes with a king who was considered shy and introverted and did not like appearing in public or fulfilling ceremonial duties. In parallel, the liberal political system and its political elites lost respect. The march to Fiume organized by the poet–soldier Gabriele d'Annunzio with his 'legionaries' in September 1919, modelled on Garibaldi's march, came to stand for the deliberate dismantling of state authority and the new forms of myth-building and mass communication. Later totalitarian movements profited from this model. In 1919–20, the *comandante* D'Annunzio embodied the first version of this longing for a strong leader in Italian society. The rising fascist movement and Mussolini himself profited in the most diverse ways from this 'free state of Fiume' as a laboratory of modernity. This applied to Fiume as a model of Caesarist democracy and as an experimental field for forms of dialogue between people and leader. The *Duce* myth, already present in the socialist movement before 1914, was used in a targeted way by Mussolini as an instrument of rule, and was supported by numerous intellectuals of the right. It developed in the years 1920 and 1921. After the last internal party revolt in March 1922, Mussolini's claim to leadership was practically unchallenged. In view of the potential for civil war and the increase in illegality and violence, stoked up by fascism, the country was crying out for a strong hand. As the liberal conservative aristocrat, Giustino Fortunato, wrote, everyone was starting 'to call for a MAN in capital letters, who could at last lead the country back to order and legality'.[17]

Leadership, authority, and hierarchy were among the key terms of the fascist programme. *Gerarchia* was the title of a monthly review devoted to cultural politics founded by Mussolini. Fascism saw itself as a *trincerocrazia*, an aristocracy of the trenches, as the new elite of the nation, born out of the immense blood sacrifice of the war years and hardened in the *Stahlgewitter*, the brutality of the First World War.[18] In its origins, the fascist movement was strictly

[17] Jens Petersen, 'Mussolini—der Mythos des allgegenwärtigen Diktators', in Wilfried Nippel (ed.), *Virtuosen der Macht: Herrschaft und Charisma von Perikles bis Mao* (Munich, 2000), 155–70.
[18] Reference to the First World War diary by Ernst Jünger, *In Stahlgewittern: Aus dem Tagebuch eines Stoßtruppenführers*, published in 1920, which paints a picture of horrifying brutality.

republican. By moving closer to the position of the established elites, Mussolini declared himself an agnostic on the constitutional question. Modelling himself on Garibaldi, he acted as a monarchist of reason (rather than conviction). 'Can our political system be thoroughly reformed without touching the institution of the monarchy?' he asked in a programmatic speech in September 1922.[19] And he replied immediately: yes, if it lets us have power. 'The monarchy has no interest in resisting what must already be called the fascist revolution.'[20] This calculated strategy of inducements, promises, and threats created the alliance between the monarchy and fascism.

After the state and the government had, on a number of occasions, failed to confront the threat and the use of illegal fascist violence, the Facta government tried to demonstrate resolve in the face of the March on Rome at the end of October 1922. The imposition of a state of emergency, agreed unanimously by the Council of Ministers, failed on the night of 27–8 October 1922 when Victor Emanuel III refused to sign. To the present day, his motives have not been explained. Historians of the period generally agree that the use of military force would not have precipitated civil war, but that a small number of casualties would have made the fascist movement collapse. The scenario already played out at the end of 1920, when Giolitti had put an end to D'Annunzio's Fiume adventure by deploying the military, would have been repeated.

The king's capitulation created a fundamental compromise between fascism and monarchy which was renewed during the Matteotti crisis and the open transition to dictatorship in 1924–5, and outlasted all the crises of the following twenty years. Looking back in 1944, Mussolini controversially described the relationship between himself and Victor Emanuel III as a diarchy, or government by two individuals, expressed in a doubling of institutions, functions, legitimacies, and symbols: *Duce* and *Re*, the fascist Great Council and the Senate, Stemma sabauda and fascio littorio, Giovinezza and Marcia Reale, and Milizia Volontaria and the regular army. For more than twenty years, fascism and the monarchy confronted each other in a relationship of concealed tension in which the king attempted to maintain appearances. In reality, he

[19] Benito Mussolini, *Opera Omnia* (Florence, 1955), xviii. 418.
[20] Ibid.

was powerless in the face of the regime's constant initiatives, going as far as intervening in regulations governing the succession and the military supreme command. Each act in building a totalitarian dictatorship, from the abolition of political parties to the establishment of a special political court, from the introduction of fascist racial laws to the declaration of war on the Western powers, also bore the king's signature. In 1938–9 Mussolini seriously considered abolishing the monarchy. It presumably would not have survived a victory in a major war.

On the other hand, the Catholic Church, the papacy, and the monarchy continued to have an important braking effect, blocking the development of the truly totalitarian dictatorship to which radical fascism aspired. In the 1930s, the primary loyalty of important sections of the elites in the army, justice, and the *carabinieri* continued to be to the monarchy. Moreover, it was precisely the fact that monarchy and fascism stood side by side which made the Italian example so attractive to many observers from business circles, the civil service, and the aristocracy of Weimar Germany.[21] The misconception that Hitler's plans and future could be interpreted along the lines of Mussolini's model made a crucial contribution to the National Socialist seizure of power.

What was the significance of the aristocracy within the fascist movement? In the *Dizionario di Politica*, published by the fascist party in the late 1930s, we read, under the heading 'Aristocrazia', that fascism was aware of 'the value of hierarchies in the state . . . some of which have not yet exhausted themselves, some of which need renewal in order thus to create a link between the past and the present'. Fascism, we read, needs 'a new national leadership class . . . of warriors, inventors, judges, great captains of industry, great explorers, great politicians'. 'Next to the old, aristocratic values (of blood, tradition, heritage), no less select new ones have emerged', that is, fighting ability, readiness for martyrdom, and being prepared for the revolutionary struggle. This new class, 'which will never become as rigid as the old oligarchies . . . is distinguished by its impartiality, its political abilities, its strong sense of duty, and the hardness and strength of its character'.[22]

---

[21] Wolfgang Schieder, 'Das italienische Experiment: Der Faschismus als Experiment. Der Faschismus als Vorbild in der Krise der Weimarer Republik', *Historische Zeitschrift*, 262 (1996), 73–125.

[22] Carlo Curcio, 'Aristocrazia', in *Dizionario di Politica* (Rome, 1940), i. 169–72, at 172.

However, supplementing the new fascist elite and recruiting for
the future remained unresolved problems. Italian fascism did not
deliberately select elites like the Nazis with their Teutonic orders
and educational institutions. As early as 1929, Hermann Heller, a
teacher in constitutional law, had asked polemically whether
fascism intended to wage war periodically in future in order to
fulfil its claim to represent the *trincerocrazia*, the new warrior aristocracy.[23] The regime very clearly postulated the primacy of the
new fascist elite. A dictionary of the fascist leadership elite, edited
by Mario Missori twenty years ago, permits a few observations
on our topic.[24] This handbook, containing about 1,000 names,
lists the members of the Gran Consiglio, the party leadership and
its subdivisions, as well as the secretaries of the Partito Nazionale
Fascista (PNF) in individual provinces. The period covered is, as
a rule, from the founding of the PNF at the end of 1921 to
Mussolini's fall on 25 July 1943. The selection of individuals
featured does not represent the complete leadership cadres of the
PNF. It does not cover the militia, the unions, the sports and
leisure organizations; nor does it contain all the pro-fascist
fiancheggiatori from industry, the civil service, justice, and the
armed forces not represented in the party organization but who,
like Arturo Bocchini, Alberto Beneduce, Felice Guarneri, and
Pietro Badoglio, played a significant part in the regime. None the
less, the selection does offer a representative picture of the fascist
leadership elite. Of the 1,003 people listed, 63 were aristocrats.
Seventeen of these had not received their titles until the fascist
period. This group of the recently ennobled contained such
prominent figures as Volpi di Misurata, finance minister from
1925 to 1928; Cesare M. De Vecchi, *quadrumvir* in the March on
Rome; Costanzo Ciano, a highly decorated naval officer and
later president of the Chamber; and Dino Grandi, foreign minister from 1929 to 1932 and later justice minister, who played a
central role in overthrowing Mussolini. A number of aspiring
noblemen chose to take the path via the Vatican which, under
certain circumstances, could be simpler. Anyone ennobled by the
pope could count on being acknowledged by the Italian state
within a few years. This was the path chosen, for example, by

---

[23] Hermann Heller, *Europa und der Fascismus* (Berlin, 1929), 52.
[24] Mario Missori (ed.), *Gerarchie und statuti del P. N.F., Gran Consiglio, Direttorio nazionale,
Federazioni provinciali, quadri e biografie* (Rome, 1986).

Dino Alfieri, propaganda minister and later ambassador to Berlin; Alessandro Chiavolini; justice minister Alfredo Rocco; Luigi Federzoni, long-serving president of the Senate; and Pietro Fedele. If we deduct the recently ennobled, aristocrats accounted for less than 5 per cent of the fascist leadership elite.

Among aristocrats, by far the most prominent was Mussolini's son-in-law, Galeazzo Ciano, who was 25 years old when his father was ennobled. In 1939, on his father's death, Galeazzo Ciano himself became a count. The mechanisms that came into play in the process of ennoblement can be studied well in the case of Badoglio. This son of a small landowner from Piedmont had had a brilliant and rapid career during the First World War. As deputy general chief of staff in 1918, he had risen to become the closest associate of General Diaz (ennobled to become Duca della Vittoria in 1922). Badoglio, who had been promoted to general chief of staff, was ennobled in 1928 as Marchese di Sabotino. After the conquest of Abyssinia, he was to receive the title Duca di Addis Abeba in 1936. Pointing to Marshall Diaz in 1922 as a precedent, Badoglio demanded a heritable title, and a title for his eldest son. A protracted tug-of-war with the heraldry commission ended in a compromise: the son received the title Ducca dei Badoglio di Addis Abeba. In addition, Badoglio was granted for life the salary that he had received as supreme commander in north-east Africa.[25]

How did the representation of the aristocracy in the Chamber and the Senate change during the fascist period? Under assault from the new mass democracy, the aristocracy fell to a historic low of 5.3 per cent in 1919. According to Musiedlak's research, it slowly increased its share in subsequent legislative periods: 26th legislative period (1921–4) 6.6 per cent; 27th legislative period (1924–9) 9.6 per cent; 28th legislative period (1929–34) 12.5 per cent; 29th legislative period (1934–9) 12.0 per cent.[26] In the Camera dei fasci e delle Corporazioni, created in 1939 and comprising almost 1,000 members, the proportion of aristocrats fell below the 10 per cent mark.[27] The aristocratic presence in the Senate was much stronger. Of the 613 senators who were active between November 1922 and 1932, 29 per cent were members of

[25] Piero Pieri and Giorgio Rochat, *Badoglio* (Turin, 1974), 713–15.
[26] Musiedlak, *Lo stato fascista e la sua classe politica*, 137 ff.
[27] Ibid. 140.

the aristocracy. This figure dropped to 25 per cent between 1933 and July 1943.[28]

The fascist regime attempted to standardize the still extremely varied aristocratic landscape of Italy and to 'nationalize' the aristocracy. After yet another reorganization, the Consulta araldica was created in 1930. It consisted of fourteen members, including the presidents of the High Court of Appeal and the Senate Council, two members of the fascist State Council (Consiglio di Stato), two deputies from the Chamber, three representatives of the aristocracy, and three historians. In June 1943 the number of members of the Consulta was increased to eighteen.

The *Ordinamento dello stato nobiliare italiano*, passed in 1929, was intended to be a sort of basic law of the aristocracy.[29] It brought together and thus cancelled out numerous older decrees. Ennoblement continued to be an act of grace by the crown and a sign of the royal prerogative (*atti sovrani di grazia*). At the same time, however, the state ensured that it had the important right of control and confirmation through the person of the prime minister (*atti governativi di giustizia*). This ordinance provided, for the first time, for the loss or temporary suspension of an aristocratic title. Thus the older notion of nobility as an irrevocable distinction conferred by birth was abandoned. Those convicted of crimes against the king, the pope, or the prime minister were to lose their titles, as were those who 'gave up their Italian citizenship, or who were deprived of it'. It seems unlikely that any of these regulations was ever invoked. But it is clear that the world of the aristocracy was to be instrumentalized for the purpose of securing the regime. Among the anti-fascists who emigrated were such prominent aristocrats as Count Carlo Sforza, who resigned from his position as ambassador in Paris in October 1922 in protest at Mussolini's appointment. After his emigration to the USA, Sforza was among Mussolini's most dangerous journalistic opponents. As Italy's foreign minister from 1947 to 1951 and a close associate of De Gasperi, Sforza was to play a significant role in the rebuilding of Europe. In all these precautions, the aristocracy was granted 'a political–administrative role which the liberal state would never have wanted it to have'.[30]

---

[28] Musiedlak, *Lo stato fascista e la sua classe politica*, 140.

[29] Reprinted in Spreti (ed.), *Enciclopedia storico-nobiliare italiana*, vii. 60–74.

[30] Giorgio Rumi, 'La politica nobiliare del Regno d'Italia 1861–1946', in *Les Noblesses européennes*, 577–93, at 583.

In essence, the regime used the aristocracy as a symbol for the hierarchical model but did not regard it as a strategic factor. How useful the regime found the reflected brilliance of high aristocratic names is demonstrated by the fact that in both Milan and Rome, the majority of mayors and governors during the interwar period were drawn from local aristocratic families.

It can be assumed that for many Italian aristocratic families the 1920s and 1930s were a time of greater openness towards training, professional life, and integration into bourgeois society. In his study of the Piedmont aristocracy, Cardoza investigated the membership of the Turin Società del Whist, which included large sections of the regional aristocracy among its members and was so exclusive that it accepted hardly any bourgeois members (before 1914: 6 per cent; after 1922: 13 per cent). Lists of new admissions give some indication of the professional reorientation of the younger members of the aristocracy. Of the 292 aristocratic new admissions between 1919 and 1940, 38 (13 per cent) were employed in banking or industry. The proportion of members who had a university education rose from 28 per cent (1893–1914) to 46 per cent (1919–40). The most popular subject studied was law (27 per cent), but engineering and economics together accounted for more than 16 per cent. The number of marriages with non-aristocrats increased steadily. Industrial magnates such as Leumann, Mazzonis, and Rossi di Montelera married their daughters to the sons of the Piedmontese aristocracy.[31]

The Piedmontese aristocracy took a distanced, wait-and-see attitude to early fascism. None of its members were among the 'fascists of the first hour', and few aristocrats are to be found among the *fascisti antemarcia*, that is, those who joined the party before the march on Rome in October 1922. As the dictatorship stabilized after 1925, the Piedmontese aristocracy embarked on a course of cooperation. Eighty-six of the aristocratic members of the Società del Whist accepted political office. These included twenty-four mayors (*podestà*), four deputy mayors, ten provincial secretaries of the PNF, four secretaries of local *fasci*, fifteen members of industrial corporations (*corporazioni*), and twenty-nine in other functions.[32] The offices listed here suggest that the aristocrats involved were concerned mainly to secure local and

---

[31] Cardoza, *Aristocrats in Bourgeois Italy*, 220 ff.
[32] Ibid. 222.

economic positions of power. The Società del Whist granted Mussolini an honour denied to all Italy's liberal prime ministers: it made him an honorary member in 1928.[33]

Despite their renewed political prominence, the aristocrats who entered public life during the interwar period differed in important respects from their nineteenth-century predecessors. Measured by the traditional standards of their class, they were considerably less wealthy, leisured, service-orientated, and socially exclusive than their parents and grandparents. Unprecedented numbers of nobles no longer possessed the financial means to support their old genteel way of life. And even those titled families who remained financially well-off were much less likely still to constitute a landed aristocracy with their wealth and status in the countryside. By the late 1930s, the figure of the aristocratic landed gentleman of leisure had become much more the exception than the rule.[34]

On the whole, the aristocracy played a very modest, even marginal role in the fascist leadership. With the exception of a few names such as Gonzaga, Foscari, and Di Robilant, no members of the old Italian aristocratic families featured as representatives of the new system. We gain the impression that most regional aristocracies kept their distance from—or even openly rejected—fascism.

Historians of the period are aware of a number of aristocratic 'renegades' who, in the late nineteenth century and during the first half of the twentieth century, left the protection of their background for political or moral reasons. One of the most influential figures in this connection is Count Ranuccio Bianchi Bandinelli (1900–75), who belonged to an old aristocratic family from Siena. The *conte rosso* was considered the most important Italian archaeologist of his time, and as a Communist, was among the most prominent intellectuals of the Party, which he served as a member of the Central Committee for a number of years. Bianchi Bandinelli, who on his mother's side was descended from a German count's family, was considered to be one of Italy's most knowledgeable experts on Germany. In May 1938 he acted as guide to Mussolini and Hitler on their art history tours of Rome and Florence. In 1948 Bianchi Bandinelli published a diary which came out in a third, greatly expanded

---

[33] Cardoza, *Aristocrats in Bourgeois Italy*, 223.
[34] Ibid.

edition in 1996. It bears the programmatic title *Diario di un borghese*.[35] In these writings, it is possible to trace in detail how he left the world of the aristocracy. The provincial nature of the aristocratic world of Siena filled him with horror. Although he was considered one of the most eligible bachelors in the town, he married a bourgeois woman and bore with equanimity the resulting social ostracism and his exclusion from the Circolo dei nobili which his father had led as president. As a 23-year-old, Bianchi Bandinelli noted: 'inherited wealth is a dreadful thing. How can one have the courage to accept it? And how can one keep it without committing a hateful and cowardly act in one's own eyes and in those of thousands of the disinherited?'[36] After attending secondary school he resolved to study archaeology and to pursue a profession. The study of Antiquity seemed to him, who had rejected fascism from the start, to offer a suitable refuge and hiding place. 'I need to earn my living, and then I need . . . an official status behind which I can hide in order to be what I am, namely, someone as good as unsuited to the society in which I live.'[37] He regarded the future of the aristocracy with great scepticism. In 1931 he noted: 'the destruction of agricultural prosperity which is taking place in Italy at present, or is to be expected in future . . . will form one of the most significant watersheds in the Italian social constitution.'[38] When he inherited the family property on the death of his father in 1930 and gained an insight into the finances, he saw himself compelled to make crucial decisions. The considerable fortune inherited from his mother's side had already been dissipated by the inflation in Germany, and now the family was facing bankruptcy. That is why the palace in Siena was sold, but the profit realized hardly covered the outstanding debts. Bianchi Bandinelli concentrated what was left of his legacy on the family's country seat, the Villa Geggiano, which is still in the possession of the family today.

The change in elites which, we have assumed, took place after 1918, is confirmed from another source. Between 1860 and 1980 more than 200 books on manners and conduct were published in

---

[35] Ranuccio Bianchi Bandinelli, *Diario di un borghese: nuova edizione con i diari inediti 1961–1974* (Rome, 1996).
[36] Ibid. 17.
[37] Ibid. 23.
[38] Ibid. 27.

Italy, some of which achieved high print-runs over a long period of time. The authors were often aristocratic women such as Marchesa Colombi,[39] or E. Morozzo della Rocca Muzzatti.[40] In a society which, at the start, had an illiteracy rate of 80 per cent, this genre of literature was already being distributed by the hundreds of thousands. Norbert Elias has demonstrated the precision with which these sorts of books chart changes in social forms of behaviour. They were intended to offer the Italian bourgeoisie, which was just growing together, security in social relations, a feeling of identity, and orientation. The prescriptions for the *vera signora* and the *vero signore* were derived from the world of the aristocracy and the grand bourgeoisie, but, as a rule, were directed to the petit and middling bourgeoisie. According to Gabriela Turnatori, there were three clearly distinguishable periods in the impact of these conduct manuals.[41] Liberal Italy with its Victorian prudishness and decorum, and its apparent exclusion of the physical and sexual, differed markedly from the interwar period, when fascism, with its ideal of the *uomo nuovo*, postulated—and partly realized—a new lifestyle. The separation between private and public was frequently abolished, and the fascination with grand bourgeois and aristocratic lifestyles gave way to the petit bourgeois ideals of a *stile fascista*. As morals relaxed, adultery, lovers, and threesomes appeared as variants of behaviour that were tolerated. Sport, leisure, and politics also provided behavioural forms to be codified. What is interesting in our context is that during the fascist period the aristocracy lost its leading position as a model and, in the popular consciousness, was relegated to a marginal position. Instead of an aura of exclusivity and exemplariness, it was now surrounded by an air of yesterday and the antiquated. 'Today', wrote the *Enciclopedia Italiana* in l934, 'the nobility is no more than a historical memory. With few exceptions, it exists as a hereditary distinction only in states which are ruled as monarchies.'[42]

---

[39] Marchesa Colombi (pseud. for M. A. Torriani Torelli-Viollier), *La gente per bene: Leggi di convenienza sociale* (Turin, 1877; 18th edn., 1892).

[40] E. Morozzo della Rocca Muzzatti, *Signorilità* (Lanciano, 1928).

[41] Gabriela Turnatori, *Gente per bene: Cent'anni di buone maniere* (Milan, 1988).

[42] 'Nobiltà', in *Enciclopedia Italiana* (Rome, 1934), xxiv. 874.

III

The end of the monarchy came with the end of fascism. Against all expectations, Victor Emanuel III managed, at the last minute, in July 1943, to separate himself from Mussolini thanks to a successful *coup d'état*,[43] vindicating what Erwin von Beckenrath had foreseen in 1927: at a moment of deep crisis, the monarchy could act as a 'reserve of legality'. But the serious omissions in the armistice announced on 8 September 1943, and the king's and the government's precipitate and undignified flight from Rome to Brindisi put an extra burden on the dynasty, which was already deeply compromised by its decades of cooperation with fascism. The abdication of the king and a rapid transfer of the crown to his relatively uncompromised son, Umberto, might have strengthened sympathy for the monarchy in Italian society. But Victor Emanuel III offered stubborn resistance and did not transfer power to his son in the form of a regency until June 1944, when he was under the pressure of an Allied ultimatum. The anti-fascist opposition groups in exile had already switched to a republican course in 1927, in response to the fascist dictatorship sanctioned by the monarchy. Since then, the demand for an end to the monarchy had been part of the programme. That is why the vast majority of the resistance movement was republican. This division of power also shaped the committees of national liberation, on which the monarchists were not represented.

In the plebiscite of 2 June 1946, the monarchy lost, gaining 45.7 per cent as against 54.3 per cent of the votes. The south, which had a majority for the monarchy, faced a largely republican north. This vote brought old divisions and anti-Savoyard attitudes to light again. In conservative, Catholic Trentino, which had not joined Italy until 1919, the Habsburg monarchy had not been forgotten, and so the monarchy gained only 15 per cent of the vote. In Piedmont, by contrast, it gained 42.9 per cent. The only northern provinces in which a majority voted for the monarchy were also in Piedmont (Cuneo and Asti). Here the monarchy could still draw on a considerable capital of trust.

The fate of the aristocracy as an institution was sealed with

---

[43] Jens Petersen, 'Sommer 1934', in Hans Woller (ed.), *Italien und die Großmächte 1943–1949* (Munich, 1988), 23–48.

that of the monarchy. Article 14 of the transitional regulations in the constitution which came into force on 1 January 1948 reads: 'Aristocratic titles are not recognized. Titles which existed before 28 October 1922 now form part of the name. . . . The law will regulate the abolition of the Heraldic Council.' Thus after the monarchy, the nobility also quietly came to an end, almost without discussion. The planned law concerning the Heraldic Council never materialized. The institution as such continued to function for another ten years. In 1959 its archives were handed over to the Archivio Centrale dello Stato.[44] The constitutionally highly contradictory undertaking by the Italian state, based on the Concordat of 1929, to recognize aristocratic titles conferred by the pope in Italy also continued in force. An appendix to the *Gazzetta Ufficiale* no. 73 of 22 March 1961 lists registration costs. The notification of a *Principe* title cost 300,000 lire. A simple *Nobile* cost 40,000 lire.[45] The exiled King Umberto II, too, continued to use his right to confer titles. By 1977, he had ennobled about 170 Italians from his base in Caiscais (Portugal).[46]

It may be seen as a quasi-symbolic ending that in 1948 the Società del Whist merged with the leading bourgeois association in Turin, the Accademia Filarmonica, 'to form a great club, a meeting place for all the best elements in the city'. A few years later Turin was the setting for the brilliant wedding of the heir to the Fiat group, Giovanni Agnelli, grandson of the firm's founder, and Marella Caracciolo, an heiress from one of the oldest Neapolitan aristocratic families.

[44] Pericoli, *Titoli nobiliari*, 7.
[45] Ibid. 72 ff.
[46] Rumi, 'La politica nobiliare del Regno d'Italia', 585.

7

Aristocracy, Fascism, and the Franco Dictatorship (1931–1945)

CARLOS COLLADO SEIDEL

I *The Aristocracy and the 1931 Republic*

Until well into the twentieth century, the Spanish aristocracy enjoyed a traditional position of social and economic pre-eminence. The loss of political power in the context of liberal-revolutionary processes in the course of the nineteenth century, such as the abolition of feudal obligations, was not associated with any loss of property or reduction in the social position of the aristocracy. Enormous tracts of land, especially in the southern part of Spain, remained in its hands. The combination of a mainly agrarian traditional aristocracy and a newly created aristocracy active in the rising financial and industrial sectors meant that the aristocracy held a pre-eminent position in the country's economic life.[1] In addition, the aristocracy, whether the traditional 'purist' or the newly created which rapidly assumed and internalized the habits and behaviour of the class, had an elitist understanding of class and position. In this view, the aristocracy was entitled to a leading position in society on the basis of birth. Even Count Romanones, a leading political figure of the time who was considered a liberal in the system of the restoration period (1874–1923), held this view, justifying it by reference to atavistic features drawn from a tradition of ruling families dating back many centuries.[2]

However, despite its influential position in society and,

Translated by Angela Davies, GHIL.

[1] Among recent publications on Spanish social history, see Adrian Shubert, *A Social History of Modern Spain* (London, 1990), 57–90.

[2] Cf. Conde de Romanones, *Breviario de política experimental* (Madrid, 1974), 22–3.

increasingly, in industry, the aristocracy was under-represented in public life, with the exception of the diplomatic corps and the upper echelons of the officer corps.[3] This mismatch was noticed by contemporaries. In 1898 a member of the German aristocratic family Ungern-Sternberg pointed out:

> The Spanish aristocracy is exclusively a court aristocracy and does not find it necessary to be actively involved in state affairs. Only when an aristocrat is short of money does he try, by recommendations, to get a lucrative post. And when he has one, he sees it as almost shameful and degrading, because anyone who knows Spain must admit that work in itself is seen as socially degrading, and that the enjoyment of leisure while receiving a pension or sinecure confers the greatest respectability.[4]

Despite its wealth the aristocracy lived mainly on the fringes of society and had turned its back on everything that constituted society. Instead, the aristocracy spent its life amusing itself, seeking entertainment, and, as another contemporary pointed out, complaining about everything that could no longer be saved, without considering what might still be rescued.[5]

The aristocracy also held certain common values formed on their understanding of the social order. These were essentially drawn from the doctrines of the Catholic Church, the institution of the monarchy and the hierarchical principle inherent in it, and the concept of the family as the basis of a socio-political patriarchalism, with a strong touch of patriotism. Given that this is how the aristocracy saw itself, it is not surprising that it rejected in principle the demand of broad classes of the population for political and social participation, and did not recognize any need to reform the political system with the aim of integrating the masses. Repression was regarded as the only suitable response to the social and political articulations of the lower classes. In this view, any equalization of the social classes represented nothing less than sacrilege against the divinely willed order on earth. This revealed a clear dichotomy between the continued existence of traditional principles of order, and the processes of social change that were taking place. The aristocracy's world-view was extremely static, and it was incapable of recognizing the social reality of Spain, or

---

[3] See Shubert, *Social History*, 105–10; Pedro Carlos González Cuevas, *Acción Española: Teología política y nacionalismo autoritario en España (1913–1936)* (Madrid, 1998), 33–42.

[4] *Deutsches Handelsblatt*, 28 Aug. 1898.

[5] Cf. Francisco Fernández de Bethencourt, *Las Letras y los Grandes* (Madrid, 1914), 45 ff.

of assessing the forces that aimed, with the fall of the monarchy, to destroy the foundations of the aristocracy's social and economic power.[6]

In its first two years the Second Republic, set up in 1931, pursued a modernization programme based on the policies of the moderate leftist government of Manuel Azaña, focusing on social reform and the secularization of political life. As was to be expected, the aristocracy perceived both the setting up of the Republic and especially its modernization programme as the outcome of an unleashing of feelings of revenge and resentment on the part of an intellectual bourgeoisie that had so far lived a sad and miserable life and had now seized power. In response, the aristocracy, which had been profoundly shaken, began to radicalize and even to express itself politically. Every form of liberalism, not to mention representative democracy, was seen as a *bête noire*. In line with the logic of the aristocracy's view of itself, its political goal was to return to the order of the *ancien régime*.

The journal *Acción Española*, published by the Spanish intellectual Ramiro de Maeztu, was the mouthpiece of a movement advocating a restoration of the traditional monarchy and a return to the dominance of the aristocracy and the authority of the Catholic Church.[7] As a movement, Acción Española defined its goal as the creation of ideological foundations, described by González Cuevas as political theology, for a battle against the ideals of the Republic. Acción Española was thus a reaction to the threat that left-wing theoreticians were perceived as posing. As Ramiro de Maeztu wrote: 'We had not bothered about the soul which has to lead the swords. That is why we founded Acción Española. For us it was important first to create a feeling, ideas, and a doctrine.'[8]

The aristocracy participated in this project by providing money. Beyond this, however, for the first time some representatives of the traditional aristocracy were prepared to become actively involved. These included the Marquess of the Eliseda, the Marquess of Saltillo, the Marquess of the Marismas del

[6] Cf. Pedro Carlos González Cuevas, *Historia de las derechas españolas: De la Ilustración a nuestros días* (Madrid, 2000), 247 ff.

[7] On Acción Española see González Cuevas, *Acción Española*; id., *Maeztu: Biografía de un nacionalista español* (Madrid, 2003); Raul Morodo Leoncio, *Orígenes ideológicos del franquismo: Acción Española* (Madrid, 1985).

[8] *Acción Española*, 46, 1 Feb. 1934, quoted from González Cuevas, *Acción Española*, 148.

Guadalquivir, the Count of Rodezno, and the Marquess of Quintanar as the editor of the journal, to name just a few.[9] For Acción Española, however, it was clear that restoration could be achieved only by the use of violence, and so a conspiratorial core came into being beneath the ideological superstructure. Here Acción Española was influenced by L'Action française, and especially by the strategy developed by Charles Maurras. Acción Española therefore took up contact with subversive generals, and although as an organization it was not directly involved in the preparations for General Sanjurjo's putsch attempt in August 1932, a number of its members were, including the Marquess of the Eliseda and his father, the Count of the Andes.

After the failure of the putsch, the republican government initiated a wave of repression and passed the agrarian reform bill with clearly anti-aristocratic clauses added. As a result, preparations for a putsch were further intensified. At the end of September 1932 a group of monarchists, again including the Marquess of the Eliseda, met in French Biarritz to plan a new *coup d'état*. Subsequently, the Count of the Andes and the Marquess of Arriluce de Ibarra began collecting the money required to finance the plan. The exiled King Alfonso XIII was informed, and gave his approval. The aristocracy and members of the old, conservative establishment made a considerable financial commitment to the plan. Within a short time, the enormous amount of 20 million pesetas had been amassed.[10] According to González Cuevas, shortly afterwards this money made a crucial contribution to the birth of the Spanish fascist movement.

II *The Aristocracy and the Falange Española y de las JONS*

As in other European countries, a number of Spanish aristocrats favoured the idea of fascism, or at least, what they understood as fascism. Fascism offered itself as a political solution for dealing with the social upheavals and crises that had broken out after the First World War. In Spain, they had become especially virulent with the founding of the Republic.

Spain's first fascist circle was formed at the beginning of 1931,

---

[9] On this see Morodo Leoncio, *Orígenes ideológicos del franquismo*, 47 ff.
[10] See González Cuevas, *Historia de las derechas españolas*, 314.

that is, a few weeks before the proclamation of the Republic, and gave rise to the Juntas de Ofensiva Nacional-Sindicalista (JONS). At this time, however, it did not yet have any supporters among the aristocracy because of the nature of the political programme of this group around Ramiro Ledesma Ramos. Although full of nationalist slogans, it strongly approved of the abolition of the monarchy, and was also anticlerical. The intellectual pioneer and first theoretician of Spanish fascism, Ernesto Giménez Caballero, went so far as to see the first head of the republican government as the leader of a national revolution. Giménez was extremely hard on the aristocracy, which he saw as a useless group with no roots among the people.[11]

The second fascist group, that around José Antonio Primo de Rivera, was a slightly different case. José Antonio was the son of General Miguel Primo de Rivera, who had headed a dictatorship under Alfonso XIII between 1923 and 1930. After the death of the exiled dictator he inherited and adopted the title Marquess of Estella. His first political steps had been taken in the Unión Monárquica Nacional, which was composed largely of the dictator's former staff. Given their reservations about JONS, conservative and aristocratic circles saw José Antonio Primo de Rivera, who had turned to fascism on the Italian model and was a talented public speaker, as the ideal figure to lead a counter-revolutionary fascist party.

In August 1933, Pedro Sainz Rodríguez, a leading member of the group of monarchists who were actively working for the return of the exiled king, met José Antonio Primo de Rivera to come to an agreement about the creation of a fascist party. Thereafter, in Biarritz, Primo de Rivera met the central figures of Acción Española in order to agree on political activities. On this occasion, José Antonio was given part of the money that had previously been collected to support counter-revolutionary movements.[12] We are thus dealing with the reinforcement of the fascist movement by reactionary circles for the purpose of establishing an organization that would involve and lead the masses in order to restore the social order they wanted.

[11] See id., *Acción Española*, 200 ff.
[12] See Julio Gil Pecharromán, *José Antonio Primo de Rivera: Retrato de un visionario* (Madrid, 1996), 188 ff. (2nd edn., 2003); Ismael Saz Campos, *Mussolini contra la II República: Hostilidad, conspiraciones, intervención (1931–1936)* (Valencia, 1986), 63–4.

Fascism was considered a movement with a future, especially after Hitler's seizure of power in Germany in 1933. This is also made clear in a position paper written at the end of 1933 or the beginning of 1934, most likely by Juan Antonio Ansaldo, who soon left Acción Española to join Falange:

> Fascism has a much greater future than JONS, and for precisely this reason, we believe that it is important for us to infiltrate here because in the case of political forces it can happen that once they develop and begin to unfold a life of their own, they suddenly dispense with us. Nobody can predict what will happen when success goes to the leaders' heads. At present, this party can use us, and one day, its force will be helpful to us. But we must consider its development and growth so that we do not lose control and our position as supporters.[13]

If the idea of fascism was to spread in Spain, the restorationists wanted to be part of it and to guide developments in their own interests with the objective of abolishing the Republic. For the financiers, it was clear that the fascist party had to subordinate itself to their interests. Thus in their view the only purpose of Falange was to serve the aims of Acción Española. While the members of JONS came from the lower and middling bourgeoisie, Falange, reflecting the social background of José Antonio Primo de Rivera, contained members of the old establishment and also aristocrats from Acción Española. These included the Marquess of Eliseda, the Count of Foxá, Sancho Dávila as Count of Villafuente Bermeja, the Marquess of Merry del Val, José de la Mora Figueroa as Marquess of Tamarón, the Marquess of Zayas, and others.

At first, both Falange Española and JONS were supported by monthly payments, but the monarchists around Acción Española were not prepared to finance two fascist parties in the long term. Thus, despite resistance from the JONS leader, Ledesma Ramos, the financiers managed to achieve a fusion of the two groups to form Falange Española y de las JONS in February 1934. Thus, as an interim finding we can say that as in other European countries, during the early phase of Spanish fascism, different and sometimes contrary ideological views mingled and cooperated for a transitional period in their common struggle against liberalism, parliamentarism, and democracy—in short, the things that the Republic stood for.

---

[13] Quoted from González Cuevas, *Acción Española*, 213.

Soon however, the incompatibility between Falange Española y de las JONS and the aims of Acción Española became clear. In particular, the agnosticism and anti-monarchism of Ledesma Ramos, former leader of JONS, made the fascist party less and less acceptable to the monarchists and aristocrats. Furthermore, in his speeches Primo de Rivera put special emphasis on social justice and castigated capitalism in Spain, which alienated the traditional establishment. In addition, the Falange leader was accused of concentrating too much on rhetoric and not pushing street fighting as much as required. The monarchists, in particular, expected the Falange militias to be strengthened so that they could be used against leftist fighting units in order to destabilize and destroy the republican system.

These developments within Falange led the monarchists to attempt to overthrow Primo de Rivera in the summer of 1934, which resulted in a deep crisis of confidence between the two groups.[14] However, Falange was dependent on the monarchists, especially in financial aspects, and another agreement was reached on the basis of the understanding of August 1933. Primo de Rivera again undertook to support the political aims of the monarchists. In return, the leader of the Alfonsists, Antonio Goicoechea, promised to support the party financially. Primo de Rivera also declared that he was prepared to strengthen the paramilitary units, and even to accept a military adviser provided by the monarchists. But Primo de Rivera's refusal, a short time later, to join the National Bloc under José Calvo Sotelo, which was formed late in 1934 to unite all efforts, showed quite clearly that, ultimately, he was not ready to toe the traditionalist line.[15]

It was clear that a break was inevitable when the Falange's policy statement, issued late in 1934, lacked any reference to the monarchy, took a lay position, and announced far-reaching social reforms. In addition, the Falange emphasized that the party took precedence over all other political groups. Eliseda and other aristocrats who had joined the Falange were no longer prepared to carry on supporting the party line. Their view of the order to be set up was not compatible with the fascist idea that all components of society had to support the aims of the state, and that these took precedence even over the Catholic doctrine. Also, the ideal of a charismatic leader elevated to his position by the masses had no place in their world-view, which was derived from a hierarchical understanding of medieval feudalism. Consequently, Eliseda's 1935 assessment of Nazi ideology was that it was 'thoroughly materialistic and heathen', and that it was diametrically opposed to the Spanish character.[16] For the traditional aristocracy, fascism had provided merely an ideological framework to allow them to adapt to the demands of a capitalist society with the aim of securing the 'old order'.

The Spanish aristocracy and traditionalists therefore looked with admiration at Britain's social and political constitution. British society was perceived as strongly hierarchical. It was believed that strict limits were imposed on liberalism and parliamentarism, and that the aristocracy continued largely to control the state's use of force. The Marquess of the Eliseda had been to school in England and had studied at Oxford, with the result that he, too, was shaped and strongly influenced by English thought. A defender of corporatism and admirer of Italian fascism had made a particularly strong impression on Eliseda at the time—Harold Goad, largely forgotten today. Eliseda translated Goad's first book about the corporate state into Spanish, and published it in 1933.[17]

Ultimately, Primo de Rivera did not succeed in mobilizing the masses. Electoral success eluded him. In the elections to the Cortes held in November 1933, the first time that Falange Española took part, the result was a victory for the right-wing alliance. But the fascist party itself gained only two seats, those of Eliseda and Primo de Rivera. In addition, both owed their election to the personal patronage of the establishment and the patriarchal structures in their home constituencies. At the last elections before the outbreak of the Civil War, those of February 1936, Falange gained only 0.4 per cent of the vote.[18]

---

[16] Cf. Marqués de Eliseda, *Fascismo, Catolicismo y Monarquía* (San Sebastián, 1935), 191, 193. For Eliseda's ideological basis cf. Pedro Carlos González Cuevas, ' "Habitus" e ideología: El pensamiento político de Francisco Moreno y Herrera, Marqués de la Eliseda', *Cuadernos de Historia Contemporánea*, 18 (1996), 110.

[17] Cf. Harold Goad, *The Working of a Corporate State: A Study of National Cooperation* (London, 1933); id., *The Making of the Corporate State: A Study of Fascist Development* (London, 1932).

[18] Cf. Gil Pecharromán, *José Antonio*, 430.

III *The Aristocracy and the Franco Dictatorship*

The outbreak of the Civil War on 18 July 1936 placed fascism, and the aristocracy, into a completely new situation. Given a common enemy and a goal to which all nationalist forces could aspire, namely, victory over the republican order, the need to join forces was clear. The military leaders of the revolt achieved this, but it had lasting consequences both for the aristocracy, who wanted the restoration of the monarchy, and for the Falange.

The Falange underwent a fundamental change. The assassination of its charismatic leader José Antonio Primo de Rivera during the early stages of the revolt, and General Franco's forced merger, in April 1937, of Falange Española y de las JONS with traditionalist units whose hopes for a restoration focused on the Carlist pretender to the Bourbon throne, created a diffuse, ideological amalgam. The originally independent development of the party with totalitarian and revolutionary claims came to an abrupt end.[19] Now the party was under Franco's leadership, and it integrated and mobilized militia men and volunteers for the Front.

In fact, the Falange now experienced a popularity that had previously eluded it. It grew into a mass movement and became the most important political and paramilitary force in the 'national camp'. The Falange was the only permitted political organization and assumed key functions by controlling the press and taking over the trade union organizations and central areas of the administration, but it had to subordinate itself to the military leadership, whose position at the centre of power was now unchallenged. The Falange also had to accept far-reaching curtailments of its originally national-syndicalist, revolutionary aims. Thus the Falange was one, but by no means the most important, pillar in the power structure of the state. The Falange, in fact, had relatively little political weight in the Franco regime's power apparatus, as the party had not been a crucial instrument in helping the dictator to

---

[19] There is an extensive literature on the Spanish unitary party Falange. I shall here mention only some recent reference works: Stanley G. Payne, *Fascism in Spain, 1923–1977* (Madison, Wis., 1999); José Luis Rodríguez Jiménez, *Historia de Falange Española de las JONS* (Madrid, 2000); and Joan Maria Tomàs, *La Falange de Franco: Fascismo y fascistización en el régimen franquista (1937–1945)* (Barcelona, 2001).

achieve power. According to Stanley G. Payne, Spanish fascism never grasped power 'from below' as a mass party. At most, it attempted to penetrate the system as 'fascism from above'.[20]

The Marquess of the Eliseda and other aristocrats had been involved in preparations for the putsch. The aristocracy saw the military rising as offering deliverance from the evils of anarchy, democracy, liberalism, and other political ideals and ideologies perceived as 'un-Spanish' and destructive. In the area controlled by the rebels, in fact, the old social structure was immediately restored, the traditional values reinstated, and the central position of the Church reaffirmed. All measures that had affected the propertied elite, such as, for example, agrarian reform and expropriation proceedings, were revoked.

Even the son of Alfonso XIII and designated heir to the throne, Juan, arrived in Spain in August of 1936 to take part in the struggle as a volunteer, although General Mola, one of the leading thinkers in the putsch, forced him to leave the country. Mola and Franco wanted to avoid the national movement having a decidedly Alfonsist-monarchical character. Other members of the royal house, such as the Infantes Luis and José Eugenio of Bavaria and Borbón, fought on the side of the insurgents. Juan's brother-in-law, Infante Carlos of Borbón y Orleans, was killed in action. There were many aristocrats amongst the high-ranking generals, including several *Grandes*. As a matter of fact, however, these were mostly aristocrats of relatively recent date, and their ennoblement was usually the result of military achievements.

Thus, in addition to various Falangists, two leading monarchists sat in Franco's first cabinet, the leader of the Alfonsists, Pedro Sainz Rodríguez, as minister for education, and the leader of the Carlists, the Count of Rodezno, as minister for justice. General Franco indeed created unity which, before the outbreak of the Civil War, had been considered impossible. Thus Alfonsists, Carlists, and Falangists were united in the struggle against the Republic. Going beyond the fascism or totalitarianism debate, we can therefore appropriately use the concept of a 'reactionary coalition' to characterize the basic features of the Franco regime.[21]

---

[20] See Payne, *Fascism*, 476 ff.

[21] On this debate see Tomàs, *Falange*, 15–34, and Ismael Saz Campos, 'Fascism, Fascistization and Developmentalism in Franco's Dictatorship', *Social History*, 29 (Aug. 2004), 342–57.

However, the peace was illusory. Tensions between the Falange and the monarchists increased again as Nazism and Italian fascism gained control over Europe. The new leadership of the Falange under Ramón Serrano Suñer was given a boost by Axis victories, and aspired to expand its power base in Spain. Consequently, not only the aristocracy and the monarchists, but the Spanish generals in particular, felt that their leadership role was under threat. The tension was finally discharged in mid-August 1942, when a bomb was set off in the doorway of the chapel of Begoña near Bilbao, injuring many people. The target of the bomb plot was a group of highly placed monarchists, including army minister General Varela, who had been attending a memorial mass for deceased Spanish kings, while the plotters were from the ranks of the Falange. In the aftermath, Franco felt forced by pressure from the generals to take action against the Falange leadership. His own brother-in-law, Serrano Suñer, had to resign from his position as foreign minister and leader of the Falange.[22]

The monarchist and especially Alfonsist opposition, whose work towards a restoration of the monarchy was fully supported by the British ambassador, Sir Samuel Hoare, steadily gained power with the imminence of Allied victory. The monarchists regarded Franco as a transitional phenomenon. They conceded that he deserved great credit for his successful military leadership, but considered that now, with the end of the fascist period in sight, he would have to make way for the Alfonsist pretender to the throne.

After the death of Alfonso XIII in February 1941, Don Juan, as the dynastic heir, claimed the Spanish throne in autumn of 1942. At the beginning of March 1943 Don Juan also wrote to Franco, demanding that the monarchy quickly be restored in his person. Franco was not slow to react to the demands from Lausanne. In his speech opening the reintroduced corporative parliament on 20 March 1943, the dictator left no doubt that he would not give in to any of these demands. Franco emphasized the durability of the regime he had created, and stigmatized the traditional monarchy as politically decadent. In his written reply to Don

---

[22] Tusell was the first to point out that the reason for Serrano Suñer's resignation lay in domestic, not foreign politics. Cf. Javier Tusell and Genoveva García Queipo de Llano, *Franco y Mussolini* (Barcelona, 1985), 169.

Juan at the end of May 1943, he also made unmistakably clear that any restoration could take place only on the basis of the New State. Franco insisted on his legitimate right to lead the state, and to decide freely whether, and in what form, regime change should be introduced. The regime that he had set up, in any case, had no obligation to the monarchy, and certainly not to the Alfonsists. Don Juan, in turn, left no doubt that he was not prepared to submit to Franco's diktat or to accept a monarchy as a favour from Franco. Thus the question of the restoration seemed to move into an open confrontation.[23]

Given Franco's intractable attitude, a group of aristocrats and monarchists used the corporative parliament that had just been established, and whose composition had been determined by Franco, as a platform to air their demand for the restoration of the monarchy. In mid-June 1943 twenty-seven members of the Cortes, including the Duke of Alba as the highest-ranking Spanish nobleman, signed a petition entreating Franco to restore the monarchy before the end of the war. Franco not only did not grant this request, but he also punished those he could get hold of who had been involved in getting up the petition. The Marquess of the Eliseda, for example, who had been actively involved in gathering signatures, was banished to one of the Canary Islands for almost a year.[24] The next step was for the generals to take action. On 8 September 1943, the day on which the armistice between the Allies and Italy was announced, the former army minister General Varela handed the dictator a letter signed by himself and another seven of the highest-ranking generals. The letter urged Franco to give up the leadership of the state and clear the way for the restoration of the monarchy.[25] This initiative, too, came to nothing.

These attempts to persuade Franco to resign were motivated by the consideration that the continued existence of a regime considered as fascist beyond the end of the war would result in a threat to the status quo in Spain, which was seen as, on the whole,

---

[23] The correspondence between Franco and Juan, and further documents of central significance on this can be found in Laureano López Rodó, *La larga marcha hacia la Monarquía* (Barcelona, 1977).

[24] See González Cuevas, ' "Habitus" e ideología', 112.

[25] The letter carried the signatures of Luis Orgaz, Fidel Dávila, José Enrique Varela, José Solchaga, Alfredo Kindelán, Andrés Saliquet, José Monasterio, and Miguel Ponte. Text in López Rodó, *La larga marcha*, 43–4.

favourable. Franco, however, took the view that, as other liberated countries had shown, an over-hasty introduction of the monarchy would merely plunge Spain into chaos and civil war. Ultimately, neither the monarchists nor the generals dared to use force against Franco. While the monarchists were convinced of the need for the restoration of the monarchy in the person of Don Juan, they wanted to proceed only in agreement with the head of state and generalissimo. Ultimately, any violence against Franco was ruled out by the fear that it might give rise to general revolutionary unrest which would threaten the existing social order.

Foreign observers, too, perceived the fundamental problem faced by the monarchists. The US ambassador, Carlton Hayes, explained the regime's durability by reference to the deterrent effect of the memory of the Civil War, which was shared by conservative and even moderate republican forces alike, and tied their hands. The fear of a Communist revolution was deep-seated, he claimed, and was deliberately fomented by Francoist propaganda.[26] And, according to a British analyst, the proper-tied classes, in particular, although critical of the existing regime and the Falange, ultimately had no interest in endangering their personal situation.[27]

Just a few weeks before the end of the war, Don Juan made a last attempt to force change. On 19 March 1945, he addressed a manifesto to all Spaniards, appealing to them to refuse allegiance to Franco.[28] Don Juan and his advisers hoped for widespread support and that Franco would be cast out from the centre of the regime. The Infante Alfonso, as Juan's representative in Spain, instructed the members of the high aristocracy in Spain to resign their positions in the Francoist state.[29]

The disappointment was great. Hardly anyone responded to the appeal. On the contrary, many monarchists and aristocrats voiced their disapproval of the manifesto and justified their decision to continue supporting the regime with arguments resembling those used by the regime itself. Thus the absolute necessity

---

[26] Cf. Report Hayes to Hull, no. 3137, 26 Sept. 1944, National Archives, Washington, RG 59, 852.00/9–2644.

[27] Cf. Report Bowker to Eden, no. 681, 1 Nov. 1944, National Archives, Kew, FO 371, 39677, C 15433.

[28] The text of the manifesto can be found in López Rodó, *La larga marcha*, 48 ff.

[29] Cf. José María Gil Robles, *La Monarquía por la que yo luché (1941–1945)* (Madrid, 1976), 117.

for internal unity in the face of pressure from outside was stressed, as was Franco's achievement in saving traditional values. Franco's work, it was argued, would merely be endangered by over-hasty action. Above all, however, widespread disapproval was expressed of Don Juan's programme for democracy and political freedom. This programme promised a referendum on a constitution, recognition of basic human rights, a guarantee of free political activity, the creation of a parliament with legislative powers, recognition of regional differences, a general political amnesty, and far-reaching social reforms. None of this corresponded to the reactionary world-view of the aristocracy. Don Juan had outlined a programme which, in essence, promised precisely what the monarchists had supported Franco in the Civil War in order to prevent.[30]

A number of aristocrats, including Antonio Goicoechea, former representative of the exiled King Alfonso XIII, who was now governor of the Banco de España, went so far as openly to accuse the pretender to the throne of endangering the system created by Franco, which was satisfactory (except for the lack of a monarch). The majority of aristocrats shared Franco's view that the time for the return of the monarchy had not yet come, and they had even become accustomed to the idea of Franco as a regent. Political prospects without Franco seemed gloomy. Despite, or perhaps because of, the huge political pressure that was put on the Spanish regime from outside, they believed that Franco was the best guarantor of peace and order in the country.[31]

Very few resigned from their positions in response to the appeal. Those who did included the Duke of Alba, who since the Civil War had been ambassador to London, and regarded the Franco regime as a transitional solution on the way to a restoration of the monarchy. Juan's representative in Spain, the Infante Alfonso de Orleans, also resigned from his position as commander-in-chief and general of the air force region of Seville, although this step was

---

[30] Cf. joint letter from the Duke of Alcalá and the Marquess of Sotohermoso to the Infante Alfonso de Orleans [early Apr. 1945?], copy, Cambridge University Library (hereafter cited as CUL), Templewood Papers (hereafter Tem.) XIII, 27; letter from the Marquess of Villabrágima to Don Juan, 6 Apr. 1945, CUL Tem. XIII, 25.

[31] As examples cf. letter from Viscount of Rocamora to Antonio Goicoechea, 22 Apr. 1945, CUL Tem. XIII, 27; letter from Bernard Malley to Templewood, 8 May 1945, CUL Tem. XIII, 25; letter from the Marquess of Villabrágima to Don Juan, 6 Apr. 1945, ibid.

taken in response to Franco's order, and Alfonso was placed under house arrest. Once again, a wave of repression against monarchists ensued.

But the Falange had not achieved its aims in the war either, and now had to let things slip. Thus while it continued to exist, the disappearance of its main models in Italy and Germany meant that its influence suffered a severe blow, while the Church and the Catholic tradition regained almost complete dominance in Spanish society.

Apart from a small group of passionate supporters of Don Juan, the majority of the aristocracy, although they criticized the regime, had less reason than ever before to call for change. Thus shortly before his return to London, Sir Samuel Hoare,[32] who had actively worked for the restoration of the monarchy during his time as ambassador to Spain, noted with disappointment that he had never met so many people who professed to be monarchists, but in reality did not want to have a king at all.[33] In the end, the political and ideological goals of the aristocracy had been realized in the regime set up by General Franco.

[32] From June 1944, Lord Templewood.
[33] Cf. Carlton J. H. Hayes, *Misión de guerra en España* (Madrid, 1946), 342.

PART III

Central and Eastern Europe

8

'Only a dictator can help us now': Aristocracy and the Radical Right in Germany

ECKART CONZE

I

The public image of the German aristocracy during the Nazi period was long shaped by the events of 20 July and the high proportion of aristocrats involved in the conspiracy culminating in 1944. This has begun to change in recent years. It has frequently been pointed out, especially in the context of the sixtieth anniversary of the assassination attempt, how strongly aristocrats themselves were committed, after 1945, to stressing the aristocratic resistance to National Socialism. This has produced a view in which the history of the aristocracy under Nazism was practically identified with that of the resistance.[1] Additionally, a number of books have appeared—especially important among these is the work of Stephan Malinowski—in which the relationship between the aristocracy and National Socialism has, for the first time, been thoroughly examined. What has emerged is that large sections of the German aristocracy became more radically right wing after 1918. Furthermore, the ideas, expectations, and orientations that made possible the broad affinities between the aristocracy and National Socialism have been identified. These affinities must be counted among the major preconditions for the

---

Translated by Angela Davies, GHIL.

[1] Esp. important in this context is the critical debate about the role of Marion Gräfin Dönhoff in the commemoration and publicizing of resistance after 1945. On this see Eckart Conze, 'Aufstand des preußischen Adels: Marion Gräfin Dönhoff und das Bild des Widerstands gegen den Nationalsozialismus in der Bundesrepublik Deutschland', *Vierteljahrshefte für Zeitgeschichte*, 51 (2003), 483–508.

destruction of the Weimar Republic, the rise of National Socialism, and the stabilization of its power.[2]

Those aristocrats who early declared their support for National Socialism by joining the Nazi Party (NSDAP), the SS, SA, or other Nazi organizations, however, at first glance held a very different opinion of the majority of German aristocrats. Wolf Heinrich Graf von Helldorff, head of the SA in Berlin and later Berlin's police chief, had only contempt for most of his fellow aristocrats. As he wrote at the beginning of 1934:

> The majority of the aristocracy has come to accept the existing situation. Most of them came to terms with the Weimar Republic. For most of the aristocracy, and particularly the older generation, there was only the lesser evil that had to be accepted in order not to lose everything. Occasionally, on solemn national festivals, the uniforms of the old regiments would be taken out in order to keep up tradition, and tempered speeches were given to veterans' associations, expressing the hope that God would let better times return. . . . It was easier to believe that the Weimar Republic would create peace and order, and to change one's opinion a little for that sake. . . . It must be said clearly, once and for all, that the aristocracy, and especially the post-war generation, succumbed to the influences of liberalism and democracy with shocking speed.[3]

Helldorff's judgement cannot be read as a vindication of the aristocracy's honour. Helldorff himself, despite his later connections with the resistance, was one of the most evil aristocratic Nazis,[4] and is certainly not worth quoting as a vindicator. Yet his judgement indicates that the relationship between the aristocracy and the extreme right, and National Socialism in particular, cannot be reduced to a common denominator during the interwar period. This refers not only to the opposition between aristocratic opponents of the Weimar Republic and its few aristocratic supporters, or to that between aristocratic National Socialists and

---

[2] Stephan Malinowski, *Vom König zum Führer: Sozialer Niedergang und politische Radikalisierung im deutschen Adel zwischen Kaiserreich und NS-Staat* (Berlin, 2003). But cf. also various essays in Heinz Reif (ed.), *Adel und Bürgertum in Deutschland: Entwicklungslinien und Wendepunkte im 20. Jahrhundert* (Berlin, 2001), and in Eckart Conze and Monika Wienfort (eds.), *Adel und Moderne: Deutschland im europäischen Vergleich im 19. und 20. Jahrhundert* (Cologne, 2004).

[3] 'Wolf Heinrich Graf v. Helldorf', in Friedrich Christian Prinz zu Schaumburg-Lippe (ed.), *Wo war der Adel?* (Berlin, 1934), 43–8, at 45.

[4] On Helldorff see the biographical sketch by Ted Harrison, '"Alter Kämpfer" im Widerstand: Graf Helldorff, die NS-Bewegung und die Opposition gegen Hitler', *Vierteljahreshefte für Zeitgeschichte*, 45 (1997), 385–423.

members of the resistance. It also refers to the very different forms of aristocratic right-wing radicalization; to the motives behind them; the forms and paths they took; and the preconditions and shape of aristocratic contacts with the radical right, namely, the affinity between the aristocracy and the radical right.

It would be too simple to explain this wide spectrum, the many facets of the relationship between the aristocracy and the radical right, merely in terms of individual biographies. Yet the methods of individual or group biography certainly offer a good approach to the analysis of the political behaviour of members of the aristocracy after 1918. A combination of biographical and history-of-experience approaches holds the key to the explanation of political orientations and patterns of political behaviour among the aristocracy as well as others,[5] and certainly not only for the period after 1918. The history of the aristocracy need not necessarily be written as the history of its attempt, over hundreds of years, to stay 'on top', to use Werner Sombart's much quoted phrase.[6] But the political, social, and economic pressure to which the aristocracy was subjected, especially from the nineteenth century (to justify itself, to assert itself, and to conform) increased from 1918 to a previously unprecedented level. To this extent the story of the relationship between the aristocracy and the radical right is also a story of dealing with the experience of growing pressure. It is the story of the aristocracy's chances of keeping solid ground under its feet by means of cultural stability at times of fundamental political and social change—but also of the limits of this process. After the First World War, for the aristocratic individual and the aristocracy as a collective, what Reinhart Koselleck has called horizon of expectation (*Erwartungshorizont*) and experiential space (*Erfahrungsraum*) were less related to each other than ever

---

[5] Cf. e.g. Wencke Meteling, 'Der deutsche Zusammenbruch 1918 in den Selbstzeugnissen adeliger preußischer Offiziere', in Conze and Wienfort (eds.), *Adel und Moderne*, 289–321; Rainer Pomp, 'Brandenburgischer Landadel und die Weimarer Republik: Konflikte um Oppositionsstrategien und Elitenkonzepte', in Kurt Adamy and Kristina Hübener (eds.), *Adel und Staatsverwaltung in Brandenburg im 19. und 20. Jahrhundert: Ein historischer Vergleich* (Berlin, 1996), 185–218; or Eckart Conze, *Von deutschem Adel: Die Grafen von Bernstorff im 20. Jahrhundert* (Stuttgart, 2000), esp. 149–88; and, of course, Malinowski, *Vom König zum Führer, passim.*

[6] Rudolf Braun, 'Konzeptionelle Bemerkungen zum "Obenbleiben": Adel im 19. Jahrhundert', in Hans-Ulrich Wehler (ed.), *Europäischer Adel 1750–1950* (Göttingen, 1990), 87–95; Eckart Conze, 'Niedergang und "Obenbleiben"', in id. (ed.), *Kleines Lexikon des Adels: Titel, Throne, Traditionen* (Munich, 2005), 187–8.

before. Not only the traditional experiences of crisis, which the aristocracy had faced for centuries, but new types of experiences of loss and of what Peter Sloterdijk has called experiences of disturbance (*Störerfahrungen*) unbalanced the relationship between horizon of expectation and experiential space which, for the aristocracy, had been relatively stable, or at least, relatively easy to restabilize.[7]

In this essay I shall attempt to combine approaches from the history of experience with an examination of the German aristocracy's habitual and mental dispositions in order to help us to define the relationship between the German aristocracy and the radical right more precisely. The history-of-experience approach will emphasize the German perspective; the aristocratic experiential space is regarded as primarily a national experiential space, without, of course, excluding from the analysis the possibility of regional, or even local, experiences. In addition, the issue of aristocratic mental and habitual dispositions helps to explain its proximity to or distance from the radical right, provides a way out of the national bottleneck, and offers starting points or criteria for a European comparison. That, of course, is beyond the scope of this essay. None the less, it is important to identify such comparative criteria clearly so that the juxtaposition of national histories can develop into a true comparison. The analysis of transfer processes—which are also within the thematic range of this volume—is a different, but no less important challenge.

II

Even before 9 November 1918, ever since the late summer of the same year, the stab-in-the-back myth (*Dolchstoßlegende*) had begun to take shape, at first among the Prussian-German officer corps, which was still dominated by the aristocracy. The feelings that cavalry captain Andreas Graf von Bernstorff confided to his diary on 11 October were by no means unique:

---

[7] See Reinhart Koselleck, '" Erfahrungsraum" und "Erwartungshorizont"—zwei historische Kategorien', in id., *Vergangene Zukunft: Zur Semantik geschichtlicher Zeiten* (4th edn.; Frankfurt am Main, 2000), 349–75; Peter Sloterdijk, *Literatur und Organisation von Lebenserfahrung: Autobiographien der zwanziger Jahre* (Munich, 1978), 113–14.

In Germany, every truly loyal German (*treudeutsch*) man naturally hangs his head in shame that our Jewish–Social Democratic government has destroyed everything that the sword achieved. All the sacrifice in vain! The army can no longer fight willingly if there is no will for victory at home, only an anxiety that Germany should not gain anything in this war.[8]

Even before the establishment of the Weimar Republic, this attitude was a burden on it and the political forces that supported it because military defeat was interpreted as the result of an illegitimate *coup d'état*. Also, it separated the end of the monarchy and the founding of the Republic from the abuses and problems of the Kaiserreich and the actions of its ruling classes. In talk of the stab-in-the-back, which pervaded not only the early history of the Weimar Republic like a theme with variations, old and deeply rooted resentments, in the case of the aristocracy, against liberal democracy, parliamentarism, and the 'unpatriotic fellows' (*vaterlandslose Gesellen*) of the Social Democratic Party (SPD) combined with a search for explanations for the problems and troubles, the actual or imagined experiences of loss and decline in the present.[9]

Beyond this, the stab-in-the-back was also a mechanism for easing one's own burden by shifting the blame for the current situation, both individual and collective, onto others, while deflecting it from the forces and actors of one's own in-group. For those aristocrats, in particular, for whom war's end and revolution had come as a dramatic interruption of life plans and career prospects (especially in the armed forces), such attributions of blame and justifications for social decline were of central significance. The war had not, as hoped and expected, stabilized the old regime; it had not placed the political and social status of the aristocracy on a

---

[8] Andreas Graf Bernstorff (1868–1945), unpublished diary, Tagebuch, x. 57, 11 Oct. 1918.

[9] On this in general see Friedrich Freiherr Hiller von Gaertringen, ' "Dolchstoß"-Diskussion und "Dolchstoß"-Legende im Wandel von vier Jahrzehnten', in id. and Waldemar Besson (eds.), *Geschichte und Gegenwartsbewußtsein: Historische Betrachtungen und Untersuchungen. Festschrift für Hans Rothfels zum 70. Geburtstag* (Göttingen, 1963), 122–60; Detlef Lehnert, 'Propaganda des Bürgerkrieges? Politische Feindbilder in der Novemberrevolution als mentale Destabilisierung der Weimarer Demokratie', in id. and Klaus Megerle (eds.), *Politische Teilkulturen zwischen Integration und Polarisierung: Zur politischen Kultur der Weimarer Republik* (Opladen, 1990), 61–101, esp. 63–8; a recent comprehensive account is Boris Barth, *Dolchstoßlegenden und politische Desintegration: Das Trauma der deutschen Niederlage im Ersten Weltkrieg 1918–1933* (Düsseldorf, 2003).

new basis. The end of the monarchy and the Weimar Republic's numerous constitutional and legal regulations that curtailed or abolished the privileges of the aristocracy, and, from the point of view of the state, at least placed its special socio-political role in question, hit the whole of the aristocracy as a group. The arguments associated with the stab-in-the-back, and their function of consolidating a group which could see itself as a victim of defeat in war and revolution, of democracy and parliamentary constitution, should be placed in the context of the attempt to rebuild a collective identity, and to boost the solidarity and homogeneity of social groups, which was especially important for the aristocracy.

This adoption of the role of victim and the anti-republicanism it led to are significant for the political radicalization of the German aristocracy. The view that one was a victim (*Opfer*) of 'left-wing' machinations easily combined with other *Opfer* topoi: talk of the aristocracy's 'blood sacrifice' (*Blut-Opfer*) on the battlefields of the world war, which had proved to be in vain.[10] And here there were opportunities for linking up with Nazi sacrifice myths and cults of the victim and the fallen. The Prussian-German military aristocracy, in particular, the foundations of whose existence had been shattered by demilitarization after 1918, would have been attracted by the ideas of 'soldierly-militant leadership' circulating everywhere in *völkisch* national circles, but particularly in the rising Nazi movement.[11] Such ideas of a new leadership combined easily with anti-Semitism, which was an integral part of the stab-in-the-back myth. Marcus Funck has recently spoken of a 'racial-national warrior community'.[12] This goes far beyond the old thesis of the brutalization of Weimar politics and society by the experience of the Front, and the argument that the violence of war continued straight on into post-war

[10] Cf. also Marcus Funck, 'Schock und Chance: Der preußische Militäradel in der Weimarer Republik zwischen Stand und Profession', in Reif (ed.), *Adel und Bürgertum*, 127–71, esp. 139–42; and Meteling, 'Der deutsche Zusammenbruch'. The German word *Opfer* means both 'victim' and 'sacrifice'; this is a prerequisite for the widespread German *Opfer* discourse.

[11] See Marcus Funck, 'The Meaning of Dying: East Elbian Noble Families as "War Tribes" in the Nineteenth and Twentieth Centuries', in Matt Berg and Greg Eghigian (eds.), *Sacrifice and National Belonging in Twentieth-Century Germany* (College Station, Tex., 2001), 26–63.

[12] Ibid. Cf. also Marcus Funk, 'Vom Höfling zum soldatischen Mann: Varianten und Umwandlungen adeliger Männlichkeit zwischen Kaiserreich und Nationalsozialismus', in Conze and Wienfort (eds.), *Adel und Moderne*, 205–35, esp. 225–34.

society.[13] And in the present context this is of special importance because, beyond all the career opportunities which Nazi policy for war and rearmament offered after 1933, especially to the aristocracy from the regions east of the Elbe, it helps to explain the attractiveness of Nazi ideas long before 1933.

Scholars have repeatedly pointed to anti-Bolshevism as the force driving the right-wing radicalization of the aristocracy,[14] and this is not to be denied. But in the years after the First World War, anti-Bolshevism was not specific to the right—neither the old nor the new variant. Rather, we can speak of a basic anti-Bolshevik consensus in the Weimar Republic, shared by all political and social groups except the extreme left. Thus anti-Bolshevism is more than a simple explanation for the closeness between the aristocracy and National Socialism. While there was a specifically aristocratic-agrarian anti-Bolshevism, centred on the issue of expropriation of land,[15] it must soon have become clear to the German landowning aristocracy that a German revolution would not be a copy of the Russian one. Friedrich Ebert was not Lenin. If, nevertheless, the October revolution was repeatedly invoked as a threat by the aristocracy, among others, this was because soon after 9 November the spectre of Bolshevism was a weapon effectively deployed in the political debate to defame political opponents and justify particular interests and intentions. The most radical opponents of the Republic and democracy could hide behind the basic anti-Bolshevik consensus; anti-Bolshevism could camouflage the most radical goals, which could be made to look attractive and presentable.[16]

---

[13] Cf. e.g. Gerhard Schulz, *Aufstieg des Nationalsozialismus: Krise und Revolution in Deutschland* (Frankfurt am Main, 1975), 286–8; George L. Mosse, 'Der Erste Weltkrieg und die Brutalisierung der Politik: Betrachtungen über die politische Rechte, den Rassismus und den deutschen Sonderweg', in Manfred Funke et al. (eds.), *Demokratie und Diktatur: Geist und Gestalt politischer Herrschaft in Deutschland und Europa. Festschrift für Karl Dietrich Bracher* (Düsseldorf 1987), 127–39, or Bernd Hüppauf, 'The Birth of Fascist Man from the Spirit of the Front: From Langemarck to Verdun', in John Milfull (ed.), *The Attractions of Fascism: Social Psychology and Aesthetics of the Triumph of the Right* (New York, 1990), 45–76.

[14] As examples cf. Heinz Reif, *Adel im 19. und 20. Jahrhundert* (Munich, 1999), 52–3; Iris Freifrau von Hoyningen-Huene, *Adel in der Weimarer Republik: Die rechtlich-soziale Situation des reichsdeutschen Adels 1918–1933* (Limburg, 1992), 106–7.

[15] Important on this is Shelley Baranowski, *The Sanctity of Rural Life: Nobility, Protestantism, and Nazism in Weimar Prussia* (New York, 1995).

[16] For more detail on this see Conze, *Von deutschem Adel*, 29–50. More general: Heinrich August Winkler, *Weimar 1918–1933: Die Geschichte der ersten deutschen Demokratie* (Munich, 1993), 33–68.

Finally, we have to look at the decline of the monarchy, and at the abdication of the Kaiser and the German princes as an aristocratic experience of loss which drove the process of political radicalization forward. Could a monarchism whose political aim was to restore the monarchy which had existed in Germany before 1914 build bridges between the aristocracy and the radical right? To see monarchism and attempts to restore the monarchy in Germany as a characteristic feature only of the conservative, 'old' right is inadequate.[17] It was not only the call to establish the *Vaterlandspartei* (Patriotic Party) in 1917 that climaxed in a declaration of loyalty to the Kaiser and the Reich.[18] At first, large sections of the *völkisch* right could not imagine replacing the Weimar Republic with anything but a restoration of the monarchy, and this form of monarchism was associated with ideas of a charismatic leadership. Exactly this provided the bridge for the aristocracy, and especially for the younger generation, born around 1890/1900, which denounced the decadence of Wilhelminism. This generation could not see a monarch like Wilhelm II as a model and, after the Kaiser's flight and abdication, accused him of betraying the people.[19] Of course, neither Crown Prince Wilhelm of Prussia, the Kaiser's eldest son, nor other Hohenzollern princes were suitable new monarchs in the eyes of these aristocrats. This led increasingly to a search for a replacement monarch, for a different charismatic *Führer* figure who, with a strong hand, would not only restore the lost order, but also unify the people behind him and lead the Reich to new greatness. 'Only a dictator can help us now', wrote Andreas von Bernstorff in 1928, 'someone who will sweep away this international bunch of parasites with an iron broom. If only, like the Italians, we had a Mussolini!'[20] The German aristocracy's reception of Italian fascism is a topic that

---

[17] On monarchism in the Weimar Republic see, in general: Friedrich Freiherr Hiller von Gärtringen, 'Zur Beurteilung des Monarchismus in der Weimarer Republik', in Gotthard Jasper (ed.), *Tradition und Reform in der deutschen Politik: Gedenkschrift für Waldemar Besson* (Frankfurt am Main, 1976), 138–85, and Hermann Schreyer, 'Monarchismus und monarchische Restaurationsbestrebungen in der Weimarer Republik', *Jahrbuch für Geschichte*, 29 (1984), 291–320. For aristocractic monarchism more specifically see Malinowski, *Vom König zum Führer*, 247–59, 504–16.

[18] Heinz Hagenlücke, *Deutsche Vaterlandspartei: Die nationale Rechte am Ende des Kaiserreichs* (Düsseldorf, 1997).

[19] Cf. Martin Kohlrausch, 'Die Flucht des Kaisers: Doppeltes Scheitern adelig-bürgerlicher Monarchiekonzepte', in Reif (ed.), *Adel und Bürgertum*, 65–101.

[20] Bernstorff, Tagebuch, xviii. 27, no date (*c*.1 Mar. 1928).

merits closer investigation. Bernstorff's position, however, suggests that Mussolini's seizure of power in Italy helped to dissolve traditional monarchism among the German aristocracy, especially as the establishment of the fascist dictatorship did not formally put an end to the Italian monarchy. The Count Bernstorff quoted here, born in 1868, also shows us that the alienation from the Hohenzollern empire and monarchy, and from monarchism as such, was not, as is often claimed, limited to the younger generation of aristocrats. The restoration of the Hohenzollern was a political project whose aim was to transform the Republic in an authoritarian way, and the longer the Republic lasted, the greater the political significance of this project became. This political monarchism was largely promoted by aristocratic politicians, especially those in the Deutschnationale Volkspartei (DNVP; German National People's Party). Its primary aim, however, was to sweep away the Republic, not to restore the Hohenzollern dynasty.

This glance at aristocratic monarchism and its mutation into a search for a charismatic *Führer* would be incomplete, however, if we did not mention that monarchist attitudes could also be an obstacle to a rapprochement between the aristocracy and the Nazi movement. This was especially true in the case of the Bavarian aristocracy, which made up a significant proportion of the monarchist and legitimist movement in Bavaria. It is typical that plans for a monarchist *coup d'état* in Bavaria in February–March 1933 aimed to prevent a Nazi dictatorship, not to strengthen it.[21] Monarchism as such thus neither encouraged friendly relations between the aristocracy and the radical right, nor prevented them. Thus our analysis must look at the individual monarchists involved, and ask what the motives behind their monarchism were. Was their primary goal to restore the monarchy, or to abolish the Republic? What were the sources feeding their monarchism?

---

[21] On Bavarian monarchism see Robert S. Garnett, *Lion, Eagle, and Swastika: Bavarian Monarchism in Weimar Germany* (New York, 1991); Karl Otmar Freiherr von Aretin, 'Die bayerische Regierung und die Politik der bayerischen Monarchisten in der Krise der Weimarer Republik 1930–1933', in *Festschrift für Hermann Heimpel zum 70. Geburtstag am 19. September 1971*, Veröffentlichungen des Max-Planck-Instituts für Geschichte, 36 (Göttingen, 1971), 205–37; Erwin Freiherr von Aretin, *Krone und Ketten: Erinnerungen eines bayerischen Edelmannes* (Munich, 1955); and Rudolf Endres, 'Der Bayerische Heimat- und Königsbund', in Andreas Kraus (ed.), *Land und Reich, Stamm und Nation: Probleme und Perspektiven bayerischer Geschichte. Festgabe für Max Spindler zum 90. Geburtstag* (Munich, 1984), iii. 415–36.

In seeking an answer to this question, the religious-denomina-
tional argument quickly comes to hand. For our wider thematic
context, too, the literature and the Catholic aristocracy have
repeatedly pointed to the significance of denomination. It is
claimed that the Protestant aristocracy had a greater affinity for
Nazism,[22] while the Catholic aristocracy kept their distance, at
least relatively.[23] More recent studies, however, suggest that this
argument is too simplistic. What may have been true for most of
the Bavarian Catholic aristocracy certainly did not apply to the
Catholic aristocracy of Westphalia.[24] After the First World War,
significant sections of the Westphalian aristocracy broke their ties
with their Catholic milieu and its political representative, the
Zentrumspartei (Centre Party), and, as Larry Jones has put it,
became 'integral components of the alliance that Hitler and the
Nazis forged with Germany's conservative elites'.[25] However,
this is simply asserted, rather than explained. Does the fact that
Westphalia was part of Prussia for a hundred years provide a key
to the explanation of the behaviour of the Westphalian aristocracy, which was undoubtedly on the extreme right-wing fringe of
the Catholic aristocracy? The most radical members of the
Westphalian aristocracy did not allow themselves to be outdone
in distancing themselves from the Prussian-East Elbian aristocracy. Perhaps nineteenth-century nation-building and nationalization processes could provide an explanation. After all, they
penetrated deeper into the aristocracy of northern and western
Germany—whether Catholic or Protestant—than into that of
the south and south-west. Correlations can be drawn between
the north–south divide among the German aristocracy in terms
of material wealth, and differences in fundamental political and
ideological positions. And finally, what part did proximity to, or
distance from, the people play, in a role which the aristocracy
claimed for itself? In the course of the nineteenth century, for

---

[22] See e.g. Baranowski, *The Sanctity of Rural Life*.

[23] See e.g. Friedrich Keinemann, *Soziale und politische Geschichte des westfälischen Adels 1815–1945* (Hamm, 1975), and id., *Vom Krummstab zur Republik: Westfälischer Adel unter preußi-scher Herrschaft 1802–1945* (Bochum, 1997); cf. also Gerhard Kratzsch, *Engelbert Reichsfreiherr von Kerckerinck zur Borg: Westfälischer Adel zwischen Kaiserreich und Weimarer Republik* (Münster, 2004).

[24] On this see esp. Malinowski, *Vom König zum Führer*, 385–94.

[25] Larry E. Jones, 'Catholic Conservatives in the Weimar Republic: The Politics of the Rhenish-Westphalian Aristocracy, 1918–1933', *German History*, 18 (2000), 60–85, at 85.

example, the Westphalian aristocracy had developed a closeness to the people in order to stabilize its political and social status. Did this closeness, including anti-Semitic elements, create a greater predisposition towards a radical right-wing orientation than an emphasis on social hierarchies and aristocratic superiority, which even paternalism could not change?[26] The explanatory power of the sectarian argument which, in the context of German history since the Reformation, seems to have acquired the qualities of a passe-partout, here approaches its limits.

III

For a moment it seemed that even the aristocracy could be reconciled with the Republic in Germany. When Hindenburg was elected president in 1925, it was not only members of the East Elbian, Protestant aristocracy, such as Andreas Graf Bernstorff, who regarded this as 'salvation'.[27] The family of the Westphalian aristocrat and Centre Party politician Kerckering zur Borg wrote: 'We are very happy that Hindenburg has been elected and have hung a black, white, and red flag out on the roof.'[28] Hindenburg was a figure with whom the nationalist right, and with it, large sections of the German aristocracy, could identify in the mid-1920s, however much this was to change later. In his person, the aged president brought together the expectations, hopes, and ideas of both the 'old' and the 'new' right. He could be considered a representative of the defunct Prussian-German empire, of the Hohenzollern family, or of old Prussian traditions, primarily military ones. Yet at the same time he stood for the idea of a military monarchy or military dictatorship with mass support, for the ideals of a soldierly charismatic leadership, and, thus, if not for the abolition of the Weimar Republic, then at least for a different republic.[29]

---

[26] On this see Heinz Reif, *Westfälischer Adel 1770–1860: Vom Herrschaftsstand zur regionalen Elite* (Göttingen, 1979), 398–456; and id., 'Der katholische Adel Westfalens und die Spaltung des Adelskonservatismus in Preußen während des 19. Jahrhunderts', in Karl Teppe and Michael Epkenhans (eds.), *Westfalen und Preußen: Integration und Regionalismus* (Paderborn, 1991), 107–24.

[27] Bernstorff, Tagebuch, xvii b. 40, no date (*c*.1 May 1925).

[28] Quoted from Kratzsch, *Engelbert Reichsfreiherr von Kerckerinck zur Borg*, 153.

[29] On this see Wolfram Pyta, 'Paul von Hindenburg als charismatischer Führer der deutschen Nation', in Frank Möller (ed.), *Charismatische Führer der deutschen Nation* (Munich, 2004), 109–47.

Hindenburg's election and the temporary political and economic stabilization of Germany that it brought about allowed the animosity towards the Weimar Republic of the aristocracy, and other social groups, to fade into the background for a time. However, this should not obscure the fact that a social and cultural anti-modernism—which, incidentally, long predated the Weimar Republic—was by no means moderated, let alone eliminated, by Hindenburg's presidency. The individual elements of this socio-cultural anti-modernism, ranging from hostility to big cities to anti-Americanism and anti-capitalism, continued and were constantly reconfirmed by the aristocracy's perceptions of the times. This aristocratic anti-modernism was not only a parallel phenomenon to the *völkisch* anti-modernism of the 'new right', but closely connected with it. The crucial link was anti-Semitism, which was increasingly being enlisted by the aristocracy, among others, not only to explain political developments (such as the 1918 revolution), but also to interpret social and cultural perceptions of crisis, and thus to confront the aristocracy's own experiences of loss and decline. From here it was but a small step to crude *völkisch* anti-Semitic conspiracy theories. 'Jewish morality equals the decline of the *Volk* and racial decay,' Andreas von Bernstorff stressed.[30] And further: 'The Jewish Moloch works constantly at our destruction. This is not the individual Jew, but international Jewry with enormous financial resources, the Jews as a race.'[31] This was neither an 'upper-class anti-Semitism' nor a specifically aristocratic anti-Semitism, but the *völkisch*-racist anti-Semitism of the radical right,[32] which, recent research has revealed, had already infiltrated a number of German aristocratic organizations in the years just before the First World War;

---

[30] Bernstorff, Tagebuch, xvii a. 162, 14 June 1924.

[31] Ibid.

[32] Aristocratic anti-Semitism is mentioned by Heinz Reif, 'Antisemitismus in den Agrarverbänden Ostelbiens während der Weimarer Republik', in id. (ed.), *Ostelbische Agrargesellschaft im Kaiserreich und in der Weimarer Republik: Agrarkrise, junkerliche Interessenpolitik, Modernisierungsstrategien* (Berlin, 1994), 379–411, esp. 381; Christof Dipper speaks of 'upper-class anti-Semitism', in his essay, 'Der Widerstand und die Juden', in Jürgen Schmädecke and Peter Steinbach (eds.), *Der Widerstand gegen den Nationalsozialismus: Die deutsche Gesellschaft und der Widerstand gegen Hitler* (3rd edn.; Munich, 1994), 598–616, esp. 599. The anti-Semitism of, for example, Andreas Graf Bernstorff and the DAG cannot be described as specifically aristocratic or as 'upper-class anti-Semitism'. We should be wary, in this context, of introducing distinctions that do not fully stand up to scrutiny and may make light of the phenomenon. On this cf. Conze, *Von deutschem Adel*, 160–3.

above all, the Deutsche Adelsgenossenschaft (DAG), which in terms of numbers was the most significant of these organizations.[33] What Shulamit Volkov has called the 'anti-Semitic code' in the interpretation of the world and the times among large sections of the German aristocracy, and among the *völkisch*-nationalist right, was identical.[34] For large parts of the German aristocracy, the Nazis' racial anti-Semitism was neither new nor something they had to get used to.

The 'new aristocracy' that repeatedly turned up in the drafts for a social order drawn up by the *völkisch* right, in particular, when the political and social elites were being discussed, was also defined in racial and biological terms. The discourse on the new aristocracy as such was not an invention of the 'new right'. Since the nineteenth century, ideas about the creation and composition of a German elite had repeatedly circled around the idea of a 'new aristocracy'. Of course, the weakness or the actual or assumed disappearance of the old aristocracy was the precondition for the lasting search for a 'new aristocracy', a 'true aristocracy', or a 'real aristocracy'. The notions of a new aristocracy that arose against the background of revolution and the founding of the Weimar Republic were not only anti-republican, anti-democratic, and anti-pluralist; they also combined a conservatism that, to start with, was primarily orientated towards restoration and monarchism with the authoritarian social models of the 'new right'.[35]

The redefinition and reconstruction of the aristocracy as an elite was especially strongly influenced by the *völkisch* stock of ideas for a number of reasons. Under the conditions of a republic, it had become difficult to revert to the orientation towards the state that had dominated among the aristocracy before 1918. Precisely because the aristocracy had so long seen itself as a class

---

[33] On anti-Semitism in the DAG, see esp. Malinowski, *Vom König zum Führer*, 157–70, 321–57.

[34] Shulamit Volkov, *Antisemitismus als kultureller Code: Zehn Essays* (2nd edn.; Munich, 2000).

[35] On the discourse of the new aristocracy in the nineteenth century see Heinz Reif, 'Adelserneuerung und Adelsreform in Deutschland 1815–1874', in Elisabeth Fehrenbach (ed.), *Adel und Bürgertum in Deutschland 1770–1848* (Munich, 1994), 203–30; on the twentieth century see Eckart Conze, 'Adel unter dem Totenkopf: Die Idee eines Neuadels in den Gesellschaftsvorstellungen der SS', in id. and Wienfort (eds.), *Adel und Moderne*, 151–76, esp. 155–65; for a summary see Eckart Conze, 'Neuadel', in id. (ed.), *Kleines Lexikon des Adels*, 183–6.

that supported the state, thereby legitimizing both itself and the many privileges it had enjoyed right to the end of the monarchical state, it was now unable suddenly to transfer its loyalty to a democratic republic. If, however, the line of continuity of orientation by the state and service to it had broken in 1918, all that was left for the aristocracy, and especially for the many anti-republicans among its ranks, was the *Volk*, the people, at whose head and in whose service they could look beyond the caesura of 1918, and understand and legitimize their own position. The *Volk* was not a new point of reference, but something that had always been there, and this appealed to the aristocracy's sense of history and continuity.[36]

Beyond this, the *völkisch* orientation gave its aristocratic supporters a wide field of associates who shared their aversion to the Republic. In an attempt not to be marginalized within the heterogeneous *völkisch* camp or the 'new right', and indeed, to maintain their traditional claim to leadership, the continued use of the term 'aristocracy' as a synonym for a political and social elite seemed helpful. If the 'aristocracy' functioned as a symbolic leadership elite and model for a new elite, then why should the historical aristocracy not form at least part of the 'new aristocracy' that was being talked about everywhere? After all, the aristocracy had been putting *völkisch* principles into practice for centuries both in its view of itself and its existence from generation to generation. Since the nineteenth century at the latest, the aristocracy had regarded the land that it controlled (though increasingly less exclusively), farmed, and lived on, as the central pillar of its identity; indeed, as a defining aristocratic feature. And it was not only aristocrats with *völkisch* affinities who thought so. Ewald von Kleist-Schmenzin, one of the last representatives of an Old Prussian conservatism who was completely untainted by any suspicion of *völkisch* affinities and was murdered by the Nazis in 1944, wrote in 1926:

There is one area where the aristocracy must preserve its position with special care, and that is the land. The roots of its power lie in the

---

[36] At regional level this popular orientation had been developed in the nineteenth century in order to give the regional aristocracy a recognized status and to legitimize its power as a regional elite. Cf. e.g. on Westphalia, Heinz Reif, 'Mediator between Throne and People: The Split in Aristocratic Conservatism in Nineteenth-Century Germany', in Bo Strath (ed.), *Language and Construction of Class Identities* (Göteborg, 1990), 133–50.

possession of a large estate, and that is where they will always lie. The aristocracy must never lose its leadership on the land, otherwise, in the long or short term, its existence will be threatened, for powers which rejuvenate the body and the soul stream constantly from the land. Ultimately, that is the origin of most of the Prussian-*Junker* world view, which is totally opposed to the modern world, and which is destined to save our people.[37]

This quotation clearly identifies the points of contact with *völkisch* thinking. The links were anti-modernism, anti-industrialism, and anti-urbanism, that is, the central elements of the agrarian romantic thinking that had emerged since the second half of the nineteenth century.[38]

In addition to its attachment to the land, the aristocracy's specific family awareness also created points of contact with the stock of *völkisch* ideas. This started with the aristocracy's awareness of lineage, and carried on with its selection of partners, marriage patterns, and reproductive behaviour, which was governed by the maxim: 'maintain the aristocratic stock and name'. Instilled by education and socialization, this maxim dictated aristocratic behaviour for generations.[39] Consciousness of belonging to a social order or Estate directed towards the reproduction of the aristocratic family—did this not, *in nuce*, point in the same direction as thinking that demanded purity of race and blood, was orientated by principles such as selection and selective breeding, and developed racial hierarchies based on biology and blood? Quite a few aristocrats saw it in these terms. And conversely, a number of adherents of *völkisch*-racist thinking saw the aristocracy, or, at least, the principle of aristocracy, as the model of a leadership class at least potentially formed by breeding.[40]

Examination of such soft factors should not, of course, obscure the fact that throughout the Weimar Republic, but especially

---

[37] Quoted from Bodo Scheurig, *Ewald v. Kleist-Schmenzin: Ein Konservativer gegen Hitler* (Oldenburg, 1968), 32.

[38] Still an important work on the German agrarian romantic thinking is Klaus Bergmann, *Agrarromantik und Großstadtfeindschaft* (Meisenheim, 1970).

[39] Heinz Reif, 'Erhaltung adligen Stammes und Namens: Adelsfamilie und Statussicherung im Münsterland 1770–1914', in Neithard Bulst et al. (eds.), *Familie zwischen Tradition und Moderne: Studien zur Geschichte der Familie in Deutschland und Frankreich vom 16. bis zum 20. Jahrhundert* (Göttingen, 1981), 275–309.

[40] This also applied to the SS, which saw itself as a new aristocracy defined by race. In its conception of this new aristocracy, the SS referred back to the model of the old, historical aristocracy. On this cf. Conze, 'Adel unter dem Totenkopf'.

during its closing phases, there were also hard political factors and common interests that made emergent National Socialism more attractive for the aristocracy, and helped to remove its reservations about the Nazi movement. In this context, I shall merely refer to the significance of the agrarian crisis, which became more acute from 1929, for the politicization and radicalization of the aristocracy (as part of the politicization and radicalization of the country as a whole).[41] In this context, anti-Bolshevism should also be mentioned. From 1930, it experienced a resurgence against the background of quasi-civil war in Germany, and drove the aristocracy, among others, into the arms of the Nazi Party (as members or voters). Individual events which created connections between the aristocracy and the radical right should also be mentioned, such as the referendum of 1926 on the expropriation of the princes,[42] quite apart from such general and overarching factors as the Versailles syndrome. (From the perspective of aristocratic history, relations between ideas of national honour and a genuinely aristocratic understanding of honour need to be investigated.)[43] The latter point, of course, shows that hard and soft factors cannot always be clearly distinguished, and recent cultural

[41] On this see, among others, Pomp, 'Brandenburgischer Landadel'; Stephanie Merkenich, *Grüne Front gegen Weimar: Reichs-Landbund und agrarischer Lobbyismus 1918–1933* (Düsseldorf, 1998); Wolfram Pyta, *Dorfgemeinschaft und Parteipolitik 1918–1933: Die Verschränkung von Milieu und Parteien in den protestantischen Landgebieten Deutschlands in der Weimarer Republik* (Düsseldorf, 1996); and Mechthild Hempe, *Ländliche Gesellschaft in der Krise: Mecklenburg in der Weimarer Republik* (Cologne, 2002).

[42] On this see Ulrich Schüren, *Der Volksentscheid zur Fürstenenteignung 1926: Die Vermögensauseinandersetzung mit den depossedierten Landesherren als Problem der deutschen Innenpolitik unter besonderer Berücksichtigung der Verhältnisse in Preußen* (Düsseldorf, 1978); Norbert Stieniczka, 'Die Vermögensauseinandersetzung des Volksstaates Hessen und seiner Rechtsnachfolger mit der ehemals großherzoglichen Familie 1918–1953', *Archiv für hessische Geschichte und Altertumskunde*, 56 (1998), 255–308; and Karl Heinrich Kaufhold, 'Fürstenabfindung oder Fürstenenteignung? Der Kampf um das Hausvermögen der ehemals regierenden Fürstenhäuser im Jahre 1926 und die Innenpolitik der Weimarer Republik', in Markus A. Denzel and Günther Schulz (eds.), *Deutscher Adel im 19. und 20. Jahrhundert: Büdinger Forschungen zur Sozialgeschichte 2002 und 2003* (St Katharinen, 2004), 261–85.

[43] On the Versailles syndrom see Hagen Schulze, 'Versailles', in Étienne François and Hagen Schulze (eds.), *Deutsche Erinnerungsorte* (Munich, 2001), 407–21; more recently Thomas Lorenz, ' "Die Weltgeschichte ist das Weltgericht!"—"Versailler Vertrag" und "Revision" als Diskurs- und Zeitgeistphänomene der Weimarer Republik 1919–1925' (Ph.D. dissertation, University of Marburg, 2005). On the aristocratic understanding of honour see Ute Frevert, *Ehrenmänner: Das Duell in der bürgerlichen Gesellschaft* (Munich, 1991), and the brief outline by Marcus Funck, 'Ehre', in Conze (ed.), *Kleines Lexikon des Adels*, 70–3.

history approaches have contributed to at least relativizing these boundaries. We could also point to the significance of the idea of the Reich for the affinity which developed between the old aristocracy and the new right. The concept of the Reich was an important bridging element in the relationship between the aristocracy and the new right, as well as in that between Catholicism (right-wing Catholicism in particular) and National Socialism.[44]

It would, of course, be going too far to describe the aristocracy as a whole as an integral component of the radical right in Germany, although this certainly applies to individual groups such as the DAG. It makes more sense to stress the reciprocal relationship between the aristocracy and the radical right, to identify opportunities for political, cultural, or intellectual affinities, and to analyse the path they took. The approach did not come exclusively from an aristocracy that, after 1918, felt it had come down in the world. Its social decline had, in many cases, turned into free fall, and not only in its own perceptions. The organizations of the radical right also made moves in this direction, in particular, the rising Nazi Party, which quite openly courted the aristocracy for a number of reasons. They saw recruiting the aristocracy with its opinion-forming role as a way of gaining the support of new groups of rural voters, for example. They also saw it as potentially providing a corrective to the image of the Nazi Party and its organizations as a vulgar, brutal, lower-class movement, and as a way of adapting to the ideal of a racially defined *Volksgemeinschaft*.

The aristocracy's, or individual aristocrats', proximity to or distance from the radical right cannot be explained only in terms of the extent of social and economic or material decline after 1918. It was not only members of the 'aristocratic proletariat' who turned to National Socialism, although they represented the largest group.[45] Agreement on national politics and common

---

[44] On the political significance of the idea of the Reich in the Weimar Republic see, among others, Klaus Reimus, ' "Das Reich muß uns doch bleiben!" ' Die nationale Rechte', in Detlef Lehnert and Klaus Megerle (eds.), *Politische Identität und nationale Gedenktage: Zur politischen Kultur in der Weimarer Republik* (Opladen, 1989), 231–53; and recently, with important observations on Catholicism, Vanessa Conze, *Das Europa der Deutschen: Europaideen in Deutschland zwischen Reichstradition und Westorientierung (1920–1970)* (Munich, 2005), 44–63.

[45] On the attractiveness of National Socialism for the high aristocracy and members of the former ruling dynasties see Jonathan Petropoulos, *Royals and the Reich: The Princes of Hessen in Nazi Germany* (Oxford, 2006).

patterns of cultural perception (especially interpretations of modernity and modernization processes) should be mentioned here. Similarly complex is the analysis of barriers between the aristocracy and the radical right. I have attempted to indicate this using the example of monarchism, but it also applies to religious arguments. Here we can at most suggest tendencies or make statements about probabilities. Social, economic, political, or cultural predispositions for an aristocratic turn to the right needed a profound crisis (individual, group, or national) to activate them, and required a view of the future which matched the radical right's offers of ways to overcome the crisis.

If we base our observations of the history of the aristocracy on the concept of crisis, perceptions of crisis, the experience of crisis, or an attempt to overcome crisis,[46] then we gain an analytical perspective that allows us to place our findings, derived from an examination of the interwar period and limited to this timeframe, into a wider temporal context: crisis becomes a leading concept in the history of the aristocracy. At the same time, we are creating a conceptual starting point for a European comparison, in particular, with respect to the interwar period. In recent years we have heard much of the 'crisis of Europe', 'democracy in crisis', the 'crisis of the European democracies', and the 'crisis of the liberal system',[47] and these concerns have already given rise to a number of outstanding studies, in particular, Andreas Wirsching's investigation of political extremism in Paris and Berlin.[48] The concept of crisis does not cover up national differences and peculiarities, but this is not the point of comparative studies. It does, however, create a precise *tertium comparationis*, which is essential for comparative works. Furthermore, it offers a

---

[46] On 'crisis' as a general concept see Reinhart Koselleck, 'Krise', in Otto Brunner et al. (eds.), *Geschichtliche Grundbegriffe: Historisches Lexikon zur politisch-sozialen Sprache in Deutschland* (Stuttgart, 2004), iii. 617–50.

[47] 'Crisis' is an important term in Horst Möller's survey, *Europa zwischen den Weltkriegen* (Munich, 1998). But cf. also Edward H. Carr, *The Twenty Years' Crisis, 1919–1939* (New York, 1964); Ernst Nolte, *Die Krise des liberalen Systems und die faschistischen Bewegungen* (Munich, 1968); Karl Dietrich Bracher, *Die Krise Europas seit 1917* (Frankfurt on Main, 1993); and Detlev J. K. Peukert, *Die Weimarer Republik: Krisenjahre der Klassischen Moderne* (Frankfurt am Main, 1987).

[48] Andreas Wirsching, *Vom Weltkrieg zum Bürgerkrieg? Politischer Extremismus in Deutschland und Frankreich 1918–1933/39: Berlin und Paris im Vergleich* (Munich, 1999); but see also Manfred Kittel, *Provinz zwischen Reich und Republik: Politische Mentalitäten in Deutschland und Frankreich 1918–1933/36* (Munich, 2000).

concept that allows for both 'hard' and 'soft' factors. And this is even more important and promising for the history of aristocracy than for other areas of research.

9

Genteel Nationalists: Nobles and Fascism in Czechoslovakia

EAGLE GLASSHEIM

In the early years of the twentieth century, the Bohemian nobility still occupied the heights of Habsburg society and government. Around 300 families of the high aristocracy owned almost a third of the Bohemian crown lands, not to mention vast investments in finance and industry. Though forced to share power with the emperor and increasingly assertive popular forces, Bohemian nobles regularly served as prime ministers, generals, bishops, and representatives in the upper house of parliament. All this would change in 1918. Weakened by defeat in war and the nationalist demands of its eleven subject peoples, the Habsburg monarchy dissolved as the First World War drew to an end. The leaders of the new nation-state of Czechoslovakia were decidedly hostile towards the nobility they inherited, seeing Bohemian aristocrats as emblems of Habsburg feudalism and authoritarianism. In 1919 Czechoslovakia passed a massive land reform, intended to redistribute noble land to Czech and Slovak peasant farmers. As the Social Democrat František Modráček put it: 'the aristocracy formed a vital pillar of the former Austro-Hungarian Empire.'[1] Land reform aimed to destroy the landed basis of noble power and prevent support for a Habsburg resurgence.

Though at first marginalized politically, Bohemian nobles retained a good deal of economic and social influence in interwar Czechoslovakia. In order to minimize the economic disruption of the land reform, legislators decided not to confiscate land outright. Instead, they empowered a Land Office to review large estates case

---

This essay is based on Eagle Glassheim, *Noble Nationalists: The Transformation of the Bohemian Aristocracy* (Cambridge, Mass., 2005).

[1] Národní shromáždění, Meeting 46: 16 Apr. 1919. Text at <www.psp.cz/cgi-bin/win/eknih>, accessed 13 Sept. 2004.

by case, redistributing some land to peasants and leaving some to
its original owners. Redistribution was a long and deliberate
process, and nobles managed to hold on to almost half their land
(much of it forest) until 1938. As the passions of the 1918 revolution
receded and land reform moved ahead, nobles found by the mid-
1920s that they could regain a modicum of political influence
through behind-the-scenes lobbying and bribery. In the 1930s,
some Bohemian nobles were active in Czechoslovak and foreign
conservative circles. In the late 1930s many embraced various
forms of fascism, with some drawing on their 'conservative revolutionary' ideals to support Nazi German expansion in Central
Europe and others invoking Czech nationalism in opposition to
Hitler. This essay examines the twenty-year transformation of the
Bohemian nobles from supra-national, conservative Habsburg
stalwarts to increasingly nationalistic conservative revolutionaries,
many of whom were sympathetic to fascism.

I *From Empires to Nation-States*

The nobility was not the only group that feared marginalization
in post-imperial Central Europe. With the collapse of the
Habsburg monarchy, millions of linguistically diverse people
became minorities in new nation-states. Czechoslovakia, a
country of thirteen million inhabitants, had over three million
citizens who identified themselves as German. Sensing the possible disaffection of large minorities, the victorious Entente pressed
Czechoslovakia, Poland, and other new states to accept League of
Nations minority protection treaties. Though these treaties at first
helped to ease tensions between nationalizing states and separatist minorities, they also increased the political salience of
national identification. Domestic national conflicts over resources
became internationalized and often intractable, as minorities
petitioned the League of Nations in opposition to discriminatory
legislation. The inception of nation-states and minority treaties
had the effect of institutionalizing national identifications, extending a process of nationalization that had taken hold in the late
nineteenth century.[2]

---

[2] For a useful examination of the nationalization of politics and interests in the late
nineteenth century see Jeremy King, *Budweisers into Czechs and Germans: A Local History of*

Czechoslovakia's 1919 land reform became a central battle-ground of the embryonic nation-state against an aggrieved ethnic minority. Seeing German-held 'national property' as vital to their existence, Sudeten German nationalists teamed with sympathetic nobles in appealing to the League of Nations against anti-German discrimination in the land reform.[3] As a vocal landowner, Wilhelm Medinger, declared in 1922: 'The German nation has already recognized that the threat to German large landowners is at the same time a threat to Germans' national, *völkisch* existence.'[4] But nobles were by no means united in following this national strategy for opposing the reform. Already in 1919, a substantial faction of the nobility created a landowner protection organization to defend noble land on an economic and corporate, but not explicitly national basis. Many of these nobles openly professed loyalty to the new Czechoslovak state, even going so far as to claim deeply rooted Czech national credentials. 'In the [Czechoslovak] republic', Bedřich Schwarzenberg declared to his colleagues, 'only an association with a Czech leadership can prosper. One with a German tint is incapable of survival.'[5]

By the mid-1920s, nobles increasingly saw their interests in national terms. The Czechoslovak landowner association argued that loyalty should bring lenience, and that nobles were effective stewards of agricultural property. In contrast, the German landowner association fought land reform by protesting discrimination to the League of Nations. Both strategies had some effect, as the Land Office sometimes favoured perceived Czech patriots and occasionally moderated redistributions of the property of vocal German critics. Though interwar Czechoslovakia was in many ways a vibrant democracy with equal legal rights for all male citizens, there was little question among contemporary

Bohemian Politics, 1848–1948 (Princeton, 2002). On nation-states and minority treaties, see Eagle Glassheim, *Noble Nationalists: The Transformation of the Bohemian Aristocracy* (Cambridge, Mass., 2005).

[3] See Mark Cornwall, '"National Reparation"? The Czech Land Reform and the Sudeten Germans 1918–38', *Slavic and East European Review*, 75/2 (Apr. 1997), 259–80.

[4] 'Bericht über die am 11. Juli 1922 stattgefundene Sitzung der Grossgrundbesitzer-verbände zur Abwehr gegen die Kündigung.' Státní ústřední archiv (SÚA), Svaz Česko-slovenských velkostatkářů (SČV), carton 7 no. 117.

[5] Protokoly o schůzích představenstva SČV (Minutes of meetings of the directorate of the SČV), 3 June 1919. Státní oblastní archiv (SOA) Třeboň, rodinný archiv (RA) Schwarzenberg Sekundogeniture, carton 332 no. 1571.

observers that a zero-sum nationalism inflected political and social life. Though steeped in class-based cosmopolitanism, the nobility, too, became increasingly nationalized, a tendency that would lead many to embrace fascism in the 1930s.

II *Conservative Revolution(s) of the 1930s*

Self-described 'Czech' and 'German' nobles came to their conservative nationalism of the 1930s via intertwined, but distinct paths. The Czech nobility, about one-third of the total families, invoked a deeply rooted 'historic rights' ideology that posited the autonomy and integrity of the lands of the Bohemian crown.[6] In the nineteenth century (and earlier), many Bohemian nobles had proffered historic rights as a counter to the centralizing tendencies of the Habsburg monarchs. They grafted their emerging Czech identification on to this earlier tradition, identifying independent Czechoslovakia with historic Bohemian statehood. As František Schwarzenberg reported in 1934, many younger nobles now 'exhibited an unexpected Czech nationalism'.[7]

German nobles, around two-thirds of the total, identified with another well-rooted Bohemian tradition that had embraced Habsburg centralism as a brake on the centrifugal forces of nineteenth-century nationalism and democracy. They saw the Habsburg Empire (the Austrian half of the Dual Monarchy) as a fundamentally German institution, with German culture and power providing leadership for the other peoples of the monarchy. By the late 1920s, many described themselves as 'Sudeten German' nobles, identifying themselves not just with other ethnic Germans of Czechoslovakia, but increasingly with Germans throughout Central Europe. Eugen Ledebur explained: 'The hopeless political situation of the national minorities offers no possibility of a parliamentary defence . . . Only international law, in its latest form, the minority treaty, offers the possibility of an effective remedy.'[8]

---

[6] See Glassheim, *Noble Nationalists*, for statistics on Czech and Sudeten German nobilities.

[7] Kancelář prezidenta republiky (KPR) Záznam, 5 Feb. 1934. Archiv kanceláře prezidenta republiky (AKPR) T119/34.

[8] Eugen Ledebur-Wicheln, 'Bodenreform und Völkerrecht', *Wochenschrift für Kultur, Politik, und Volkswirtschaft*, 7/20–1 (14 and 21 Feb. 1925), 483. Copy of article in SOA Litoměřice (Děčín) RA Ledebur, carton 14 no. 190.

Even as they divided politically, Czech and German nobles in Bohemia maintained social and marital ties and shared a Christian conservative outlook. Their increasing national polarization in the 1920s did not diminish their class solidarity. But by the mid-1930s, divergent national identification channelled nationalism on the right in dramatically different directions, with the Germans generally in support of Nazi imperial ambitions and the Czechs in opposition to National Socialism. The two most active noble publicists influential in Czechoslovakia, Karel Schwarzenberg and Karl Anton Rohan, indicate how shared ideology had very different implications for Czech as against German nobles in the 1930s. Both criticized the political factionalism and moral decline they attributed to liberal democracy.[9] Both embraced a latter-day corporatist social and political order. Like many other nobles, both found the corporatist and authoritarian aspects of fascist ideology attractive. But only Rohan would support National Socialism, while Schwarzenberg became an outspoken critic of Hitler's expansionism.

Schwarzenberg wrote regularly for the monthly journal *Řád* (Order), the mouthpiece of the right wing of the Czechoslovak Catholic People's Party. Many Czech nobles quietly supported the Catholic Populists, who advanced a Catholic–conservative brand of Czech nationalism. Representing an illustrious line of Bohemian (and later Czech) patriots, Schwarzenberg owned three large estates in central Bohemia amounting to over 15,000 hectares. The Schwarzenberg family was one of the most progressive and wealthy in Bohemia, and before 1918 the Schwarzenbergs had been prominent in both imperial and provincial politics.[10]

In a series of polemical articles, Schwarzenberg criticized the 'modern, hypertrophic state', where centralizing and secularizing governments had diminished or destroyed autonomous political

[9] Rohan was technically a citizen of Austria, though he was actively involved in noble political and social life in Czechoslovakia. His brother Alain Rohan inherited the family estate in northern Bohemia.

[10] On the Schwarzenbergs see Herman Freudenberger, 'The Schwarzenberg Bank: A Forgotten Contributor to Austrian Economic Development, 1788–1830', *Austrian History Yearbook*, 27 (1996), 41–64; Petr Placák, 'Duch křesťanství a duch otroctví: Karel Schwarzenberg (1911–1986)', pt. 1: *Střední Evropa*, no. 85 (1998), 43–58; Robert Sak, 'Der Platz der Schwarzenberger in der tschechischen Politik der zweiten Hälfte des neunzehnten Jahrhunderts', *Opera Historica Editio Universitatis Bohemiae Meridionalis*, 2 (1992), 107–10; and Zdeněk Bezecný, 'Karel V. ze Schwarzenberku', *Opera Historica*, 4 (1995), 281–95.

and social bodies.[11] He identified this centralizing tendency with the Enlightenment and more particularly the French Revolution, which had subordinated the Church and other autonomous bodies to the secular state. The ever-expanding state had taken over more and more prerogatives in society, creating 'the state school, which incorporates the mind into the state (*zestátňuje*), conscription, which incorporates the body into the state, and socialism, which incorporates property into the state'.[12]

Schwarzenberg's writings displayed an implicit nostalgia for the old feudal order, in which the nobility was an autonomous estate and served to check the power of the state. Supposedly untainted by the liberal trinity of materialism, individualism, and secularism, nobles and their peasant subjects had lived in organic harmony with a healthy respect for morality, religion, and community. In contrast, 'American principles' of atomization and individualism were undermining the old order. 'A vocation is no longer an estate (*stav*), a lasting quality inherent in a person', Schwarzenberg wrote, 'but rather a chance circumstance of the moment.' He mourned the loss of 'Christian hierarchy, social order, and economic stratification', which had given way to 'capitalism, industrialization and the modern method of forced schooling'. Europe had become nothing more than a decadent 'playground for upstarts, swindlers, adventurous women, and dishonourable people'.[13]

Schwarzenberg saw the historic rights tradition as an alternative to the interventionist state. A historian by training, Schwarzenberg considered Bohemia's autonomy (preserved by the conservative nobility) preferable to the centralizing and modernizing tendencies of the Habsburg emperors since the eighteenth century. In the post-imperial age, Czechoslovakia needed to carry on the tradition of Bohemia's historic rights, resisting German imperial expansion and the dehumanizing influence of global capitalism and socialism. Rejecting materialism of all sorts, Schwarzenberg considered Catholicism the only

[11] Karel Schwarzenberg, *Obrana svobod* (Prague, 1991), 32. Original article appeared as 'Kato čili o svobodě plněním zákonů', *Řád*, 2 (1935), 551–9.

[12] Jindřich Středa (Karel Schwarzenberg), 'Svoboda a totalita', *Řád*, 4 (1937), 363. See also Schwarzenberg, *Obrana*, 27–37.

[13] Schwarzenberg, *Obrana*, 62–5. Original article appeared as 'Konce křesťanské společnosti', *Řád*, 3 (1936), 234–41.

legitimate universalist ideology. Invoking the papal encyclical Quadragesimo Anno (1931), Schwarzenberg called for a return to a corporate order, where different groups such as labourers, farmers, and landowners would have rights and privileges connected to their station. Such a system would be both decentralized and de-ideologized, as self-regulating corporations took back many of the roles claimed by the modern state. The corporate bodies under feudalism had maintained freedom from the tyranny of the state, Schwarzenberg argued. In a 1935 article in *Řád*, Schwarzenberg claimed that corporatism would usher in a more just economic and political order, a true democracy, in which all citizens could participate 'in that field of life into which fate has placed them'.[14]

These arguments resonated with the emerging national Catholic conservatism of Czech noble landowners. Corporatism appeared to promise an end to class conflict and socialism, while institutionalizing a 'natural' hierarchy, in which paternalistic upper classes coexisted harmoniously with docile workers. Popular democracy, which had sapped the power of the nobility, would give way to a democracy of estates, in which large landowners would regain some of the power lost to mass-based political parties. Corporatism seemed capable of reversing the moral and political rot that nobles associated with liberalism, but it would protect private property, the continuing bedrock of noble wealth and status. Finally, it was soundly rooted in conservative Catholic doctrine and had the support of the pope.

Writing in his Austrian-based journal, the *Europäische Revue*, Rohan shared Schwarzenberg's critique of liberalism and judgements about moral and spiritual decline. Rohan praised national man, who embraced the entire national community (*Volksgemeinschaft*), in contrast to the selfish class politics of socialist or bourgeois man. Without national solidarity, 'we would quickly sink into an unstructured chaos of wild opportunism and personal battles of all against all, whose first warning signs we can already see today . . . in large cities'.[15] A real nationalist was conservative,

---

[14] Schwarzenberg, *Obrana*, 32–5.

[15] Karl Anton Prince Rohan, 'Inventar der politischen Grundhaltungen im heutigen Europa (1929)', in id., *Umbruch der Zeit, 1923–1930: Gesammelte Aufsätze eingeleitet von Rochus Freiherr von Rheinbaben* (Berlin, 1930), 41. Individual articles in this collection originally appeared in Rohan's journal *Europäische Revue*. Dates of original publication are in parentheses.

upheld 'an orderly family . . . a patriarchal relationship to his employees', loyalty to the state, ruler, and God. Now that the old conservatism of the Habsburg monarchy was irrevocably lost, Rohan wrote, a new generation of revolutionary conservatives had appeared to take its place.[16]

Rohan's vision of a new conservative movement was similar to that of the Austrian writer Hugo von Hofmannsthal, who spoke in 1927 of a 'conservative revolution'.[17] Fritz Stern has described the supporters of Hofmannsthal's revolution as 'disinherited conservatives, who had nothing to conserve, because the spiritual values of the past had largely been buried and the material remnants of conservative power did not interest them. They sought a breakthrough to the past, and they longed for a new community in which old ideas and institutions would once again command universal allegiance.'[18] Rohan called for the creation of a conservative ideology that would incorporate elements from both the past and present. Like Schwarzenberg, Rohan looked back to a corporate social and political order, but one that acknowledged the industrial and mass political reality of the present. Rohan hoped this latter-day corporatism would engender a 'new sense of community . . . an organically organized society' that would overcome conflicts between classes and nations.[19] The new conservatives were not fundamentally opposed to democracy, Rohan wrote, but they objected to the French revolutionary idea that the people equalled 'the sum of separate, equal individuals'. Rather, 'the representatives of the re-formation of democracy understand by "the people" (*Volk*) an organically grown unity, made up of differentiated limbs and parts'.[20] The 'modern people's state (*Volksstaat*)' would act 'not for the benefit of a single party, but in the name of the national community'.[21]

As Schwarzenberg's and Rohan's writings indicate, aristocratic elitism, corporatism, anti-socialism, and anti-liberalism

---

[16] Rohan, 'Inventar', 42.

[17] Hofmannsthal first used the phrase 'conservative revolution' in a speech to students in Munich in 1927. See Jeremy Noakes, 'German Conservatives and the Third Reich: An Ambiguous Relationship', in Martin Blinkhorn (ed.), *Fascists and Conservatives: The Radical Right and the Establishment in Twentieth-Century Europe* (London, 1990), 80. Note that Hofmannsthal was an occasional contributor to Rohan's *Europäische Revue*.

[18] Fritz Stern, *The Politics of Cultural Despair* (New York, 1965), 6–7.

[19] Rohan, 'Inventar', 56.

[20] Rohan, 'Krise der Demokratie (1930)', in id., *Umbruch der Zeit*, 173.

[21] Id., 'Der moderne Rechtsstaat (1930)', ibid. 179.

drew many nobles to fascism. Like many right-wing supporters of the Czechoslovak Christian People's Party, Schwarzenberg joined the Czech fascist group Vlajka in the mid-1930s. Rohan, too, embraced fascism as an energetic alternative to liberalism and socialism. Already in the mid-1920s, Rohan celebrated 'the new *Lebensgefühl* that fascism has created—heroic-tragic, young-revolutionary and traditional at the same time, unideological-activist, noblesse in the devotion to a supra-individual ideal'.[22]

Rohan was ecstatic when Hitler founded a seemingly 'revolutionary conservative' regime in 1933. Rohan considered the triumph of National Socialism to be a double revolution: the victory of the leadership principle and the realization of a genuine community that elevated the nation above the individual. In Rohan's view, the Nazis replaced the unnatural idea of equality with the rule of a 'new type of human being . . . Thus have all aristocracies begun,' Rohan wrote. 'This revolution seeks to create a new elite, perhaps a new nobility.'[23] The leader and the new elite personified the national community, which brought together the national and social principles. National Socialism and fascism would reverse the disintegrating forces of liberalism, strengthening the community by incorporating social identity within national identity. With Hitler's rise, Rohan saw the triumph of a 'conservative revolution'.[24]

In contrast, Schwarzenberg considered Hitler the worst possible democrat, the nadir of the French revolutionary tradition. Intrusive Nazi edicts on education, family policy, and labour were a radicalized version of the centralizing state Schwarzenberg abhorred. Hitler's *Gleichschaltung*, the Nazification of organizational life, was a further example of the state destroying the autonomy of non-governmental institutions. 'The Hitlerites are no more than national socialists', Schwarzenberg wrote. 'Like all socialists, they are the heirs and consummation of liberalism . . . They adopted the equality of citizens; they assumed the whole apparatus of state tyranny; they escalated centralization into totality; they intensified the party system into dictatorship.'[25] To

---

[22] Id., 'Fascismus und Europa (1926)', ibid. 31.

[23] Rohan, 'Europäische Revolution', *Europäische Revue*, 9/2 (July–Dec. 1933), 523.

[24] Ibid. 527. For more on the connection between a 'third way' and 'conservative revolution', see George Mosse, *Germans and Jews: The Right, the Left, and the Search for a 'Third Force' in Pre-Nazi Germany* (New York, 1970), ch. 5.

[25] Středa, 'Svoboda a totalita', 362–3.

Schwarzenberg, Hitler was the ultimate democrat, not a genuine fascist.

Rohan's and Schwarzenberg's ideologies were shared by many Bohemian nobles, who would come out for or against National Socialism during Hitler's moves to dismantle Czechoslovakia in 1938 and 1939. Many nobles openly or clandestinely backed Konrad Henlein's fascist-leaning Sudeten German Party in the mid-1930s. After France, Britain, and Germany forced Czechoslovakia to relinquish the Sudetenland in 1938, many nobles welcomed the arrival of German forces. Typical of many of his fellow nobles, Alfons Clary-Aldringen vowed: 'We will never forget the jubilation and our deep, heartfelt joy when the first soldiers of the German *Wehrmacht* arrived as liberators; nor will we forget above all the overflowing feeling of thanks for our great *Führer*.'[26]

On the other hand, a significant portion of the Bohemian nobility followed Schwarzenberg in opposing the destruction of Czechoslovakia and the eventual Nazi occupation of Bohemia. A bold 1938 declaration, drafted by Karel Schwarzenberg on behalf of twelve prominent noble families, urged Czech national unity against the looming Nazi threat.[27] These nobles claimed that 'all estates and classes of our nation' opposed 'the violation of the historic borders of our state'. The proclamation noted the Czech nobility's deep attachment to the Bohemian historic rights tradition and support for the Czech national movement in the nineteenth century. As self-described 'Czech national' nobles, they rejected Hitler's revolutionary intention to redraw the map of Central Europe, including the destruction of the ancient Kingdom of Bohemia.

---

[26] Alfons Clary-Aldringen, 'Kameraden und Kameradinnen der Gefolgschaft der Turner Brauerei!' (n.d. [Oct. 1938]). Text of speech located in SOA Litoměřice (Děčín), RA Clary-Aldringen, carton 445.

[27] Declaration of members of the historic nobility, delivered 17 Sept. 1938 to President Edvard Benes. Copy in AKPR, D3038/40. The declaration was signed by Karel Schwarzenberg, Jan Lobkowicz, Zdeněk Radislav Kinský, František Kinský, Zdeněk Kolowrat, Rudolf Czernin, Leopold Sternberg, W. Colloredo-Mannsfeld, Karel Parish, Jindřich Dobrzensky, Hugo Strachwitz, and Karel Belcredi. The full text appears in translation in Glassheim, *Noble Nationalists*. Though only twelve nobles signed the declaration, many more supported its contents. See František Schwarzenberg, letter to the editor, *Svědectví*, 20/79 (1986), 707. A more complete tally of Czech noble loyalists can be drawn from a second noble declaration in 1939, which bore sixty-nine signatures. See 'Prohlášení příslušníků historické šlechty, předané v září 1939 prezidentu dr. Emilu Háchovi'. AKPR D3038/40.

III *Conclusion*

Given the centrality of nationalism to fascist ideology and practice, nothing approaching a unified fascist movement emerged in Europe, even at the height of Hitler's domination of the continent. It is no surprise, then, that Czech and Sudeten German fascists found little common cause in the late 1930s. Though their anti-democratic, anti-liberal, and anti-Semitic rhetoric was similar, their primary value was the so-called national community, a bounded and exclusive entity. In theory, this centrality of nationalism should have alienated members of the Bohemian nobility, who had a long tradition of cosmopolitanism and class solidarity. On the other hand, there was much about fascist ideology that appealed naturally to nobles: its opposition to Bolshevism, liberalism, and equality; its embrace of a modern-day corporatism; and its resonance with certain traditional values, including the patriarchal family and paternalistic labour relations. The Bohemian nobility had come to embrace nationalism too, in its organized opposition to land reform in the 1920s. But Czech and German nobles drew on different Bohemian traditions—historic rights federalism and Viennese centralism— to justify their newfound nationalism. Consequently, the two groups differed in their views of Hitler and German imperial expansion.

During the occupation of Bohemia from 1939 to 1945, Czech nobles faced tremendous pressure to renounce their Czech nationalism and Germanize. But few did so, and dozens of the most prominent families had their estates sequestered in retribution. Several spent time in prison. Sudeten German nobles, on the other hand, prospered, at least until Hitler's war turned bad. Many served as officers in the *Wehrmacht*, while others socialized with the elite of the German occupation authorities. At the end of the war, the tables were turned. In 1945 and 1946, Czechs expelled Czechoslovakia's three million ethnic Germans, including hundreds of German noble families. Czech nobles regained their lost property in 1945, only to lose it again when the Communists seized power in 1948. The Communist regime did not care about the national credentials of Czech nobles, seeing them only as a hostile feudal remnant. Most remaining nobles went into exile, though a few remained as managers and tractor drivers on their confiscated estates. In 1948, the Bohemian nobility ceased to exist as a distinct social group.

10

Nostalgic Agnostics:
Austrian Aristocrats and Politics,
1918–1938

Lothar Höbelt

Jedes Volk wird seine Reaktion erhalten; das eine sie härter, das andere sie gelinder erfahren; kurz gesagt, jedes Volk bekommt die Reaktion, die es verdient.

(Every people will have its reaction; some will have a harsher experience, some a milder one; in short, every people will get the reaction it deserves.)

Prince Aloys Liechtenstein, *Das Neue Reich*, 6 July 1919

I *Revisionists without a Cause*

The end of the Austro-Hungarian monarchy left the (German-) Austrian republic with thousands of ennobled officers and civil servants. It can only be surmised that their politics were similar to those of the middle classes in general, which is why this essay will focus on the few dozen aristocratic families who were either large landowners or belonged to the charmed circle of families which had held hereditary seats in the old Austrian upper house. Any notion that these aristocrats had reason to regard the constitutional and territorial arrangements of 1918–19 with anything other than distaste can safely be discounted. In terms of longings and frustrations, they were probably more estranged from their political environment than any other noble society in Europe except for that of Bohemia, and thus more right wing. Yet political action is not about wishful thinking, but about constraints and incentives. Initially there were few incentives, but there were many constraints.

Compared with the Bohemian aristocracy, they had no agenda. Bohemian aristocrats had clear-cut grievances: they had been hit by land reform, shared the resentment of Sudeten Germans at a world turned upside down, and did not relish the influence of left-wing parties in the Prague government. To that extent, Austrians were better off, although not usually economically. Land reform was talked about but never actually carried out;[1] there were no more ethnic disputes in the rump state of Austria; and the Socialists had left the government for good in 1920. Their losses were of prestige, status, and political potential. Thus their revision-ism had no obvious and clear-cut goals. Aristocrats were under-standably nostalgic about the world they had lost, but 'all the King's Horses and all the King's Men couldn't put Humpty-Dumpty together again'. The Habsburg monarchy could not be reconquered; optimists might hope that sooner or later people would repent and see reason, but that required patience, and there was little that could be done to hasten the process. That is why they can accurately be described as nostalgic agnostics.

In the meantime, there was little left for conservatives to defend or 'conserve', at least psychologically. The old state had not simply changed colours, but broken apart. The ABC that had upheld aristocratic influence before 1918, despite universal suffrage, army, bureaucracy, and court, no longer worked. The safeguards that had held democracy in check before 1918 no longer existed. The mass parties had started to partition the state among themselves, leaving little room for deference to tradition. Aristocrats had often been proud of their position above party, and few had stood for election to the lower house after 1907.[2] That left them without a safe power base, or even a line of retreat, after 1918. Their old social standing was a position not to defend, but to reconquer.

Referring to the monarchy in veiled terms, Ignaz Seipel, the new leader of the Christian Social Party, who had been a minis-ter in the last imperial government and who took over as chan-cellor in 1922, summed up the situation in a fashion that was

[1] Franz Bernreiter, 'Die Entwicklung des Großgrundbesitzes in Österreich von der Jahrhundertwende bis 1938' (Ph.D. thesis, University of Vienna, 1979); Ernst Metz, 'Großgrundbesitz und Bodenreform in Österreich 1919 bis 1924' (Ph.D. thesis, University of Vienna, 1984).

[2] Those who did were Aloys Liechtenstein for the Christian Social Party and Karl Auersperg for the Nationalverband. Count Leopold Kolowrat, who married an American heiress and was the father of Austria's pioneer of film, was elected for a German Bohemian constituency in 1907, but died soon after.

fitting, and yet almost too glib for a Catholic priest: 'The fallen ones of the war will not return. I believe in the resurrection of the dead, but only on Judgement Day.'[3] In 1918 Seipel had made himself unpopular with the dynasty for publicly suggesting a way out that would enable tender consciences to support the Republic. His policy was clearly to defend substance rather than symbol, and to sacrifice the monarchy in order to prevent a real revolution.[4] Geopolitically, neither of the two options available to Austria, namely, *Anschluß*, the merger with Germany, or a Danubian federation, was feasible at the present time. Of course, it was possible to consider a synthesis at a higher level than the Danubian Federation. Count Richard Coudenhove-Kalergi[5] and his pan-European sect might be seen as the prophets of such a project; at a different level, Seipel's confidant, later to be adviser to the underground Nazi party, Prince Karl Anton Rohan, who used the same publisher as Coudenhove, would toy with European ideas in a different context. But both were clearly outsiders, and were often seen as dangerously affected by the *Zeitgeist*.

A restoration of the Habsburgs within the limits of the Alpine rump state alone seemed a let-down. As Count Adolph Dubsky put it, a Habsburg would surely disdain to return as a small princeling (*Duodezfürst*) to the town where his ancestors had ruled as Caesars.[6] Similarly, Starhemberg and his followers argued that the whole question of legitimism was irrelevant unless it offered an opportunity to transform the Central European land-scape, because the crown would act as a magnet.[7] At the beginning, of course, restoration was not quite such an attractive option either, but for different reasons. Relations between the

[3] Ignaz Seipel, 'Die Wege zum Frieden', *Europäische Revue*, 1 (1925), 20.

[4] The only concession to dynastic loyalty that Vienna's Christian Socials (but not their farming brethren) made was to leave the chamber when the expropriation of the Habsburg family fortune was voted through unanimously in April 1919. Peter Böhmer and Ronald Faber, *Die Erben des Kaisers: Wem gehört das Habsburgervermögen?* (Vienna, 2004), 34.

[5] Richard Nikolaus Coudenove-Kalergi, *Adel* (Leipzig, 1922), 28, 39, argued that perse-cution had provided the best possible selection for the Jewish race. For a biographical sketch, see Anita Ziegerhofer-Prettenthaler, *Botschafter Europas: Richard Nikolaus Coudenhove-Kalergi und die Paneuropa-Bewegung in den zwanziger und dreißiger Jahren* (Vienna, 2004).

[6] Adolf Dubsky, *Die Anschlußfrage im Rahmen einer mit österreichischen Legitimisten geführten Diskussion* (Salzburg, 1934), 9.

[7] Hoyos Archive, Schloß Horn, F. 348/110b, diary Count Rudolph Hoyos, 23 Jan. 1936. (The meeting had taken place on 12 Jan.)

Habsburgs and the political elite had no longer been quite so amicable even before the break-up of the monarchy. Francis Joseph, who died in 1916, had of course commanded their unswerving loyalty. But in the crisis that blew up in 1918 over his successor's contacts with the French, known as the Sixtus affair, the majority of the aristocracy clearly sided with his foreign secretary Count Ottokar Czernin against the blessed Charles I.[8] The Vienna Jockey Club, focal point of the social whirl, would heatedly defend Czernin's reputation during the 1920s.[9]

Some of his no longer quite so uncompromisingly faithful followers might also hold the Emperor's refusal to fight for his throne in November against him. After all, when the game was over in Germany, the general staff told the Emperor to take the blame and abdicate; in Austria, Charles received offers to march on Vienna and turned them down.[10] Joseph M. Baernreither, a clever if obsequious follower of aristocratic politics, hinted at a conspiracy when he commented upon his sovereign's inaction in November 1918: 'The Emperor leaves us in the lurch and punts on anarchy . . . Once confusion has become general, with the Entente willing, he may return. Thus, after the flood, once again the old Habsburg ark. Dumba says that is too Machiavellian. Maybe for the Emperor, but not for his entourage.'[11] Comments made by the Emperor a few months later lend some plausibility to that suggestion. Perhaps Baernreither underrated him.[12]

In any case, by 1922 Charles was dead, and the heir to the

[8] For Charles's personal views see the documents in Elisabeth Kovacs, *Untergang oder Rettung der Donaumonarchie?*, ii. *Kaiser und König Karl I. (IV.): Politische Dokumente aus Internationalen Archiven* (Vienna, 2004).

[9] Haus-, Hof- und Staatsarchiv, Vienna (hereafter cited as HHStA) PA I 1092a, Czernin Papers. In 1924, the seconds nominated by Czernin were Prince Starhemberg, Ernst Rüdiger's father (1861–1927), and Prince Croy. Baernreither claims that Czernin's popularity topped even Lueger's in his best days. (HHStA, Baernreither Papers, box 7, vol. xix, fo. 26) He certainly counted Schönburg as a great fan of Czernin's (fo. 45).

[10] For hints about offers from his generals see Ernest Bauer, *Der Löwe vom Isonzo: Feldmarschal Svetozar Boroevic de Bojna* (Graz, 1985), 126–7.

[11] HHStA, Baernreither Papers, box 7, vol. xix, fo. 75. Alexander Lernet-Holenia documented the same idea in his novel *Die Standarte* (1934), in which his hero burns the banner he has brought back from the wars when the Emperor leaves Schönbrunn without listening to the entreaties of his faithful followers.

[12] Ursula Prutsch and Klaus Zeyringer (eds.), *Leopold von Andrian (1875–1951): Korrespondenzen, Essays, Notizen, Berichte* (Vienna, 2003), 509, report an audience with the exiled Emperor in June 1919: 'Open Bolshevism would survive only a short time—finally the Entente would have had to intervene and then the monarchy's turn would come much more quickly.'

throne was not yet 10 years old. It was some time before he would start to grow out of the shadow of his mother. The Empress Zita was as strong-willed as she was controversial, as pious as she was suspect because her Bourbon relatives had been implicated in the Sixtus affair. For the time being, clearly, restoration was out of the question. Strangely enough, given their pre-war histories, there was an active legitimist movement in Hungary, but only a splinter group advocating the same cause in Austria. The bulk of crypto-legitimist opinion took shelter with the Vereinigung katholischer Edelleute (Association of Catholic Nobles) or the Reichsbund der Österreicher (Austrian Imperial Alliance) and bided their time.[13]

Service to the Republic was no longer a given. Few risked their fortunes to represent Mr Renner abroad, or felt any obligation to do a tour of duty in the no longer royal Dragoons of the *Volkswehr*, the Red-tinted professional army. Ten years after the end of the monarchy, apart from Baron (later also Sir) George Franckenstein in London,[14] there was a lone Prince Orsini-Rosenberg in the Republic's foreign service, stationed, appropriately enough, at the Legation in Prague. The first aristocrat did not graduate from the Military Academy in Wiener Neustadt until January 1934. This date is symbolic but less significant than it seems, as he must have entered the Military Academy in 1930; in 1934 the authoritarian regime, with Prince Aloys Schönburg-Hartenstein as minister of war, did exert a pull, as evidenced by the half dozen aristocratic cadets who entered Wiener Neustadt that year—only to graduate into the German *Wehrmacht* in 1938.[15]

Yet great landowners, responsible for extended family and retainers, were pragmatists. After all, regimes come and go, but they had to find ways of ensuring the survival of their estates. Liechtenstein tempered the fury over the terms of the peace treaties by pointing out that they were absurd. This was precisely why they should be signed, he argued, as after a number of years

---

[13] *Das Neue Reich*, 12 Oct. 1919.

[14] Franckenstein who, unlike many barons, came from an old Rhenish family with a title dating back to 1670, was cold-shouldered by some of his acquaintances for continuing to serve the Republic. Sir George Franckenstein, *Facts and Features of my Life* (London, 1939), 213.

[15] The class included Emil Spannocchi, commander of the Austrian Army in the 1970s; Ferdinand Coreth; Nikolaus Chorinsky; Eduard Walderdorff; Prince Thurn und Taxis; and Baron Franz Sternbach, all from strongly Catholic families.

no one would put up any money to uphold them.[16] Prince Max Egon Fürstenberg, whose residence in Lana was now inhabited by Masaryk, wrote: 'One simply has to adapt to circumstances, try to co-operate and write off those things which simply cannot be helped right now. But that does not mean that one has to abjure one's principles.'[17] One revolution later, after the *Anschluß*, Count Rudolph Hoyos, Austria's largest landowner, would echo Fürstenberg's sentiments: 'Considering my responsibilities to my family, my retainers, and the public, I cannot afford to indulge in a pointless negativism.'[18] Politically, too, aristocrats could live with an imperfect constitution because they had never been enthusiastic about any of them. After all, for the fervently Catholic wing, even the nineteenth-century version of the good old days had already smacked of heathen enlightenment and social engineering. Moreover, while few sympathized with a Godless, egalitarian party which had pledged to do away with property rights, there was no other party that they would willingly have called their own. Late in 1918, Schönburg plaintively asked: 'Is there any party in German Austria that one could sympathize with?' Could they even run for parliament without jettisoning all their principles? In the end, Schönburg did not enter politics, but let himself be persuaded to gather the faithful into the Vereinigung katholischer Edelleute.[19]

In the old Austrian upper house, Schönburg had been leader of the Centre Party, and Max Egon Fürstenberg the leader of the left, of the Verfassungspartei (Constitutional Party). Most of the aristocratic families in the rump state of Austria had belonged to these two closely allied parties. True, up to 1918 half the upper house had belonged to the Catholic right, but fewer than a third of the hereditary peers who lived in what became the Republic of Austria did.[20] With the upper house gone, many members of the

---

[16] *Das Neue Reich*, 15 June 1919. Liechtenstein, a lifelong critic of liberalism, retained a touching belief in the rationality of capitalism: 'Nichts auf Erden ist so kühl objektiv wie das Kapital' (Nothing on earth is as coolly objective as capital), ibid. 12 Oct. 1919.

[17] Fürstenberg Archive Donaueschingen, Max Egon Fürstenberg, 'Politik im Kriege: Briefe', letter to Baernreither, 12 Mar. 1920.

[18] Hoyos Archive, F. 348/110 b, diary Count Rudolf Hoyos, 27 Mar. 1938.

[19] Kriegsarchiv Vienna (hereafter KA) B:762, unpublished memoirs of Prince Aloys Schönburg-Hartenstein, p. 295 (10 Dec. 1918).

[20] A rough count of the party affiliation of members of the 1918 upper house whose estates were located primarily in the Republic of Austria gives twenty-six *Verfassungstreue* (supporters of the 1867 constitution) and Centrists against ten members of the right.

Constitutional Party found it difficult to find a political home. In theory, they had been the 'Whigs' of Austria, allied to the Liberals, that is, the motley collection of free-traders and protectionists, Jews and pan-Germans, whose strongholds lay in the Sudeten areas. Yet that connection owed more to their opposition to the centrifugal and pro-Slav tendencies of the right than to any great appreciation of the troublesome middle-class parties with their strident anticlericalism. As one of the Constitutionalist counts put it, tongue-in-cheek: 'Even if I do not believe in God, I still believe in the Catholic Church.'[21] In terms of domestic politics, many saw the Christian Socials as the lesser evil, an impression that was heightened by the realization that they represented the only bulwark against Socialism. Yet, the relationship between the aristocracy and the mass parties lacked real warmth. On the right, it is true, membership of such Catholic lay organizations as the Volksbund provided an additional link with the Christian Socials. Aloys Liechtenstein had been formal leader of the Christian Social Party since Lueger's death in 1910. Yet even Catholic conservatives found the democratic and populist impulses of the Christian Socials unsettling. Liechtenstein's appraisal of his own party's stand in 1918 and its 'charming indifference' to property rights was far from complimentary. They behaved, he said, like 'Socialists who continue to attend mass out of habit'.[22]

Late in 1917 aristocrats had founded a lobby group, the Waldbesitzer (Association of Forest Owners), which served to camouflage some of their activities in the First Republic.[23] The Waldbesitzer dealt with economic grievances, such as the export duties levied on wood that the desperate Republic, prompted by

[21] Count Adolf Dubsky, according to his great-nephew, Baron Christoph Thienen-Adlerflycht.

[22] *Das Neue Reich*, 30 Nov. 1919. 'For one and a half years the parliamentary leadership of the Christian Social Party gathered the courage to show their fear of the Social Democrats in public: *urbi et orbi*, the Viennese street cliques, and the world' (ibid. 29 Feb. 1920). Liechtenstein admired Lenin as 'a Thomas Müntzer, an Anabaptist of the biggest dimensions' (22 June 1919), and urged his readers to show pity, not hate for his Austrian camp-followers (8 Feb. 1920) who had created an army in their own image. As a result, it did not obey them (29 June 1919).

[23] Fürstlich Fürstenbergisches Archiv Donaueschingen, Max Egon 'Div. Korrespondenzen '14–18', first meeting 9 Oct. 1917, chaired by Althan, with Leopold Berchtold, Franz Liechtenstein, Nikolaus Revertera, and Rudolf Traun; in Jan. 1918 Traun was already rounding up members (Allgemeines Verwaltungsarchiv, FA Harrach, box 860, 8 Jan. 1918).

the paper-mills, had invented as a ready source of revenue. They easily sidetracked the none-too-serious attempts at land reform. Some may have suffered from rent control, a wartime expedient introduced in 1917 that survived half a century of political upheaval remarkably unchanged. Beyond that, the Waldbesitzer—like the Reichsverband der Industrie—did their best to persuade the middle-class parties to present a united front against the Red threat.[24] All *Kulturkampf* issues were to be avoided at any cost. 'Today, when it is a question of to be or not to be for our centuries-old estates, we have to avoid anything that might disunite the Christian and conservative elements as a Socialist majority would surely dispossess us with the same *desinvolture* as the bourgeois regime in Czechoslovakia.'[25]

Only Charles's personal followers felt obliged to keep a travesty of a monarchist movement alive. In 1923, Seipel agreed to place Baron Wense on the Christian Social ticket as a representative of the Party of Austrian Monarchists. He resigned his seat when revisionist activists within the movement disowned the pact with the Christian Socials in the autumn of 1924. Reportedly, the aristocrats prominent within the party, ex-Prime Minister Heinrich Clam and Field Marshal Viktor Dankl, would have liked to continue the liaison. They were right, as on its own the party soon disappeared into absolute irrelevance. Fervent believers among the nostalgics formed the Kaisertreue Volkspartei (Loyalist People's Party) which henceforth represented legitimism to the general public. It was a pitiful association of cranks, led by a mere colonel, Gustav Wolff, and its only two members with any sort of name recognition were Count Arthur Polzer-Hoditz, Charles I's personal secretary, and 'Montschi' Sternberg, a colourful eccentric who was at daggers drawn, almost literally, with most of his peers.[26] When he finally came of age in late 1930,

---

[24] Count Rudolf Colloredo-Mannsfeld and Baron Ehrenfels started the first election committee of estate owners 'to influence the elections against the Socialists' in late 1918. AVA, FA Harrach 861, 1 Jan. 1919; Metz, 'Großgrundbesitz und Bodenreform', 151–60.

[25] Gräflich Abensberg und Traun'sches Zentralarchiv (Schloß Maissau), Box 325, Franz Liechtenstein to Rudolph Traun, 17 Oct. 1930. Traun had caused offence with a comment about marriage reform.

[26] Politisches Archiv des Auswärtigen Amtes (Berlin), Pol. Abt. II, Pol. 11/2, reports of 13 Mar. and 23 July 1926 provide a survey of legitimist activities and organizations; see also Friedrich Wagner, 'Der österreichische Legitimismus 1918–1938, seine Politik und Publizistik' (Ph.D. thesis, University of Vienna, 1956) and Stephan Neuhäuser, 'Der österreichische Legitimismus in der Ersten Republik (1918–1938) unter besonderer

Otto von Habsburg would gently chide Colonel Wolff and advise against any partisan activities. The Habsburg cause had to be above party.[27]

II *The Heimwehr*

Thus in the early years of the First Republic, aristocrats followed a policy of wait and see. This also applied to the early stages of the home guard movement (*Heimwehr*) that had started as a set of local self-defence forces in disputed border areas.[28] In the hinterland, if there were any paramilitary forces on the right, it was the war veterans' federation (*Frontkämpferbund*) with its down-to-earth agenda of pensions that was led by unemployed career officers, many of whom would, of course, count as nobles, but few of whom were aristocrats. Things changed after the mid-1920s. These were the quiet and almost prosperous years of the First Republic after the consolidation, both politically and financially, that Seipel had achieved by forming a solid centre-right coalition in 1922. By that time the revolutionary wave that had swept over Europe had spent itself. Self-confidence had returned. Neighbouring Hungary and fascist Italy had returned to a firmly right-wing foundation.

Yet the Social Democrats issued a challenge. Unlike in Germany, their supporters had briefly dominated the small professional army that Austria was obliged to set up under the terms of the peace treaties. After 1922, when Reds began to be purged from the army, Social Democrats founded the *Schutzbund*, officially called Republican *Schutzbund* ('Resch') to emphasize its

Berücksichtigung seiner Organisationen' (Master's thesis, University of Vienna, 1991); 'Montschi' Sternberg's pre-war memoirs have recently been edited by Hans Rochelt as *Adalbert Graf Sternberg 1868–1930: Aus den Memoiren eines konservativen Rebellen* (Vienna, 1997). In Mar. 1922, Sternberg was ballotted out of the Jockey Club. (HHStA, Albert Mensdorff-Pouilly Papers, box 4, diary, 12 and 20 Mar. 1922.)

[27] August von Lovrek, 'Die monarchistische Bewegung' (1997), 2. I am grateful to Albert von Pethö for a copy of this unpublished manuscript. Wolff had first drawn attention to himself by holding a black-and-yellow flag aloft in front of the parliament building on the day Austria was declared a republic (12 Nov. 1918). In 1931, the motley monarchist associations came together under an umbrella organization called the Iron Ring and led by the diplomat Friedrich von Wiesner.

[28] Schönburg (KA, B:762, p. 298) had been asked to assume the leadership of the early *Heimwehr* in 1920 by Kunschak (Christian Socials) and Dinghofer (Greater German People's Party), but had refused. For contacts abroad see Lajos Kerekes, *Abenddämmerung einer Demokratie: Mussolini, Gömbös und die Heimwehren* (Vienna, 1966).

defence of the republican constitution in line with Germany's *Reichsbanner*. Yet the *Schutzbund* was clearly an exclusively partisan affair, and, what is more, apparently did its best to proselytize in the countryside. Talks about a rival organization to the 'Resch' led to a revival of the *Heimwehr* or *Heimatschutz* ('Hasch') with a domestic agenda. The Vienna riots of July 1927, often erroneously described as a putsch, followed by a railway strike which the fledgling home guards helped to defeat, is generally, and probably rightly, seen as a catalyst.[29] The impact of rhetoric at the Social Democratic party conference in November 1926 with wild, if hypothetical, talk about the proper context for the dictatorship of the proletariat, is also often cited as a trigger for the more philosophically minded.[30] The result of the 1927 elections with their disappointing result for the anti-Socialist *Einheitsliste* (single list) should probably also be regarded as a pointer towards strong-arm tactics. Similarly, Socialist obstruction at the committee stage of parliamentary debates gave ammunition to those who argued that the Reds saw no reason to take democracy seriously either, unless it suited their purpose.[31]

The *Heimwehr* was anti-Socialist, yet supposed to be above party, as its leaders pointed out—neutral and open to all comers, legitimists and pan-Germans, clericals and liberals, anti-Semites and Jews.[32] In Germany, Hugenberg proudly proclaimed that he preferred a hard-core party to a catch-all porridge of politics

[29] The conflict that sparked the Justizpalast riots centred on a *Frontkämpfer* who had fired shots, not members of the home guard. When the Christian Social leaders had discussed the paramilitaries exactly one year earlier, Vaugoin reported that the 'Resch' were training their members to throw hand grenades in the Prater, a park in Vienna; Kunschak at that time still spoke of 'our' *Hakenkreuzler* (swastika men). (AVA, Christlichsoziales Parteiarchiv, Klubvorstand, 15 July 1926.)

[30] Walter Wiltschegg, *Die Heimwehr: Eine unwiderstehliche Volksbewegung?* (Vienna, 1985), 39.

[31] See Robert Lukan, 'Der Kampf um den Mieterschutz in der Ära Seipel 1922–29' (Ph.D. thesis, University of Vienna, 2005); Social Democrats, too, toyed with corporatist ideas e.g. only city-dwellers to be qualified to vote on rent control (*Arbeiter-Zeitung*, 1 Aug. 1924).

[32] The three most prominent supporters of the *Heimwehr* with Jewish backgrounds were Rudolf Sieghart, director general of the Bodencreditanstalt that collapsed in 1929, Jacob Lippowitz (1865–1934), owner of *Neues Wiener Journal*, and Fritz Mandl (1900–77), owner of the Hirtenberg Small Arms Company who reluctantly emigrated to the Argentine in 1938 accompanied by Count Maximilian Thurn-Valsassina. See Ronald C. Newton, 'The Neutralization of Fritz Mandl', *Hispanic American Historical Review*, 66 (1986), 541–79.

('Block, nicht Brei').[33] Austrians combined the two elements. Ideologically, the *Heimwehr* was as heterogeneous as it was possible to be, yet at the same time it was much more militant than anything Hugenberg could come up with. Party representatives tried to supervise the home guards' organization, and sat on its board, yet the initiative was taken by community leaders, unaffiliated with parties or dissatisfied with them. It was a heaven-sent opportunity for the old elites who had been crowded out in the post-war competition for jobs, not just by the Reds, but also by upstart busy-bodies, civil servants' shop stewards, and officials of farmers' cooperatives, who were prominent among the right-of-centre parties. Renner diagnosed correctly: 'In a Marxist perspective, the whole of the *Heimwehr* is a revolution against bourgeois leadership.'[34]

For a brief period, at least, the *Heimwehr* movement, apolitical and ultra-political at the same time, was the sort of party aristocrats had always hoped for. Not least among its charms was that it was not really a party. The list of its rural representatives read like an excerpt from *Gotha* or a parody of the *Ascot Gavotte*: 'Every duke, and earl, and peer is here; Everybody who should be here, is here.' For the lesser fry, one assumes, it was indeed a 'smashing, positively dashing spectacle' to pay back the Reds in their own currency and 'be received everywhere'. Left-wing intellectuals might scoff at the gathering of the backwood clans, and *Heimwehr* propaganda might reinforce that image by its denunciation of post-war decadence, but the movement clearly appealed to the smart set, from flying aces and racing heroes to actresses and pioneers of radio.[35]

This sort of gregarious, top-down civil society was perhaps reminiscent of the reaction to the 1926 strike in Britain. At the beginning, rural grandees cooperated, but took something of a back seat. The cutting edge of the early years was clearly provided by the input of industrialists, whose economic background in

[33] Thomas Mergel, 'Das Scheitern des deutschen Tory-Konservatismus: Die Umformung der DNVP zu einer rechtsradikalen Partei 1928–1932', *Historische Zeitschrift*, 276 (2003), 323–68, at 344.

[34] Quoted in Wiltschegg, *Die Heimwehr*, 15 n. 7.

[35] The top Austrian flying ace of the First World War, Captain Brumowski, was an active *Heimwehr* member who fought in the civil war of 1934 (*Heimatschutz in Österreich*, 31, see n. 40 below); Starhemberg married the Burgtheater actress Nora Gregor after the dissolution of his first marriage in 1937.

heavy industry and pan-German orientation might be likened to the Hugenberg wing of the Deutschnationale Volkspartei (DNVP, German National People's Party) in Germany. The difference was that in Germany this sort of militant strategy had the effect of crowding out old-style conservatives;[36] in Austria, it split and weakened the civil service-dominated Großdeutsche Volkspartei (Greater German People's Party), arguably the DNVP's sister party in Austria. But it also provided an opening for the old elites to re-enter politics on a new ticket, one, moreover, that enjoyed the support of Austria's priestly version of Gustav Stresemann, Ignaz Seipel. Seipel, who had resigned as chancellor in early 1929, used the *Heimwehr* as a dual-purpose weapon to frighten the Socialists and, at the same time, to put pressure on his obstreperous smaller coalition partners, whose supporters among the small-town middle-class often moved to the *Heimwehr*.

In 1927, when the *Heimwehr* actually had to run the trains, the vigilantes of the Alpine Montan conglomerate had done the dirty work. Their fame and ability to fight the Socialists on the shop floor made the *Heimwehr* a worthwhile investment. When the *Heimwehr* next entered politics, in 1929, aristocrats were once again conspicuous by their absence. It seems that they had developed an instinct for spotting lost causes early on. As Johannes Schober, the chief of police turned chancellor in 1929, told the eager putschists: 'I ought to arrest you but your plans are so ridiculous that you will have to be acquitted on any charge of treason.'[37] Moreover, *Heimwehr* activism—unlike the mass appeal of Nazism, but like Hugenberg's takeover of the DNVP in late 1928—was a pre-Depression phenomenon. When financial difficulties arose in the autumn of 1929 (and the Austrian Bodencreditanstalt crisis actually preceded Black Friday by a few weeks), it had a dampening effect on their activities. It was

[36] For Germany, see, apart from Mergel, 'Das Scheitern des deutschen Tory-Konservatismus'; Larry Eugene Jones, 'Catholic Conservatives in the Weimar Republic: The Politics of the Rhenish-Westphalian Aristocracy, 1918–1933', *German History*, 18 (2000), 60–85; for East Elbians see Mario Niemann, 'Die Stellung der mecklenburgischen Großgrundbesitzer zum Nationalsozialismus und zur Mitgliedschaft in der NSDAP', in Ernst Münch and Ralph Schattkowsky (eds.), *Festschrift für Gerhard Heitz zum 75. Geburtstag* (Rostock, 2000), 309–35; Stephan Malinowski, *Vom König zum Führer: Deutscher Adel und Nationalsozialismus* (Berlin, 2003) actually provides more material on the pre-Nazi period and tends to gloss over the importance of exactly when people joined the party.

[37] Diary Hans Glaser, editor of the *Salzburger Volksblatt*, 4 July 1930 (the episode referred to 20 Aug. 1929, however).

rumoured that the march on Vienna had been cancelled after Baron Rothschild had confessed to Schober (or warned him?) that he could not guarantee the Schilling in the case of further disturbances.[38]

Schober managed to persuade the Social Democrats to cooperate with a watered-down version of constitutional reform that fell far short of *Heimwehr* demands. It was after this first disappointment, when the *Heimwehr* felt that it had been used by the centre-right coalition as a convenient bogeyman without getting what it actually wanted, that a representative of the aristocracy finally took over the movement. Prince Ernst Rüdiger Starhemberg, a colourful figure, was a descendant of Vienna's defender against the Turks 250 years earlier and a famous ladies' man whose most amazing female conquest, it might be added, turned out to be a posthumous one.[39] Under Starhemberg's leadership the movement turned itself into a party that regarded Schober and the cluster of small law-and-order parties that supported him as traitors for his refusal to countenance a *coup d'état*, and looked towards an alliance with Seipel's Christian Social Party. There was disagreement, however, about the best way to maximize the impact of such an alliance. Should they present a joint list, or should the *Heimwehr* run on a separate ticket as a reservoir for anticlerical voters? Ideally, they could march separately but fight together. Yet when the *Heimwehr* did so, the electoral results were disappointing (only 6 per cent of the vote).

The *Heimwehr* represented an unstable combination held together by the dynamics of a movement. Once a setback occurred or stagnation set in, its heterogeneous elements were prone to start fighting each other. This is what happened on a large scale in 1932. (In the heartland of Lower Austria, the split came even earlier.[40]) This was not a two-way, but a three-way split. One part of the movement stayed with the Christian Socials, while another drifted towards the Nazis, who made big

---

[38] PA/AA, Pol 2, no. 3 (Heimwehr), 21 Nov. 1929.

[39] See Gudula Walterskirchen, *Starhemberg oder die 'Spuren der 30er Jahre'* (Vienna, 2000). Vienna owes the only mention of an aristocratic title in a street name to him: Graf Starhemberg-Gasse, named after Vienna's defender against the Turks in 1683, in order not to be confused with his controversial descendant, who had the title of prince which the family had been given during the Napoleonic period.

[40] The PR volume *Heimatschutz in Österreich*, published in the summer of 1934 by the propaganda department of the *Heimwehr* leadership, offers surprisingly candid summaries of these internal disputes.

gains in 1931–2. But the aristocratic elements, including most of the officers, stayed loyal to Starhemberg, both when he turned away from the Christian Socials early in 1931, and when he returned to an alliance with them early in 1932.[41] These were the people not accustomed to seeing themselves as part of politics at all, and thus not committed to either camp, even if their middle-class followers could not be restrained from manning the old ideological fault-lines.

Styrians tried to copy Mussolini in the autumn of 1931, when Pfrimer staged an abortive 'march on Vienna'. Starhemberg distanced himself from the *coup,* not because it was a *coup* but because he had not been informed in advance.[42] It is not necessary to impute an exaggerated sense of legalism to *Heimwehr* leaders. It might sound ironic but was perfectly logical that the *Verfassungstreuen,* named after their loyalty to the constitution of 1867, should be so dismissive of its republican replacement. After all, they might well have subscribed to the theory that the whole order of things after 1918 was illegitimate anyway. Yet a sense of what was practical cautioned against some of the wilder flights of fancy indulged in by hotheads. The way in which authoritarian rule came about in 1933, as a defence of established authority rather than as a rebellion, with a suitable explanation attached about the failure of parliaments, was reassuring because it read just like 1897, or 1902, or 1914.

III *The Ständestaat*

When Dollfuß took a great leap forward and established his authoritarian *Ständestaat* (corporate state), the *Heimwehr* briefly came into its own. The *Heimwehr* proudly pointed to its record in fighting the two rebellions or civil wars of 1934, the Socialist rising in February, and the Nazi putsch in July. Yet, with hindsight, it seems that the army was quite capable of doing so on its own. The *Heimwehr* was not important because of its armed

---

[41] Raab's paper listed the leaders of the *Heimatschutz* The eleven men who made up the executive committee included one count, three barons, two more officers, and a manager from industry. Two more counts (Friedrich Karl Schönborn and Anton Attems) had run on their ticket in the 1930 election. *Niederösterreichische Heimwehr,* 20 Jan. and 3 Feb. 1931.

[42] Josef Hofmann, *Der Pfrimer-Putsch: Der steirische Heimwehrprozeß des Jahres 1931* (Vienna, 1965).

strength. But the movement, spearheaded at this time by a highly decorated bourgeois major, Emil Fey,[43] in charge of the police, acted as a catalyst, and persuaded reluctant Christian Socials that there was no alternative but to forge ahead. Socialist militants played into their hands when, against the entreaties of their Vienna leadership, they staged a rising in February 1934, exactly when the tug-of-war between Dollfuß's new *Heimwehr* friends and his old constituency among the Lower Austrian farmers threatened to reach dangerous proportions.[44] The uprisings led to a closing of ranks behind Dollfuß; in the short run, the *Heimwehr* got what it wanted. One of Starhemberg's loyalists exulted: 'Today only the *Heimwehr* has a say. Dollfuß and his like have to follow along, like it or not.'[45] In the long run, however, the establishment of an authoritarian regime, paradoxically, lessened the government's dependence on the *Heimwehr*.

In the meantime, the structure of the *Heimwehr* had also changed. Many of the early militants had defected to the Storm Troopers. Those who stayed were recruited as auxiliary police units after 1933. This meant that middle-class volunteers who had participated in weekend rallies were often replaced by the unemployed, whose ideological commitment was overshadowed by material incentives. Within the leadership, however, the aristocratic element had become more visible, especially during the mobilization against the Nazi risings in July. A track record of this sort came in useful after 1945, if not before. In any case, that antagonism was dictated by geography, not ideology. Few of the movement's aristocratic protectors lived close to the council housing where the fighting took place in February, but many owned castles in the Styrian and Carinthian countryside where

[43] Georg Mautner Markhof, *Major Emil Fey: Heimwehrführer zwischen Bürgerkrieg, Dollfuß-Mord und Anschluß* (Graz, 2004). Fey was awarded a Maria Theresa Cross in the 1920s for his wartime exploits; theoretically, in the days of the monarchy, that would have conferred noble status.

[44] The February rising was a traumatic event in Austrian history, celebrated for the first fifty years culminating in a big exhibition in 1984; since then, historians seem to have lost interest in the interwar years, except for British scholars who, during the Thatcher years, discovered the Austrian militants as a role model, thus providing valuable insights into the labour movement in the countryside. For Styria, see Jill Lewis, *Fascism and the Working Class in Austria, 1918–1934: The Failure of Labour in the First Republic* (New York, 1991); for Upper Austria, see Charlie Jeffrey, *Social Democracy in the Austrian Provinces 1918–1934: Beyond Red Vienna* (London, 1995).

[45] Hoyos Archive, F. 348/113 b, letter 23 Feb. 1934.

the Storm Troopers flexed their muscles in July. Aristocratic *Heimwehr* leaders poured scorn on the Austrian Nazis, led by a former Communist, Theo Habicht, who sided with Socialists and Czechs against the Dollfuß government. Hitler's Germany, one of them wrote, was not a fascist state, but 'something chaotic, steadily getting Redder, and increasingly dependent on the mobs in the street.'[46]

The *Heimwehr* has appropriately been called a 'would-be fascist' movement. It was a vehicle of the old elites, and although it achieved a certain resonance after 1927, it was not a real mass movement. In Italy, and to some extent also in Weimar Germany, it seems, parts of the old elites tried to use fascists as shock troops against the revolution, but then had to defend their own turf against the newcomers. In Austria, the old elites themselves built a surrogate movement that sufficed for the job—and then went on to defend their position against their more plebeian and vibrant rivals. Fascism, after all, is a post-democratic phenomenon. If democracy had never been taken seriously anyway, a mass movement was not needed to turn the clock back. As Hoyos asserted: 'We have thoroughly broken with the democratic past and cease to take the masses seriously. Not so the Nazis. Unwittingly they cling to old liberal and democratic ways of thinking. Thus their fawning on the favour of the mob.'[47] The Habsburg monarchy had, after all, often ruled by decree, even if this unavoidably ran counter to the wishes of the overwhelming majority of its subjects. Or perhaps Austria fascism was home to the 'Frank Sinatra doctrine' of Fascism: 'I'll do it my way . . . ' Even those who proudly claimed to be fascists defined it in curious ways: authority, as Hoyos took good care to remind Schuschnigg, must not be confused with executive licence. On the contrary, the point of an authoritarian government was to protect the state from the vagaries of party democracy, and not to be swayed by the whims of the moment. Theirs was supposed to be a fascism that did not allow the state to become omnipotent, balanced budgets, and regarded the monarchy as essential.[48] (Otherwise continuity could not be guaranteed.)

[46] Regional Archive (Statni oblastni archiv, hereafter SOA) Leitmeritz/Tetschen, RA Clary-Aldringen 711, Rudolf Hoyos to Sophy ('Foffa') Clary, 24 Feb. 1934.

[47] Hoyos Archive, F. 348/113b, letter to Lori Ledebur, 7 May 1934.

[48] Ibid., letter to Marietta Starhemberg, 13 Dec. 1933; Hoyos diary, 17 Oct. 1936; 'Grundsätzliche Ansichten über Heimatschutz und Verfassungsänderung' (Oct. 1933).

Aristocrats presumably liked the corporatist idea, as they had never been wholly comfortable with laissez-faire doctrines, intellectually at least. One of their number, Count Ferdinand Westphalen, was an adherent of Othmar Spann, the fashionable proponent of that idea.[49] But they shied away from totalitarian aspirations that required giant bureaucracies to put them into practice, and it would probably be correct to say that they disliked all '-isms'. Any mention of secular value systems is beside the point in their case: aristocrats had the dynasty (or rather, they no longer had it); they had *esprit de corps* and a code of honour from their army days; and they had the Catholic Church. Those were the things that lasted. As for the rest, Prince Alois Auersperg probably spoke for most of his fellow aristocrats when he wrote: 'Emotionally, I have regarded all political developments after 1918 with distaste, or at best indifference.'[50] Their approach to constitutional blueprints or economic doctrines was a purely functional one. As has been written about their even more unfortunate comrades from another defunct empire: 'The White leaders were not as reactionary as the Cossacks feared, not so much because they held progressive political opinions as because they had almost no political opinions at all.'[51] Bohemian nobles required stronger medicine to topple 'their' republic, but Austrian aristocrats were content with the *Ständestaat* and generally did not see any reason to rock the boat. 'We have finished the Reds—better and more thoroughly than anywhere else, including the Third Reich.'[52] Lujo von Toncic-Sorinj, a youthful admirer of Fey who became Austrian foreign secretary in the 1960s, summed it up when describing his feelings about the

'Möchtegern-Faschismus' is Wiltschegg's term. Helmut Wohnout, *Regierungsdiktatur oder Ständeparlament? Gesetzgebung im autoritären Österreich* (Vienna, 1993), 434, rightly points out that 'Austro-fascism'—a term sometimes used for the *Ständestaat* as such—was a term the *Heimwehr* liked to use for their agenda.

[49] Spann was unlucky in his politics; the *Ständestaat* regarded him as a Nazi sympathizer until he turned up on Hoyos's doorstep three weeks before the *Anschluß* to help defend Austria against the 'un-German and anti-Christian fools Hitler and Rosenberg'—which promptly earned him banishment from his academic career by the Nazis. Horn, F. 348/113 b, Hoyos to Schuschnigg, 26 Feb. 1938. In 1937 Westphalen was denied a professorship at the University of Innsbruck, but later appointed to the Bodenkultur (Agricultural College) in Vienna. (Hoyos diary, 5 Feb. and 28 Apr. 1937).

[50] Alois Auersperg, 'Menschen von gestern und heute' (privately circulated manuscript, Salzburg, 1982), 88.

[51] Paul Robinson, *The White Russian Army in Exile 1920–1941* (Oxford, 2002), 5.

[52] Rudolph Hoyos to 'Foffa' Clary, 24 Feb. 1934, as in n. 46.

Ständestaat: 'If one did not choose to think ahead, it was a good time. Finally we who were on the right had had our say, too.'[53] Once he had outgrown his mother's shadow, young Otto might even come into his own, one day. Legitimism had lost the stigma that had long attached to it. It was noted that the *Ständestaat* had jettisoned Austria's designation as a 'republic'. Dollfuß's successor, the Tyrolean Kurt von Schuschnigg, certainly harboured legitimist sympathies. Legitimists gained an official foothold in the political hierarchy when a *Traditionsreferat* (department of tradition) was created and entrusted to one of their spokesmen, Zessner-Spitzemberg, that 'good natured super-Austrian'.[54] Austrian army uniforms returned to the cut they had had during the First World War. Rival leaders from Hitler to Benes had not quite overcome a lurking fear that, given the chance, people might easily slip back into the mould of loyalty to the Habsburgs. If, with hindsight, this seems an exaggeration, it was not for nothing that Hitler's emergency plan for Austria was famously entitled Operation Otto. Early in 1936, Schuschnigg and the *Heimwehr* leaders, meeting in the chambers of the old Imperial War Council, agreed on a joint approach to Otto. Restoration was the ultimate goal, but one to be pursued with caution. 'Will you not come back again'—but not right now. Starhemberg was supposed to visit Otto on his return from King George V's funeral, but diplomatic pressure forced him to cancel the visit.[55] The antics of the legitimist ultras under Friedrich von Wiesner, an ex-diplomat and Jewish convert, were in any case suspect to the *Heimwehr* leaders. Perhaps as an interim solution, Archduke Eugene, a popular army leader, could be elected president?[56]

[53] Lujo Toncic-Sorinj, *Erfüllte Träume* (Vienna, 1982), 71–2.

[54] Helmut Wohnout, 'Das Traditionsreferat der Vaterländischen Front', *Österreich in Geschichte und Literatur*, 36 (1992) 65–82.

[55] Horn, F. 348/110 b, Hoyos diary, 23 Jan. and 15 Feb. 1936. In particular, it was the Yugoslav members of the Little Entente who were, at the same time, believed to have signed a pact with Germany in order to prevent a restoration. See also Arnold Suppan, *Jugoslawien und Österreich 1918–1938: Bilaterale Außenpolitik im europäischen Umfeld* (Vienna, 1996), 1196–200.

[56] Hoyos diary, 25 Apr. and 5 May 1937. Prince Karl Emil Fürstenberg, the top-ranking leader of the legitimist group, told Hoyos he had proposed such a solution to Otto, but received no reply. Eugene also agreed with Hoyos that an anti-German policy—as advocated by Wiesner's adherents—was impossible and would serve only to drive even more people into the Nazis' arms. For comments on Wiesner's crowd see ibid. 18 Oct. 1936, 19 May 1937.

The flurry around the monarchist revival proved to be the high-water mark of aristocratic influence in the interwar years— and Starhemberg's parting shot. In May 1936 he lost his position in the government, and in October 1936 the *Heimwehr* was dissolved. Starhemberg's group,[57] probably the one most representative of aristocratic sentiment, was increasingly unhappy with the drift of things. They realized that they would have to come to an agreement with the pan-Germans at home and the Third Reich abroad.[58] The ratification of the Franco-Soviet pact and the outbreak of the Spanish Civil War only served to rouse their anti-Communist instincts.[59] Starhemberg fondly spoke of a fascist entente between himself, Mussolini, and Goering, but Hitler and Schuschnigg refused to be sidelined. The *Heimwehr* disliked Schuschnigg's way of replacing them with Nazi go-betweens, and they liked his volte-face of March 1938, with its overtures of an anti-Nazi Popular Front, even less. During the *Anschluß* crisis, Revertera, for example, disregarded Vienna's order to distribute arms to former Socialist workers.[60] After the *Anschluß*, crypto-monarchist opinion leaders offered to publish a statement accepting the new order. Vienna *Gauleiter* Bürckel thought that their text was too tepid and contained a *reservatio mentalis*; when it was redrafted, some legitimists thought it went

[57] Starhemberg's group included Rudolph Hoyos, Peter Revertera, the Upper Austrian director of security, and Botho Coreth, another Upper Austrian; Kottulinsky and Thurn-Valsassina were close collaborators; in Lower Austria Edmund Hartig and Friedrich Tinti should be added. Of the five people who had a final showdown with Schuschnigg on the night he dissolved the *Heimwehren*, three were counts (Hoyos, Revertera, and Stürgkh), the other two *Heimwehr* leaders from the West (Hoyos diary, 9 Oct. 1936). Fey, with whom Starhemberg had fallen out, and the lower-ranking nobles Berger-Waldenegg and Neustädter-Stürmer, who in 1936 advocated a complete break with the Schuschnigg regime, followed different paths. See also Egon Berger-Waldenegg and Heinrich Berger-Waldenegg, *Biographie im Spiegel: Die Memoiren zweier Generationen* (Vienna, 1998), 466.

[58] Contrary to post-1945 myth, one of the chief complaints of *Heimwehr* leaders about Schuschnigg's July 1936 agreement with Berlin was that the Chancellor had stolen their clothes (Hoyos diary, 5 June and 1 Oct. 1936). During the Rhineland crisis Starhemberg's sympathies were with Germany: at such a critical juncture, he argued, one could not take a stand against the German nation and the Reich, even if one did not want to succour its regime. Austrian aristocrats were unhappy with Otto's pronouncements in the French press; to preserve his chances of yet ruling over a great Mitteleuropa, they suggested, Otto should be marketed as a 'German prince' (ibid. 15 July 1936).

[59] When Hitler gave his first speech on Spain, Hoyos noted: 'Something unbelievable has happened. I agreed with him almost totally' (10 Sept. 1936). Peter Revertera's brother fought as a volunteer on Franco's side.

[60] Hoyos diary, 9, 11, and 23 Mar. 1938.

too far. In the end, nothing came of the idea ⎯perhaps this was just as well, as Hoyos thought.[61]

IV *The Third Reich*

A look at the aristocracy, like a closer look at any other group, demonstrates the futility of the Manichaean view of the world as neatly divided into Nazis and resisters. Both terms allow for an infinite variety of different shades of grey. Unfortunately, it seems, with the passing of time morally loaded denunciations and apologetics have increased in volume rather than faded away. Thus, when dealing with the relationship of the aristocracy to the Third Reich, a certain amount of hyperbole has to be discounted. This difficulty is compounded by the tendency of post-1945 propagandists to mistake loyalty to Old Austria for a particularist patriotism centred on the Republic of 1918 that was unbeloved of all true conservatives.

There is no reason to exaggerate aristocrats' opposition to National Socialism, or their prescience of ills to come. Yet their very reactionary nature enabled them to recognize the left-wing elements of the National Socialist movement that were plebeian and heathen, and subversive of the old order. Prince Adolph Schwarzenberg, at the very top of the magnates' pyramid, more an Old Austrian than a new one, summed up his impressions of the first few months of the Third Reich: 'It looks very much like a sort of national Bolshevism . . . The power of the lower classes seems to be increasing and if the famous Hitler is not able to push the lower classes down, then Bolshevism might come sooner or later.'[62] Even more, Hitler might pretend to be a good Catholic at times, and he had certainly signed his version of the Lateran Pacts in 1933. But his local followers, the Austrian Nazis, were clearly steeped in a priest-baiting anticlerical tradition, and

[61] Hoyos diary, 30 and 31 Mar., 5 Apr. 1938.

[62] Letter to Roy Home, 7 May 1933, quoted in Sarka Lellkova, 'Ztraceny raj: Farma knizete Adolfa Schwarzenberga v Africe' (Paradise Lost: Prince Adolph Schwarzenberg's Farm in Africa). This as yet unpublished manuscript forms part of a series of papers on the aristocracy in Bohemia that will be edited by Ivo Cerman and Lubos Velek. Rohan agreed that the German revolution 'had two faces, a national and a Communist one', and that 'the national pincer of the German Revolution must not be broken', but 'made useful for the state', *Europäische Revue*, 9 (1933), 32.

their experiences with the supposedly Catholic *Ständestaat* only served to heighten that feeling. Aristocrats probably preferred the German take-over in 1938 to a pseudo-independent Austria run by the local Nazis who would be far more radical.

Yet fighting the local Nazis often meant firing at former *Heimwehr* comrades; fighting Germany meant firing at former comrades from the First World War. If provoked, they were prepared to do it, but few liked the idea. Schuschnigg was right when he refused to give the order to shoot in 1938. Resistance was a crazy idea that might have turned Austria into another Spain, with a civil war raging down to the last village,[63] and conservatives ground to pieces between a Popular Front and the Nazis. While many hoped that Hitler could somehow be contained, few were willing to pay the price of another defeat for German-speakers in Europe, quite apart from the fear that such a war would necessarily benefit Stalin. Aristocrats had certainly learnt the lessons of 1914–18. Chamberlain's Munich agreement was welcomed: 'For he is a jolly good fellow and so say all of us.' If envy of perfidious Albion rang a bell with middle-class nationalists, aristocrats never lost sight of the Bolshevik menace—and Britain was their favourite country. But only Schwarzenberg was far-sighted enough to buy a farm in Kenya as an insurance policy. After all, his prophecy that 'a great war is sure to end in Bolshevism' turned out to be right in his case, and it stopped only a few miles short of many of his relatives' estates.[64]

In Bohemia, where political orientations were linked to ethnic disputes, aristocratic society was deeply split between Czech and German partisans, and some old friends were reputedly no longer on speaking terms after 1938.[65] In Austria, polarization was far less advanced. There was no reason why one should not socialize with the Rothschilds and Hermann Goering at the same

[63] Hoyos diary, 9 and 11 Mar. 1938.

[64] Hoyos diary 30 Oct. and 13 Nov. 1938; Schwarzenberg's letter to Home, 28 Mar. 1938.

[65] HHStA, Nl. Berchtold 5, transcripts of his diary, 25 Oct. 1933, 28 July 1934. Berchtold himself, true to his charming image, remained on good terms with all and sundry; however, a Lobkowicz reputedly refused to speak to a Czernin while the latter wore a German uniform (interview with Rudolf Czernin); Count Gerulf Coudenhove, Richard's brother, tried to explain to *Reichsstatthalter* von Neurath that aristocratic families who preserved their Czech loyalties after 1939 were in fact only demonstrating old Teutonic feudal virtues (information from Christoph Thienen). This ingenious explanation did not cut any ice with Heydrich, however.

time. Many aristocrats were sceptical or opposed to the Nazis, but also liked or supported some of the regime's measures.[66] There were different shades of grey. Known hard-core legitimists of the Wiesner–Wolff persuasion were singled out for persecution,[67] as were the Hohenberg family (Franz Ferdinand's sons), whereas Franz Ferdinand's last head of Chancellery, General Karl von Bardolff, welcomed the *Anschluß*.[68] The Nazis were less 'bolshie' about Old Austria than has sometimes been suggested. After all, for all the Nazis' anti-Habsburg credentials (and vice versa), a luminary such as Field Marshal Archduke Eugene, Grand-Master of the Teutonic Knights, was treated with at least as much respect by the Third Reich as by the First Republic.[69] Captain Georg von Trapp of *Sound of Music* fame simply happened to be on the wrong side of the border when war broke out—and made the best of it.[70] In other cases, *Heimwehr* connections or family ties that transcended political cleavages served to soften the blow. Hoyos was arrested for three months but took the incident in a sporting spirit. Left-wingers certainly did their

[66] The same holds true for business opportunities. Participation in the 'Aryanization' of Jewish businesses was by no means confined to fanatical Nazis; nor, it has to be added, would keeping a virtuous distance from these admittedly sordid transactions have helped Jewish owners forced to sell in a buyers' market.

[67] Gudula Walterskirchen, *Blaues Blut für Österreich: Adelige im Widerstand* (Vienna, 2000), 68.

[68] In 1923, however, the young Duke Maximilian of Hohenberg had asked Bardolff to assume a more active part in the Association of Catholic Nobles. KA, B:207 Bardolff Papers, x.

[69] KA, B:3/10 Dankl Papers. In Apr. 1939, Dankl, who as legitimist leader was certainly not in favour with the regime, was still asked to provide a bust of himself for the Vienna Military Museum; see also Peter Broucek (ed.), *Ein General im Zwielicht: Die Erinnerungen Edmund Glaises von Horstenau* (Vienna 1983), ii. 67, 672; Thomas Grischany, 'Der Österreicher Adolf Hitler' (Master's thesis, University of Vienna, 1994), 110–11. The same was true in reverse: Prince Ulrich Kinsky, denounced as a Nazi sympathizer by Countess Sternberg in her memoirs, Cecilia Sternberg, *Es stand ein Schloß in Böhmen* (Hamburg, 1979) because of his support for Henlein, in 1930 headed a fund-raising drive for the upkeep of Emperor Charles's burial chapel in Madeira. (Copy of his appeal in Traun Archive, box 324.)

[70] The invitation to sing at Hitler's birthday that the Trapp family is supposed to have rejected does not speak of hostile intentions. The Trapps did sing for Mussolini, as the Austrian submarine hero had opted for Italian citizenship after the First World War. Trapp was not—or only distantly—related to the Counts Trapp. However, he was related to the upper crust through his first wife, a Whitehead. Before his second marriage he had apparently once been engaged to Karl Anton Rohan's sister Mary. Elisabeth Monarth, 'Mythos und Wirklichkeit: Die Trapp-Geschichte aus verschiedenen Blickwinkeln', in Ulrike Kammerhofer-Aggermann and Alexander G. Keul (eds.), *'The Sound of Music'—zwischen Mythos und Marketing* (Salzburg, 2000), 67–90.

best to advertise the charms of the Third Reich for the old elite,[71] which was often reinforced by a little bit of self-delusion. In 1938 a story made the rounds that Goering had apologized, in a way, for the 1934 putsch, and was even looking for a way to bring Starhemberg back into the fold.[72] During the war, military instincts resurfaced. Some easily adapted the old slogan to 'Gott, Führer und Vaterland'. Many aristocrats, as cavalry men, served with the nostalgics from further east, the anti-Bolshevik Cossacks.

To be sure, there were a number of aristocrats who had supported the NSDAP all along. In general (if there is such a thing as general rules when dealing with such limited statistical samples) it was progressives who were a little more respectful of the twentieth century and yearned for an *aggiornamento*, who persuaded themselves to see the Nazis as representatives of the true people. Like most other Nazi supporters, they tended to be young. Moreover, many of those who joined the party early were younger sons. This might be seen as part of a traditional survival strategy: 'Never put all your eggs in one basket!' If that was the result, it seems to have been unintentional in most cases. It also seems that aristocrats who were divorced or married divorcees or commoners were more likely to look upon the Nazis with kindly eyes.[73]

Interestingly, most of the aristocrats who joined the National Socialists came from Lower Austria, not Styria or Carinthia where the movement was strongest, and many members of what was known as 'second society', that is, ennobled businessmen and civil servants, clearly had strong sympathies for the Nazis.[74] Perhaps the proximity of Vienna highlighted the limitations of the *Ständestaat*; perhaps economic grievances contributed to their

[71] See the postscript to Alfred Zweig's novel *Einsetzung eines Königs* (Amsterdam, 1937), in which he remarked: 'It was not forseen that the old ruling class would succeed in returning to power even before the story of their defeat had been written' (573).

[72] Hoyos diary, 9 Apr. 1938.

[73] Hardegg was divorced and remarried; Traun married a divorcée; in Bohemia, Prince Kinsky had also been ostracized for divorcing his wife in the 1930s and remarrying. Cecilia Sternberg, *Es stand ein Schloß in Böhmen* (Hamburg, 1979), 58, 165. Contrary to the impression given in her book, Cecily continued to be a frequent visitor at the Kinsky home, as the entries in the guest-book show.

[74] The two barons implicated in the rising, Helmut von Reinsdorff and Berndt von Gregory, were Prussian immigrants; the family of Otto von Wächter, who had masterminded the Vienna putsch, had been ennobled only in 1918. Kurt Bauer, *Elementar-Ereignis: Die österreichischen Nationalsozialisten und der Juliputsch 1934* (Vienna, 2003), 228, 299.

disaffection. The clumsy attempts of the *Ständestaat*, in its corporatist guise, neatly to pigeonhole landowners according to their sources of income opened an easy way out for Alpine aristocrats. They withdrew into the forestry section, which they dominated. There was no such way out for Lower Austrian *Gutsbesitzer* (estate owners), whether Jew or Nazi, who owned less land, but more productive acres.[75] Interestingly, the two foremost examples of Austrian aristocratic heirs who counted as Nazi *fiancheggiatori* belonged to that category. In 1937 they signed a petition for a reconciliation with the national opposition but wielded no great influence.[76] The only aristocrat who played any part in the final takeover in 1938 was Count Peter Czernin, younger son of the foreign secretary of 1916–18, who threw in his lot with the Carinthian SS leaders who outflanked the plodding SA leadership.

One reason why some aristocrats were more willing than others to advocate an understanding with the Third Reich was rooted in foreign policy. Austrian aristocrats with interests in non-German countries tended to appreciate the re-emergence of Germany as a great power. The foremost example of this tendency was the Grusbach circle of Austro-Bohemian nobles (Count Adolph Dubsky, Count Karl Khuen-Belasi, Prince Karl Anton Rohan, and Baron Wolfgang Thienen, who had married Prince Franz Thun's only daughter). The Grusbach circle, named after Khuen's castle in Moravia, was close to Henlein and the Sudetendeutsche Partei (SdP) in Czechoslovakia. They wanted Germany and Austria to stop bickering and cooperate in putting pressure on Czechoslovakia. A *coup d'etat* and the mere magic of the Habsburg name were not enough to rebuild Europe

---

[75] Hoyos diary, 19 June 1936; Gräflich Abensberg und Traun'sches Zentralarchiv (Maissau), box 323, contains correspondence between Hoyos and Hans Traun's father Rudolf, concerning that question at that time. This is not to say that the disagreements that centred on the role of the Landwirtschaftsgesellschaft fed into automatic support for the Nazis. On the contrary, the Landwirtschaftsgesellschaft's president, Rudolf Colloredo-Mannsfeld, incidentally Karl Anton Rohan's brother-in-law, was himself targeted by the Nazis after the *Anschluß*. Walterskirchen, *Blaues Blut für Österreich*, 139. But it does highlight a problem that was particular to Lower Austria, where the Christian Social farmers under Reither retained an unusual degree of influence.

[76] The list, which provides a sort of *Who's Who* of luminaries with a national touch, was published by *Die Neue Zeit* on 18 Feb. 1937. The drive was sponsored by *Heimwehr* secretary of state Neustädter-Stürmer, who lost his job soon after. A similar appeal had earlier been published in *Wiener Neueste Nachrichten*, 23 Mar. 1934.

in the time-hallowed imperial image; a truly popular movement was required. The Nazis had proved that they had the potential for this. It was not their ideology that was an incentive to join, but the very fluidity of their position that resembled 'an area of inundation with a complex of currents and cross-currents running in different directions'.[77] The Grusbach nobles did not close their eyes to the less savoury aspects of the Nazi movement.[78] But if the Nazis were a potentially double-edged weapon, that was one more reason for the old elites to exert their leadership and make sure they turned the right way. The right way to do this, in the eyes of Rohan and Dubsky, was to support the SA, the Storm Troopers, often seen as the plebeian element, against the more elitist SS, which copied monastic paraphernalia but was a heathen order. The tug-of-war between the two rival factions in Henlein's SdP only served to underline their argument.[79]

After 1938, the Grusbach circle tried, largely in vain, to make the saying about Vienna as the second capital of the Reich a reality, and resuscitate its role as a focal point for the whole of south-eastern Europe.[80] Khuen found it a difficult task to recruit suitable candidates for a Jockey Club that continued life as a mere society section of the Racing Association.[81] Even worse, their attempts to prevent the rift with Britain from escalating into war came to nothing.[82] Thus, in the end, Schwarzenberg's bleak prophecy about another war spelling the victory of Communism in Europe came true.

[77] Dubsky, *Die Anschlußfrage*, 13.

[78] Ibid. 14, concerning the sins of Nazi propaganda; see also Rohan's articles in *Europäische Revue* (1932), 454–9, where he talks about the superior talents and high moral standards of Judaism.

[79] Ralf Gebel, *'Heim ins Reich!': Konrad Henlein und der Reichsgau Sudetenland* (Munich, 1999), 49–52.

[80] SOA Litomerice/Leitmeritz, pob. Decin/Tetschen, RA Clary 616, Karl Khuen to Alfons Clary-Aldringen, 24 Oct. 1938. Dubsky wrote a memorandum early in 1940 defending the reputation of the Habsburg monarchy and the term 'Austria' versus 'Ostmark' (copy in Borodajkewicz Papers, KA, B/1251/36).

[81] Ibid. letters 11 and 28 Feb. 1939; see also RA Clary 615, Karl Egon Fürstenberg to Alphons Clary, 14 Sept. 1938.

[82] Fascinating glimpses of these attempts can be found in Group Captain Christie's correspondence with Prince Max Hohenlohe, deposited in Churchill College, Cambridge.

11

The Hungarian Aristocracy and its Politics

IGNÁC ROMSICS

The Hungarian aristocracy of the interwar period comprised about 300 to 350 families or clans. A more precise estimate of their number cannot be given because of intermarriages, both domestic and international, and various colligations of family names. Of these families, approximately half held the title of baron; the other half were counts. Only ten clans were titled *herceg* (prince), and a single family, related to the House of Habsburg-Lorraine, bore the title of archduke. Some of the clans were relatively large, at times comprising thirty to forty households, each headed by a title-holder, while there were also examples of the opposite extreme, when a clan comprised only three or four—and sometimes even fewer—adult males. The aristocracy, therefore, hardly exceeded a few thousand in number, meaning that it made up less than 0.1 per cent of the country's population of almost nine million. Most clans had received their respective titles after 1541: only two families held titles dating back to medieval times.[1]

Centuries of dividing lands up between heirs and the massive loss of estates entailed by the Trianon Treaty meant that the aristocracy was far from homogenous in terms of wealth. While some continued to rank among the richest in the land, an ever-increasing number were forced to work for their living. In the 1940 census, seventy-nine people reported an income exceeding 200,000 Pengős. Of these, eighteen individuals or 22 per cent were aristocrats. The next statistical group, comprising 290 individuals with incomes between 100,000 and 200,000 Pengős

---

[1] Ernő Lakatos, *A magyar politikai vezetőréteg 1848–1918* (Budapest, 1942), 18–21; János Gudenus and László Szentirmay, *Összetört címerek* (Budapest, 1989), 72–3; Gábor Gyáni and György Kövér, *Magyarország társadalomtörténete* (Budapest, 1998), 193–4.

counted only twenty-four aristocrats (8 per cent), while among
the 1,010 taxpayers earning between 50,000 and 100,000 Pengős,
the aristocracy made up only a small minority of thirty-three
individuals or 3 per cent.[2]

The affluence of the aristocracy had traditionally been ensured
by the ownership of large latifundia. In 1935, the 1,171 estates
exceeding 1,000 yokes in size accounted for 30 per cent of all the
land in agricultural use.[3] Of the owners of these large estates, 687
(62 per cent) were members of the aristocracy. As with incomes,
the aristocracy was most preponderant in the topmost categories,
with a progressively diminishing share.[4]

In terms of its social network, the aristocracy retained its caste-
like character as late as the interwar years. Its castles were, in a
sense, microcosms inserted into the world, with servants, precep-
tors and governesses, duennas, ceremonial dinners, hunts, horse-
races, tennis courts, and balls.

The large cream-coloured manor house of Fót, built in the Napoleonic
era, with its Doric columns, its library of 80,000 volumes collected by
my great-grandfather Joseph and his son Stephen, its mahagony
shelves, its galleries and winding stairs, its stucco-moulded ceilings and
open fireplaces, its 300 acres of park and its lake—one of them remembered this exclusive isolation—was a gilded cage that held us in splen-
did isolation from the outside word . . . Already as a small boy, I was
made to realize that I was a privileged being, a special pet of the
Almighty, who had made me heir to such great wealth. I was supposed
to expect and obtain respect and exercise authority over the less privileged, who had to be directed, governed and assisted by us. Our attitude could best be compared with that of the English in their colonies,
with the slight difference that the 'natives' were our own people.[5]

Its self-contained social networks, however, did not mean that
the aristocracy was a relatively homogeneous and unitary stratum
of society. Quite the contrary: the few hundred families with
their 4,000 to 5,000 members were differentiated by a number of
criteria, and multiple hierarchies existed. As a contemporary
sociologist noted: 'the old magnate looks down on recently titled
barons, the most ancient families even distinguish themselves

[2] Dezső Zentay, *Beszélő számok*, 13 vols. (Budapest, 1941–5), ix. 73–103.
[3] One yoke equals 1.4 acres or 0.57 hectares.
[4] Zentay, *Beszélő számok*, xiii. 72–108.
[5] Mihály Károlyi, *Memoirs of Michael Károlyi: Faith without Illusion* (London, 1956), 20.

from the other indigenous houses, the titled baron or industrialist looks down on similarly titled civil servants, yet may also despise—being more educated or productive—the ancient count.'[6] Duke Pál Esterházy, the largest private landowner in the country with more than 200,000 yokes to his name, was remembered as having a nervous fit upon having to pay a visit to the prime minister of the time, who, although one of the most successful politicians of pre-war Hungary, was not a member of the nobility.[7]

Using the criteria of when the title was granted, the size of the family fortune, ancestry, and confession, three loose groups may be identified among the aristocracy as a whole. The Transdanubians—so-called because of the geographical location of their estates—were in close contact with the imperial court in Vienna, linked to the supranational aristocracy of the empire, often by marriage, belonged to the Catholic Church, and had accumulated very considerable wealth over the centuries. A second distinct group consisted of the predominantly Calvinist Transylvanian aristocrats, whose material means were more modest (very modest, at times), and who usually married within their own group. The 'barons' made up the third group, this term referring to those who had received their titles for military or civic services, or for their economic achievements, largely in the nineteenth and early twentieth centuries. They were usually called soldier barons, industrial magnates, and so forth, all denominations reflecting their distinct status. The 'historical' baronial titles, whose holders usually socialized with the similarly ancient counts, are therefore not included here, but they were a small minority. In the period between 1849 and 1918 alone, emperors Francis Joseph and Charles I granted 204 titles to Hungarian nationals, all but a few of them baronial. A considerable number of generals and civil servants raised to the status of baron were of German origin and of relatively modest means, while extremely wealthy Jewish entrepreneurs made up the bulk of the industrial magnates. Even in the interwar years, these Jews failed to gain admittance to the exclusive circles of the historical aristocracy.[8]

---

[6] István Weis, *A mai magyar társadalom* (Budapest, 1930), 145.

[7] Mihály Károlyi, 'Emlékezés az úri Magyarországra', *Valóság*, 1(1946), 8.

[8] Lakatos, *A magyar politikai vezető réteg*, 19–23; Gyáni and Kövér, *Magyarország társadalomtörténete*, 194–8.

The influence of the aristocracy, like its finances, remained considerable between the two world wars, although it decreased by comparison with what it had been in the previous century. A statistical investigation of the legislature and executive provides clear evidence of this. The upper house of parliament, for instance, was always made up predominantly of aristocrats— before 1918 their share never sank below 70 per cent. When the upper house was reorganized in 1926, however, it was by and large conceived on corporatist grounds, and consequently only 28 per cent of the seats were held by aristocrats, with their share remaining relatively constant in the following years. Of the 240 to 250 representatives, 42 sat as delegates of the aristocracy, while a further 20 to 25 aristocrats held seats as a result of their public functions or in recognition of their services.[9]

The aristocracy had never had a comparable influence in the lower house, which was elected by 6–7 per cent of the population before 1918, and by 30 per cent after 1920. Its share lay between 8 and 16 per cent before the First World War, but the high watermark of 15 per cent in 1910 had fallen to 5 per cent by 1920, before stabilizing at around 10 per cent for a decade and a half in 1922, and finally decreasing to 8 per cent in 1939. In a sense, then, there was no significant decline in the representation of the aristocracy in the lower house, yet the number of seats held by aristocrats was also less significant in the first place.[10]

A much more significant loss of ground can be registered in terms of offices in the executive. During the half-century before 1918, ten out of sixteen prime ministers had been aristocrats, while of the fifteen heads of government between 1919 and 1944, only three held an aristocratic title. A similar decrease can be observed in government portfolios: the average of 34 per cent from the pre-war decades fell to a meagre 7 per cent between 1920 and 1944.[11]

The ministry with the greatest appeal for the aristocracy had traditionally been the foreign office. Among Hungarian nationals working at the Austro-Hungarian foreign ministry before the war, 16 per cent were members of the aristocracy. Yet if we take the actual administrative grades, the figure jumps to 26 per cent,

[9] Levente Püski, *A magyar felsőház története 1927–1945* (Budapest, 2000), 11–31.

[10] Lakatos, *A magyar politikai vezetőréteg*, 29; *Nemzetgyűlési és Országgyűlési Almanachok, 1910–1944* (Budapest, 1910–39).

[11] József Bölöny, *Magyarország kormányai 1848–1975* (Budapest, 1978); Gyáni and Kövér, *Magyarország társadalomtörténete*, 199.

superseded only by a staggering 63 per cent within the exclusive branch of the diplomatic service. This contrasts sharply with the interwar Hungarian ministry for foreign affairs, where the aristocracy provided 7 per cent of the total number of employees, accounting for 17 per cent of the administrative, and 26 per cent of the diplomatic service branch.[12] In sectoral ministries such as agriculture and commerce, which required more specialized professional training, the aristocracy's share was considerably smaller than these figures in both periods.

There are at least two reasons for this loss of position. The overall process of democratization meant that an ever-increasing number of gentry and non-noble young people gained a college-level education and diploma, which enabled them to enter the service of the state and reinforced their political ambitions to join the legislature. 'Democracy looks past the institutions and the people of yesteryear, and forgets about what the Hungarian nation can thank its aristocracy for', complained one of them in 1929.[13] Also, and no less importantly, the half-hearted compromise reached on the question of monarchy meant that Horthy, a Calvinist petty noble, became Regent of Hungary, while Charles and, later, Otto von Habsburg were prevented from taking the throne, also because of a prohibition by the Great Powers. This disheartened and alienated much of the Transdanubian aristocracy, which tended to look upon Horthy with disdain. Some aristocrats followed their hearts and joined royalist conspiracies of various sorts, while others simply abstained from public affairs in the interwar years. Passivity in public life was especially characteristic of the very upper stratum, the richest counts and the few dukes in the country. Those who did take up government positions came predominantly from Eastern Hungary, Transylvania, or Upper Hungary, and were usually of limited means. It is typical of this phenomenon that of the three aristocrats who held the office of prime minister in the interwar years two, counts István Bethlen (1874–1946) and Pál Teleki (1879–1941), were Transylvanian. Bethlen, in particular, was Calvinist and well-nigh penniless, as the Romanian land distribution law had left him with a mere 40 yokes of his 5,000-yoke estate.[14]

---

[12] Pál Pritz, *Magyar diplomácia a két háború között* (Budapest, 1995), 19–36.
[13] Erzsébet Csekonics, 'A magyar arisztokrácia válsága', *Magyar Szemle*, 18 (1929), 162.
[14] Ignác Romsics, *Hungary in the Twentieth Century* (Budapest, 1999), 181–91.

Most aristocrats who chose to become politically active or entered the civil service in the interwar period sympathized with conservative ideas of various shades. Apart from the counter-revolutionary interlude of 1919–20 and the extreme right-wing course brought about by the German occupation of 1944, this coincided with the declared ideological affiliation of successive governments and of the governing party. Interwar Hungarian conservatism, however, can be separated into two main currents, one traditionalist-libertarian, and a more modern, anti-liberal movement. The traditionalists held on to the nineteenth-century heritage, including unconditional respect for private property, legal and civil equality, a system of pluralistic parliamentarism, and relative freedom of the press. This political vision was challenged from both the left and the right at this time. The radical left, including the Communist fringe and a section of the Social Democrats, was committed to a far-reaching transformation of society, while the leftist mainstream was working for the transformation of a liberal political system into a democratic one. The extreme right, on the other hand, was anti-parliamentary and pro-dictatorship, and its programme contained a strong anti-Semitic element. Liberal conservatives, as these traditionalists may be called, had to confront all three currents.[15]

This latter group was headed by István Bethlen, prime minister between 1921 and 1931. He had no sympathy for the parliamentary democracies that had multiplied after the First World War, and confessed himself a proponent of 'guided' or 'conservative' democracy, and 'moderate progress' or 'small steps'. In the spring of 1922, he characteristically stated: 'we want democracy, but not the rule of the masses, because the countries where the masses rule over the nation are doomed.' He regarded the aristocracy and the landed gentry as the natural elite of such a 'guided democracy', because, as he explicitly stated, these strata of society 'possess the greatest capacity to resist pressure and upheaval'. To justify his elitism while also making it compatible with the democratic discourse of the day, Bethlen drew on the contrast between

---

[15] Ibid. Cf. Miklós Lackó, 'A magyar politikai-ideológiai irányzatok átalakulása az 1930-as években', in id., *Válságok—választások* (Budapest, 1975), 318–63; and Ignác Romsics, 'Parlamentarismus und Demokratie in der Ideologie und Praxis der ungarischen Regierungsparteien in den Jahren 1920–1944', in Anna M. Drabek, Richard G. Plaschka, and Helmut Rumpler (eds.), *Das Parteiwesen Österreichs und Ungarns in der Zwischenkriegszeit* (Vienna, 1990), 19–38.

liberalism and radicalism. The former he described as 'a powerful creative force and true democracy' while equating the latter, a 'bastardization of liberalism', with 'destruction'.[16] The Hungarian political system, drawn up in the early 1920s and surviving in essence to 1944, which restricted the suffrage and prescribed open balloting for about 80 per cent of the electorate until 1939, can be regarded as a direct expression of Bethlen's views.

The general shift in the international political environment in the 1930s made Bethlen's positions appear in a different light. As prime minister, his most important challengers were on the democratic left. This position was, however, taken by the fascist or quasi-fascist formations in the late 1930s and early 1940s. It was with regard to these ideologies that he declared in 1934: 'I stand on the basis of the thousand-year-old Hungarian tradition and I will have nothing to do with uncontrolled Western democracies, just as I will have nothing to do with dictatorship.'[17] Bethlen also opposed the anti-Jewish legislation that was passed between 1938 and 1941, which he held to be in violation of the principles of civic equality. In association with an informal coalition of loyalist and pro-Horthy counts, a number of industrial magnates, and liberal democrats, he played a leading role in the founding of the anti-German and anti-dictatorial National Hungarian Circle in 1943, renamed Democratic Civic Alliance at the end of the same year. He was motivated by the conviction that this centrist democratic formation, which would only conditionally cooperate with the Social Democrats, might become a vehicle for organizing post-war society, and counter the radical left, which was expected to come more to the fore in the process. To prevent a radical redistribution of lands seemed to him of extreme importance, as this would have entailed the financial ruin of the aristocracy and the landed gentry, making a loss of prestige and societal privileges almost impossible to avoid.[18]

In its struggle against the Communist left and social and liberal democracy, liberal conservatism found a steady ally in the anti-liberal

---

[16] [No author given], *Bethlen István gróf beszédei és írásai*, 2 vols. (Budapest, 1933), i. 228, ii. 43. Cf. Ignác Romsics, 'István Bethlen et le conservatisme hongrois', in Chantal Delsol and Michel Maslowski (eds.), *Histoire des idées politiques de l'Europe centrale* (Paris, 1998), 477–88.

[17] Ignác Romsics, *István Bethlen: A Great Conservative Statesman of Hungary, 1874–1946* (New York, 1995).

[18] Ibid. 322–86.

neo-conservative current. As far as the fight against the Hungarian republics of 1918 and 1919, and especially the Hungarian Soviet Republic, were concerned, Bethlen fought side by side with Pál Teleki, one of the most important and best-known representatives of the anti-liberal neo-conservative current. They also cooperated closely in 1920, in preparation for the signing of the peace treaty, and later in setting a course for the country's foreign policy. Their opinions on the nineteenth-century liberal heritage, however, differed sharply. In the early 1920s, the heyday of right-wing radicalism and anti-Semitism, Bethlen emphasized the importance of this liberal heritage, and strove to preserve its institutions and spirit, albeit with some modifications. Teleki, at the same time, was taking a markedly clerical and anti-liberal position. Liberalism, he stated once, 'a current of the late nineteenth century, has passed and disappeared; it has died, never to return'.[19] At times, he interpreted the age of liberalism as a period of decline, seeing its inherent destructive tendencies as responsible for 'gradually eradicating national sentiment, [and] sucking the fibre of Christian morality out of society'.[20]

Teleki saw the Jews as the chief social carriers of these destructive tendencies, especially the latecomers, the imperfectly or wholly unassimilated nineteenth-century immigrants from Galicia. Whereas the Jews accounted for a mere 5 per cent of society as a whole, 30–50 per cent of university students and certain professions were Jewish. This motivated Teleki, as prime minister, to propose a law that aimed to reduce the proportion of Jewish students at universities to 5 per cent—the law of *numerus clausus*. This he pushed through parliament in 1920. In 1928, when Bethlen in his turn moved to relax the law, Teleki expressed his unaltered convictions. And during his second premiership, between 1939 and 1941, he once again initiated a movement to extend anti-Jewish legislation to include the professions as well. The so-called Second Jewish Law of 1939, which he had helped to prepare and which was passed during his period in office, set the upper limit of Jewish participation in business at between 12 and 20 per cent, and in the professions at 6 per cent. The civil service was to release all its Jewish staff within five years.[21]

[19] Pál Teleki, *Magyar politikai gondolatok* (Budapest, 1941), 34.
[20] [No author given], *Gróf Teleki Pál programbeszéde Szegeden 1919. év december havának 14. napján* (Szeged, 1920), 2.
[21] Balázs Ablonczy (ed.), *Pál Teleki: Válogatott politikai írások és beszédek* (Budapest, 2000),

A second important difference between the two currents and the two politicians touched upon their attitudes towards popular representation and party pluralism. Bethlen may have sought to constrain free competition between parties, yet he never opposed it in principle. Teleki's ideals showed a strong affinity with corporatism or the *Ständestaat*, above all its Portuguese version. He felt especially close to Salazar, volunteering to write an introduction for the Hungarian edition of his selected speeches. His programme of 1940 foresaw the transformation of the lower house, with 50–5 per cent of seats delegated by the counties, 38–42 per cent by the corporatist chambers, and a mere 6–8 per cent elected, and even these only by the select few with a college degree, or 1.2 per cent of the total adult population. The 'hunt for the voter', the competition between the parties, was to be replaced by competence, while party politics in general were to be replaced by meritocracy and professionalism.[22]

Teleki's willing acknowledgement of the achievements of dictatorial systems was surely not unrelated to his dislike of democracy and liberalism. To him, Hitler's Germany also symbolized 'what may be achieved with faith and will'. At a conference in 1933 in Paris he openly declared that 'successful dictatorships are the ones which give faith and confidence in the attainment of a goal'. At the same time, he resented the role of the popular leader, the mobilization of the masses, modern means of propaganda, and populism in general. One may surmise that the forms of modern politics as a whole were diametrically opposed to his world-view and conception of governance. His views on Germany were, in addition, also influenced by his political opposition to those National Socialist designs that he felt threatened the sovereignty of Hungary. These factors understandably reinforced his ties with the liberal conservatives.[23]

As previously stated, most aristocrats in politics subscribed to one of these two central currents, described here in terms of their most characteristic representatives. Royalists and industrial magnates, understandably, ranked with the liberals, whereas

---

200–3. On the laws and their effects cf. Mária M. Kovács, *Liberal Professions and Illiberal Politics: Hungary from the Habsburgs to the Holocaust* (New York, 1994), 189–244.

[22] Ablonczy (ed.), *Pál Teleki*, 443–63.

[23] Balázs Ablonczy, 'Eszmék és vonzalmak: Teleki Pálról fehéren—feketén', *Rubicon*, 2 (2004), 40–3.

owners of smaller estates and aristocrats in the civil service tended to sympathize with the anti-liberal direction. The affiliation of the aristocracy with each of the two conservative currents can easily be measured by taking a brief look at parliament. Of those MPs who were also members of the aristocracy, 90 per cent sat in the government party or in some other conservative formation, occasionally as independents with a conservative agenda. Few joined a democratic party and right-wing extremist movements—in all, two or three MPs for each shade of the opposition during the whole of the interwar period. If we add aristocrats without a seat in parliament to the list, as well as members of the Szálasi or Arrow Cross government of October 1944, the total number of aristocrats participating in National Socialist or related movements rises to half a dozen, but no more.[24]

The right-wing extremist party of the 1920s, the Party of Race Protection (Fajvédő Párt), had no aristocrats at all among its leaders. This was a characteristically middle-class party, which appealed to young officers, intellectuals, and professionals. The second great surge of the Hungarian extreme right, in the wake of the Great Depression and Hitler's rise to power, did recruit two aristocrats to the cause, both of whom went on to hold prominent positions on the rightist fringe of the political palette. One of them was Count Fidel Pálffy (1895–1946), a poor landowner who sold his estate in newly formed Czechoslovakia in 1921, moved to Hungary, and acquired a 600-yoke estate. During the recession, however, he became severely indebted. He founded one of the first Hungarian National Socialist parties, under the name of the National Socialist Hungarian Agrarian and Workers' Party, in 1932. Pálffy soon abandoned his own brainchild: he quit the party and founded a new one, under the name of United National Socialist Party in 1933. Pálffy essentially radicalized the anti-Semitism characteristic of anti-liberal neo-conservatism, going beyond merely restricting the Jews' civil rights and aiming to revoke their citizenship altogether. In addition, he also pursued the expulsion of 'undesirable immigrants'. As the party programme declared, citizenship or 'membership in the nation' was to be open exclusively to individuals of Turanian or Aryan origin, or alternatively, to 'Hungarians of Turanian,

[24] *Országgyűlési Almanachok*, 1931, 1935, 1939; and Miklós Lackó, *Arrow-Cross Men, National Socialists, 1934–1944* (Budapest, 1969).

Aryan, Slavic, and Latin ancestry'.[25] The lengths to which the definitions went and their vagueness highlights the absurdity of a Hungarian theory of race which was bound to fail in the face of the task of identifying a Hungarian race spread over a territory characterized by such ethnic diversity and interpenetration.

A further radical innovation of Pálffy's programme aimed to nationalize mines and larger industrial enterprises, and demanded a switch to a planned economy. The programme also foresaw the expropriation of large estate-owners, the radical distribution of the land, and aid to indebted smallholders. On these points, as on the question of race, the programme confronted conservative policies directly. The demand for universal, secret, and compulsory suffrage was also opposed by conservatives, who saw in it a vehicle for mob rule. Conservatives and right-wing extremists were in agreement, however, on the need to revoke the 1920 peace treaty and to seek the quickest and most integral reunification of Hungary possible.[26]

Pálffy went on to join several extreme right-wing formations, but he always ended up quitting to found his own party. Although he never gained a seat in parliament, his activities were acknowledged in the Third Reich, and gained him an invitation to participate at the Nuremberg party rally in 1937. Pálffy achieved his highest position by far in October 1944 when, after the abdication of Regent Horthy, he received the portfolio for agriculture in Szálasi's Arrow Cross cabinet. As a direct result of his role at the close of the Second World War, the People's Court sentenced him to death by hanging on 15 December 1945, and the verdict was carried out on 2 March 1946.[27]

The other aristocrat who experimented with founding a right-wing extremist party was Count Sándor Festetics (1882–1956). He grew up in a family that was considerably wealthier than Pálffy's, and attended elite schools. Festetics joined the imperial diplomatic service as a young man, and served on the front as an officer in the First World War. In the autumn of 1918 he held the defence portfolio for a few weeks in the new Hungarian government. After his demission, he retired to his 30,000-yoke Transdanubian estate,

[25] Jenő Gergely, Ferenc Glatz, and Ferenc Pölöskei (eds.), *Magyarországi pártprogramok 1919–1944* (Budapest, 2003), 268–73.

[26] Ibid. 314–20.

[27] Rezső Szirmai, *Fasiszta lelkek* (2nd edn.; Budapest, 1993), 170–8, 274–5.

which provided him with the means to live a true aristocrat's life. He won a seat in parliament in 1931, representing the government party, but quit the majority soon after. Festetics founded his own organization, the Hungarian National Socialist Party, in 1933, which survived, albeit with several fusions and splits, until 1938.[28] Its programme largely coincided with that of Pálffy, who was an occasional political ally. However, a new element was the demand for a presidential political system, since parliamentarism 'had not worked anywhere but in England'. It may not be too far-fetched to suspect that the term 'presidential' stood for a dictatorial form of government.[29]

Relying on name recognition and personal wealth, Festetics ran for election and won in two districts at the 1935 elections. He then resigned one of his two seats, thus securing a second representative in parliament in the person of one of his deputies. This made Festetics the only aristocrat with a right-wing extremist programme in parliament, and one of two National Socialists. His followers, however, were dwindling in number by 1938, and this as well as the rivalry characteristic of the Hungarian extreme right, cost him his seat in the 1939 elections. After his defeat, he retired from politics for a second time, and survived the Second World War in seclusion on his estate. As a result of this passivity, he was sentenced to a jail sentence after the war, and died, following his release from prison, in 1956.[30]

Another five aristocrats joined the ranks of extreme rightist organizations in the interwar period. All of them were affiliated with the Party of National Will, founded in 1935 and later renamed National Socialist Hungarian Party—Hungarist Movement. The organization, best known under its final, and most notorious reincarnation as the Arrow Cross Party, was headed throughout the period by a former general staff captain, Ferenc Szálasi who in 1944 assumed power with German help following Horthy's abdication. Szálasi's views did not differ significantly from those of Pálffy and Festetics as far as their preference for a dictatorial system over democracy or the need to 'cleanse' the country of Jews was concerned. He was more moderate on the issues of land reform and the nationalization of strategic industries, but more than made

---

[28] *Országgyűlési Almanach 1935–1940*, 257–8.
[29] Gergely, Glatz, and Pölöskei (eds.), *Magyarországi pártprogramok*, 303–13.
[30] Gudenus and Szentirmay, *Összetört címerek*, 104.

up for this by his extreme views on foreign policy, advocating a Hungarian empire, envisaged as stretching beyond the Carpathians and bearing the puzzling name of Hungaria United Ancestral Lands.[31]

Three of these five aristocrats had historical titles: Count Lajos Széchenyi (1902–63), Count Miklós Serényi (1898–1970), and Baron Gábor Kemény (1910–46). Széchenyi was the scion of a great clan; the founders of both the National Library and the National Museum were among his ancestors. He completed his studies at an agricultural college, and drew his income from his 3,000-yoke Transdanubian estate. After 1937, he ranked as one of Szálasi's less influential deputies, and gained a seat in parliament at the 1939 elections. It was at the same elections that Count Miklós Serényi also became an MP, while continuing to live off his 900-yoke estate.[32] Kemény first earned a law degree and worked in the administration as a provincial district administrator, a kind of sheriff in the English sense, before switching to journalism in 1933. He had no lands, and was highly motivated, which was perhaps not unrelated to his lack of fortune. He was caretaker of foreign relations, the official in charge of party connections, for the Arrow Cross Party from 1941 on, and joined the Szálasi cabinet in October 1944 as minister of foreign affairs. Like Pálffy he, too, was sentenced to death and executed by the People's Court after defeat in the Second World War. The new aristocracy was represented in the party by Baron Ede Temesváry (né Vest), chief of press relations to Szálasi, and Baron Gyula Stralendorff, a party propaganda coordinator. The former was of Swiss, the latter of Austrian origin.[33]

In sum, the Hungarian aristocracy's representation in politics remained considerable in the interwar years, although it had declined by comparison with the decades before the First World War. The overwhelming majority was attached to conservatism, both in world-view and in politics; the extreme right succeeded in gaining the active support of no more than seven aristocrats. All strata of the Hungarian aristocracy, however, were represented among them, with the obvious exception of the predominantly Jewish industrial magnates: historical clans as much as recently

---

[31] Gergely, Glatz, and Pölöskei (eds.), *Magyarország pártprogramok*, 321–33, 424–31.
[32] *Országgyűlési Almanach 1939–1944*, 302, 319.
[33] Gudenus and Szentirmay, *Összetört címerek*, 105.

titled aristocrats, Transdanubians and Transylvanians, wealthy and poor alike. The view, frequently encountered in the historiography of the period, that the extreme right appealed only to impoverished and déclassé aristocrats is therefore in some need of revision.

12

Aristocracy, Fascism, and the Social Origins of Mass Politics in Romania[1]*

CONSTANTIN IORDACHI

In October 1937 an impressive funeral ceremony took place in Bucharest. General Gheorghe Cantacuzino (1869–1937), a renowned war hero but controversial politician, was buried with national honours and a large public presence. A descendant of the prestigious Cantacuzino princely family (branch Prince of Wallachia Şerban Cantacuzino, 1678–88), which had roots in the Byzantine Empire, the General found glory in Romania's military campaigns during the Second Balkan War (1913) and the First World War (1916–18), and had been decorated with the highest military medal, Michael the Brave.

Yet the last years of the General's life spurred much controversy in Romania's politics. In 1933, dissatisfied with traditional parties, the old conservative politician linked his political fortune to that of the fascist Legion of 'Archangel Michael', (alternatively known as the Iron Guard), and its charismatic leader, 'the Captain', Corneliu Zelea Codreanu. Cantacuzino's subsequent activities were central to the development of the Legion, paving this organization's way to political prominence. The General's burial, heavily exploited by Legionary propaganda, gave a final electoral boost to the party All for the Fatherland, which he had founded in 1935 and led on behalf of Codreanu—just before the national parliamentary elections. In December 1937, carried also by the general's prestige, All for the Fatherland obtained a stunning 16 per cent of the total vote, sending sixty-six deputies to what was to be Romania's last freely elected parliament in over fifty years (1937–90).

In this essay I use the terms 'liberal' and 'conservative' to refer to the members of the two leading factions (later parties) in Romanian political life, without wanting to imply that their views were necessarily compatible with 'classical' liberalism or conservatism.

Although the most prominent, General Cantacuzino was but one of a plethora of Romanian aristocrats who collaborated with the Legion. What can account for this 'unholy' alliance between leading aristocrats and fascism? In order to answer this question, we will explore the wide variety of strategies of adaptation to mass politics practised by Romanian aristocrats between the wars. It is argued that the Romanian aristocracy traditionally pursued a conservative domestic social policy, but favoured tolerance towards ethnic minorities and an inclusive immigration policy. This attitude changed to some extent in the interwar period when, following the social upheaval generated by the First World War and the introduction of universal male suffrage, the Romanian aristocracy experienced a dramatic decline in social and political influence. Even though most aristocrats joined new mass political parties or collaborated with the monarchy, a few prominent aristocrats joined the anti-establishment Iron Guard in the hope of regaining political visibility. Their participation had important symbolic connotations, aristocracy being assigned an important role in the Legion's ideology of national regeneration. Based on case studies of members of two famous aristocratic families associated with the Legion, the Cantacuzinos and the Sturdzas, we underline the fusion between the fascist charismatic elite and revolutionary ultra-nationalist political ideology on the one hand, and the 'traditional' legitimacy claimed by aristocrats in the movement on the other. These two streams blended to produce a new type of 'charismatic aristocracy' concomitantly promoting a 'regressive' and 'futurist' political utopia based on the glorification of the Middle Ages but embodying the new men.

I *Aristocracy and the Social Origins of Mass Politics*

Aristocracy's link with fascism raises the more general question of the social origins of political regimes in the era of mass politics. In a pioneering study, Barrington Moore explores the social factors and conditions that shaped the evolution of modern political regimes in six major societies—those of Britain, France, the United States, China, India, and Japan.[1] Moore identifies four main paths

[1] Barrington Moore Jr., *Social Origins of Dictatorship and Democracy: Lord and Peasant in the Making of the Modern World* (London, 1966).

in the transition from pre-industrial to modern industrial society: bourgeois revolution based on 'the combination of capitalist and Western democracy', as exemplified by Britain, France, and the United States; capitalist reaction which 'culminated during the twentieth century in fascism', as exemplified by Japan (and also by Germany, a case that Moore does not analyse in detail); Communism, as exemplified by China (and also by Russia); and a fourth path, specific only to India, where the weak impulse towards modernization meant that neither capitalism nor Communism was the end result. In his view, these outcomes were shaped by 'the ways in which the landed upper classes and the peasants reacted to the challenge of commercial agriculture'.[2]

Moore's analysis does not include the small countries of Eastern and Northern Europe, South-East Asia, or the Middle East on the grounds that 'smaller countries depend economically and politically on big and powerful ones', so that 'the decisive causes of their politics lie outside their own boundaries'.[3] Despite this controversial claim, Moore's interpretative model has been creatively applied to explaining political developments in other parts of the world.[4] Pointing out that 'in a fundamental way large countries and small countries do not differ in the era of transformation', the American historian Gale Stokes provides a comprehensive account of the social origins of modern politics in Eastern Europe.[5] Stokes argues that an uneven combination of similar exogenous factors and local social configurations produced markedly different political outcomes in the region, namely, 'functioning democracy in Czechoslovakia, vigorous peasant political parties in Serbia and Bulgaria, aristocratic bureaucratism in Hungary, and authoritarian governments in Poland and elsewhere'.[6]

Romania's political regime qualifies as a mixed case within Stokes's typology. Although its social structure shared many features in common with that of Hungary—namely, a massive concentration of landed property, the emergence of a group of

---

[2] Ibid. p. xiv.

[3] Ibid. p. x.

[4] For an attempt to explain the social origins of politics in the Middle East in terms of Moore's model, see Heim Gerber, *The Social Origins of the Modern Middle East* (London, 1987).

[5] Gale Stokes, 'The Social Origins of East European Politics', in Daniel Chirot (ed.), *The Origins of Backwardness in Eastern Europe: Economics and Politics from the Middle Ages until the Early Twentieth Century* (Berkeley, 1989), 210–52.

[6] Ibid. 226.

liberal reformers originating from the gentry, a tendency towards converting cattle production into a trade in grain, and the importance of the role played by Jews in commerce, banking, and industry—the political outcome was quite different.[7] Whereas in Hungary the political system was dominated by the nobility, in Romania the economic and political preponderance of the landed aristocracy was broken by the king and the central government bureaucracy. As a result, Romanian politics was dominated by national–liberal politicians emerging mainly from the lower and middling aristocracy, and not from among the large landowners. Committed to an agenda of transforming the urban population through industrialization and expansion of the bureaucracy, the liberals relied mainly on the support of the emergent ethnic Romanian middle class. Unlike in Hungary, after an early attempt at conditional emancipation, Romanian liberals opposed the emancipation of the Jews and their assimilation into the native middle class, and were in favour of restricting their economic activities, thus preventing their potential alliance with large landlords: 'The complete lack of desire of the liberals to work out a compromise with the Jewish middle class, and the conservatives' inability to do so, left the Romanian body politic splintered and made it impossible for the landlords to control the development of social forces to the same extent as in Hungary.'[8] Another significant difference between the two countries was the strong political role played by the king in Romania, as compared to the relative political autonomy enjoyed by the Hungarian aristocracy: 'whereas in Hungary a handful of the most prominent landowners exercised ultimate control over the system, in Romania the king did so, and the old boyars were never able to sustain the same confident dominance as their Hungarian counterparts.'[9] Stoke concludes that 'the Romanian case is less clear than the Czech or Hungarian ones in view of Moore's model. A landowning class did "use a variety of political and social levers to hold down a labour force on the land", but the result, at least immediately after the First World War, was not fascism. Instead a recognizable, if weak, tendency toward democracy emerged.'[10]

This analytical framework explains why in the first interwar decade Romania did not evolve towards fascism but took

[7] Ibid.   [8] Ibid. 232.   [9] Ibid.   [10] Ibid. 233.

important steps towards building a multi-party parliamentary system, formally functioning until 1938, and thus second only to Czechoslovakia in terms of its longevity. But the social origins of mass politics in Romania in general, and the peculiar status of the nobility in particular, might also shed light on the gradual collapse of the parliamentary system in the late 1930s under the joint pressure of authoritarian tendencies from above and fascist pressure from below. To this end, building on Moore's concepts and findings as further developed by Stokes, the following analysis provides an overview of the historical origins of the Romanian nobility and the evolution of its legal and political status during the long nineteenth century and the interwar period.

1. *Landownership and Politics in Romania*

In order to understand the changes that occurred in the status of the Romanian nobility in the modern period, a brief account of its origins and history is required at this point. From the beginning of the fifteenth century to the achievement of state independence in 1878, the principalities of Wallachia (1420) and Moldova (1456) were under the protection of the Ottoman Empire and integrated into the system of *pax ottomanica* as tributary principalities. Nevertheless, compared with regular Ottoman territories in Central Europe and the Balkans, which lost their statehood and their native aristocracy under the Ottoman occupation, Moldova and Wallachia enjoyed a privileged judicial status based on treaties between the sultan and native princes called *ahdnames* or *sulhnames* (agreement acts). According to these treaties, the principalities paid the High Porte an annual tribute and renounced attributes of formal sovereignty, such as the right to conduct an independent foreign policy. In exchange, they escaped direct military occupation and managed to preserve their local nobility, the *boieri* (boyars), and their specific socio-political organization. As a result major state institutions such as the princedom, the Church, and the administration remained under the control of the local elites. Moreover, unlike other Balkan provinces, the principalities underwent neither forced population movements nor Muslim ethnic or military colonization leading to a large-scale mixing of peoples.

In the principalities of Moldova and Wallachia noble status thus had a dual basis: possession of large landed estates and appointment to rank by a prince. Unlike in Western and Central Europe, where the rights of the nobility were written down in a Magna Charta, in Moldova and Wallachia they were consecrated by tradition and regular individual written confirmation by princes. In both principalities there also existed assemblies of the Estates, which are documented from the fifteenth century. These assemblies were composed of all privileged groups, such as the nobility, dignitaries, the army, and the clergy, while the cities were irregularly represented. Assemblies were convoked only in exceptional situations, when they assisted princes in reaching major foreign or domestic policy decisions.

The Moldovan and Wallachian nobilities achieved maximum power in the seventeenth century when, taking advantage of the weakening of the central power, they transformed the assembly of the Estates into a permanent institution invested with effective control over the princedom. But the power of the nobility rapidly deteriorated in the eighteenth century as the result of a slow but steady decline in the international status of the two principalities. During the period 1711 to 1821, Moldova and Wallachia were de facto almost assimilated into the status of regular Ottoman provinces. Their internal autonomy was severely curtailed, while their ruling princes were no longer elected by the local boyars, but were generally nominated by the sultan from among the Greek families living in the district of Phanar in Constantinople (hence the name of the 'Phanariot' regime).

Phanariot princes arrived accompanied by a large personal clientele, whom they rewarded with positions in the state apparatus. This practice gave Ottoman Greeks unrestricted access to offices and ennoblement. Their penetration into the local aristocracy fluctuated during this period. Overall, foreigners made up less than one-quarter of the total number of boyars in the two principalities. Between 1715 and 1800, the most important state offices—eight in the first half of the period, and fifteen in the second half—were held by a total of eighty-nine families. Among them were thirty-seven Moldovan–Wallachian families, seven naturalized families, and forty-four foreign families, mostly Greeks. Proportionally, Moldovan–Wallachian or naturalized families made up 50.5 per cent of great office holders, and held office for a total of 512 cumulative years, while foreigners made up 49.5 per cent of the total number of office holders, but kept office for only 176 cumulative years. During the same period, 65.6 per cent of the second-rank offices were held by Moldovan–Wallachians (125 Romanian and 22 naturalized families), while 34.4 per cent of the total were held by foreigners (77 families).[11] Moldovan–Wallachian boyars still numerically dominated the nobility by a narrow margin. Although less numerous than local boyars, Ottoman Greeks in practice monopolized the most important offices of state. This gave them the upper hand in daily affairs, accounting for a significant shift in real power from local to foreign nobles. In reaction, most local nobles left the court and withdrew to the countryside, adopting an attitude to the regime of passive resistance that took 'national' overtones. The infiltration of Ottoman Greeks would later be invoked in the political struggles between the conservative and the modernizing liberal factions, the latter arguing that as a result of the Phanariot penetration the Romanian nobility had been 'denationalized', and had lost the 'purity of its aristocratic blood' and its internal cohesion.

In 1821, a military revolt of the lower nobility in Wallachia finally led to the end of the political domination of the Phanariots in both principalities, opening the way for the restoration of the noble regime. The main battle over the political reorganization of the two principalities was fought between the lower and upper strata of the nobility. This conflict was triggered by the unprecedented numerical expansion of the nobility in the last decades of Phanariot rule, mostly because of the ennoblement of officeholders and the selling of titles of nobility. Small and middle-ranking nobles formed dynamic social strata, eager to participate in state institutions and to assume political leadership.

The restoration of the regime of noble Estates was embedded in the Organic Regulations, the first constitution of the principalities adopted in 1831–2 under temporary Russian military occu-

---

[11] See Ion Ionaşcu, 'Le degré de l'influence des Grecs des Principautés Roumaines dans la vie politique de ces pays', in *Symposium: L'Epoque phanariote. 21–25 octobre 1970. Á la mémoire de Cléobule Tsurkas* (Thessaloniki, 1974), 217–27. For a statistical analysis, see Dan Berindei and Irina Gavrilă, 'Analyse de la composition de l'ensemble des familles de grands dignitaires de la Valachie au XVIIIe siècle', in *Comunicaciones al XV Congresso Internacional de las Ciencias Genealogica y Heraldica* (Madrid, 1983), i. 239–54. For small dignitaries, see Dan Berindei and Irina Gavrilă, 'Considérations sur les dignités de seconde et troisième classe en Valachie au XVIIIe siècle: Le problème de la pénétration Greco-Phanariote', in *Genealogica et Heraldica: Actos do 17 Congresso Internacional das Ciencias Genealogica e Heraldica* (Lisbon, 1989), 46–62.

pation (1828–32). The Regulations were part of a larger process of transition from medieval Estates to an oligarchic parliamentary regime that took place between 1830 and 1848 in Central Europe. The essence of the new political order was formed by the rights and privileges of the nobility, which was granted (1) complete exemption from taxation; (2) exclusive access to state offices and landed property; and (3) exclusive rights to participate in the newly created political institutions.

The Regulations reorganized the political life of the principalities. They strictly controlled access to noble status, restored the hierarchical system of attribution of noble titles, and specified the privileges attached to various ranks. The nobility was recorded statistically, noble ranks were once again hierarchically organized in a ranking catalogue called the *Arhondologie*, and a strict delimitation was implemented between boyars 'of office' and those 'of blood'. Ennoblement was possible only through the prince with the express approval of the Ordinary Assembly, a new permanent legislative body which replaced the former irregular assembly, composed solely of boyars and de facto dominated by great boyars. As such, the Regulations instituted an oligarchic system: political life was dominated by a narrow group of about 500 boyars, in their turn effectively controlled by twenty powerful families.

The incipient oligarchic parliamentary regime instituted by the Organic Regulations functioned in the principalities until 1848. The new political order was undermined by revolutionary movements for change conducted by enlightened nobles and members of the emerging intelligentsia. Initially articulated in numerous political petitions and constitutional projects, the new political vision crystallized in the programmes put forward during the 1848 revolution in Moldova and Wallachia. These documents proposed an inclusive and egalitarian definition of the national community encompassing all the inhabitants of the country, and called for mass political participation. Although the 1848 revolution was defeated, in the following decade the transition from the *ancien régime* to a modern nation-state was accelerated by European intervention in the internal organization of the principalities.

2. *The 1858 Abolition of Privileges*

The political evolution of Moldova and Wallachia was decisively shaped by the geopolitical reorganization of South-Eastern Europe by the Congress of Paris (1856) after the end of the Crimean War (1854–6). In August 1858, the Great Powers, taking into account the resolutions adopted by ad hoc consultative assemblies instituted in the two principalities under the terms of the Treaty of Paris (1856), endorsed the unification of Moldova and Wallachia, and granted them a common constitution known as the Convention of Paris, which functioned as their fundamental law until 1864. The Convention marked the formal legal division between the old and the new regimes in the principalities, abolishing all aristocratic titles, privileges, and monopolies, and instituting equality before the law. From a legal point of view, the Romanian nobility was thus formally abolished in 1858. The dismantling of noble privileges was equivalent to a genuine social revolution in both principalities, shocking even the most enthusiast aristocratic reformers.

In the political realm, the Convention instituted a nascent political system centred on the 'owner-citizen'. It replaced political representation based on social Estates with a restrictive franchise, assuring political domination by large landowners as the electoral body was made up of only 4,138 voters in both principalities. The system indicated that the Great Powers wished to compensate former nobles for loss of privileges by endorsing their complete political domination. Under the new political order, landownership was the main source of economic revenues and political rights. Thus the Romanian nobility was transformed into a landed upper class, converting their social privileges into political domination.

Although the process of state unification between Moldova and Wallachia had the consent of a large part of the political elites in both principalities, there were, nevertheless, significant ideological differences between various political factions with regard to the specific path to be followed by the new state. The main division was between a modernizing liberal political leadership, recruited mainly from boyars, members of the intelligentsia, and the urban middle strata of the population, and conservative political elites, represented mainly by landowners and members of the intelligentsia. Influenced primarily by French Romantic political thinkers such as Jules Michelet, Robert de Lamennais, and Edgar Quinet, Romanian liberal politicians—gathered around the Wallachian leaders I. C. Brătianu and C. A. Rosetti—promoted a comprehensive programme of social and political reforms. In contrast, conservative politicians, influenced mainly by German and English evolutionist theories, opposed the radical socio-political changes envisaged by the liberals, and favoured maintenance of the political status quo through limited evolutionary reforms 'from above'.

During the rule of Prince Alexandru Ioan Cuza (1859–66), the political rivalry between these two dominant factions of the Romanian political establishment was largely repressed. Unable to gain unconditional support from either the conservative or the liberal faction, Cuza based his political legitimacy on a fragile political grouping of moderate liberals. The foundation of Cuza's reform programme was the emancipation of the peasantry and its integration into the legal and political framework of the newly forged nation-state, through landownership and political participation. The ambitious scope of these reforms led to an acute political confrontation with conservative landowners. In order to ensure a large political basis for his rule, in 1864 Cuza considerably enlarged the voters' body to an estimated 570,000 voters. The new electoral law abolished the electoral colleges based on professions, simply dividing the electorate into urban and rural constituencies, and granting them proportional rights of territorial representation decided by a simple majority.

In his political confrontation with the landowning oligarchy which dominated the political system, Cuza relied on the peasantry, which he regarded as 'the State's active force'.[12] In 1864, following a *coup d'état* that suppressed political opposition, Cuza imposed a land reform abolishing peasant servitude and granting peasants small plots of different sizes, according to the size of their cattle herd. The reform reduced ownership of large estates in favour of individual small plots, redistributing a total of 1,810,311 hectares of land to 463,554 families. Although the reform transformed peasants into small landowners, the land assigned to them was not sufficient to assure economic independence, and many

---

[12] Thad Weed Riker, *The Making of Roumania: A Study of an International Problem, 1856–1866* (London, 1931), 437.

were forced to contract additional plots from large landowners under onerous terms. Landowners, in turn, lacking agricultural mechanization, were still dependent on peasant labour. In the long run, despite partial improvement in the economic situation of the peasantry, the reform thus preserved the patrimonial system it wanted to abolish, perpetuating a sharecropping peasantry working under burdensome labour contracts.

In 1866, a heterogeneous alliance between conservatives and liberals forced Prince Cuza to abdicate. Political elites nevertheless remained divided about the reorganization of the country. While the liberal faction favoured inclusive political participation endorsed by the idea of popular sovereignty, the conservatives pleaded for an exclusive and elitist understanding of the nation, composed only of educated and propertied men. Ultimately, the 1866 Constitution was a political compromise between the two dominant factions. It established a constitutional monarchy under the German prince Karl Ludwig of Hohenzollern-Sigmaringen (Carol I of Romania); provided for the separation of powers; and guaranteed fundamental rights and liberties. In order to prevent future expropriations, private property was declared 'sacred and inviolable'.

Under the new constitution, political rights were reserved only for adult males. Furthermore, the electoral law differentiated between direct and indirect voters, and grouped them according to profession, education and property. Territorial constituencies for the Chamber of Deputies—the lower house of the Romanian parliament—were divided into four colleges which assured the dominant representation of great and middling landowners (Colleges I and II, representing 1.5 per cent of the total voters, but electing 41 per cent of the deputies), and of the urban middle class and professional categories (College III, representing 3.5 per cent of the voters, but electing 38 per cent of the deputies). At the same time, the remaining 95 per cent of the electorate were confined to a single college (IV) which elected only 21 per cent of the deputies. The electorate for the Senate consisted of only 2 per cent of the voting body, grouped into two electoral colleges and recruited solely from the ranks of great landowners and high professional categories.

Until the First World War, Romania's political life was dominated by the Liberal and Conservative Parties, which had different

visions for the country's development. Preponderantly representing the political interests of middling and large landowners, the
conservatives favoured the development of agriculture as practised
on large estates, and saw Romania's well-being as based on cattle
and the trade in cereals. Although they did not necessarily oppose
the development of industry, conservatives saw it as complemen-
tary and subordinated to the needs of agriculture, and therefore
rejected plans for economic protectionism. In contrast, the liberals,
alerted by the great fluctuations in cereal prices on the international market and eager to subvert the economic influence of great
estates, regarded the creation of a national industry as vital to
Romania's long-term development. Furthermore, the liberals
favoured a policy of economic protectionism and sheltered industrialization. Romania's independence, achieved in 1879 after its
military participation in the 1877-8 Russian–Ottoman war,
enabled the ruling Liberal Party to intervene actively in the
economy. This exposed an underlying paradox of Romanian political life. Conservatives supported free trade and the emancipation
of local Jews, leading to a heterogeneous and cosmopolitan middle
class, while liberals favoured protectionism, active state intervention in the economy, and implemented legislation that effectively
excluded Jews from citizenship until 1918.

At the turn of the century, the Liberal Party intensified its
campaign for sheltered industrialization. In order to undermine
the economic efficiency of the great landed estates, the main
opponents of the policy of industrialization, the Liberal Party,
conducted a sustained campaign to emancipate the impoverished
sharecropper peasantry and transform it into independent
farmers. To this end, the liberals attempted, by active state intervention, to expand the number of schools in rural areas and to
invest them with an increased socio-cultural role. They also initiated a vast network of rural bank cooperatives, intended to
consolidate a solid stratum of middling peasantry as the basis for
a prospective internal market necessary to absorb the products of
state-sponsored industry and to generate a rural proletariat as the
workforce required for industrialization. The task ahead was
nevertheless enormous, given the concentration of landownership. (See Table 12.1.)

TABLE 12.1 *Distribution of the ownership of agrarian land in Romania, 1905*

Categories (ha)	Extent (ha)	% of total	Class of property
up to 10	3,153,645	40.29	Small (40.29%)
10–50	695,953	8.89	Medium (11.02%)
50–100	166,847	2.13	
100–500	816,355	10.43	Large (10.43%)
500–1,000	803,084	10.26	Latifundiary (38.26%)
1,000–3,000	1,236,420	15.80	
3,000–5,000	434,367	5.55	
5,000	520,095	6.65	
TOTAL	7,826,766	100.00	100.00%

Source: David Mitrany, *The Land and the Peasant in Rumania: The War and Agrarian Reform, 1917–1921* (first published Oxford, 1930; reprint New York, 1968), 186. By permission of Oxford University Press.

Large landowners, although representing only 0.56 per cent of the country's total population, owned 48.69 per cent of the land, thus effectively dominating the country's agricultural sector.[13] Medium-size landowners, representing 4.01 per cent of the total population, possessed 11 per cent of the agrarian land. At the same time, 920,080 peasant families, representing 92 per cent of the rural population, owned 40.29 per cent of the total agrarian land, distributed in small properties of up to 10 ha.

Instead of fostering a capitalist transformation of agriculture 'from below', the liberal campaign unleashed social tensions in the countryside and failed dramatically in the great 1907 peasant revolt, the last European 'Jacquerie'.[14] Challenged by the failure of their campaign for a transformation of agriculture 'from below', a new generation of liberal politicians, led by Ion I. C. Brătianu, in October 1913 launched plans for a substantial land reform and universal franchise enacted 'from above'. The liberal campaign met strong resistance on the part of conservative landowners, who saw the reforms as an attempt to subvert their economic basis and to eliminate them from political life. They argued that the great estates were the driving force behind the

[13] David Mitrany, *The Land and the Peasant in Rumania: The War and Agrarian Reform, 1917–1921* (New York, 1968), 187.
[14] Philip Gabriel Eidelberg, *The Great Romanian Peasant Revolt of 1907: Origins of a Modern Jacquerie* (Leiden, 1974).

country's economic development, providing a means of existence for a large dependent peasantry. To destroy the great estates would endanger Romania's functioning economic system. With regard to the proposed electoral system, large landowners argued that political rights were an entitlement that had to be earned through education and property; to hand them out as 'bonuses' from above would lead to despotism and mass domination of property and culture. The beginning of the First World War meant that the liberal plans for electoral and agrarian reforms could not be debated by the parliament; they served, nevertheless, as the basis for sweeping reforms in the interwar period.

3. *Aristocracy and Politics in the Interwar Period*

Romania's bipolar political system was fundamentally altered by the First World War, when the social pressure for change was increased by the mass mobilization of the peasantry. The country emerged from the war as a winner. The incorporation of the historical provinces of Transylvania, the Banat, and Bukovina from Austria–Hungary, and of Bessarabia from Russia doubled Romania's size (from 130,177 sq. km. in 1914 to 295,049 sq. km. in 1919) and population (from 7,771,341 inhabitants in 1914 to 14,669,841 in 1919), considerably strengthening its economic potential. In addition, following the great socio-political upheaval of the war, comprehensive reforms such as universal male suffrage (1919), massive land redistribution (1921), and a new liberal constitution (1923) remodelled the state into a parliamentary democracy, granting full citizenship rights to ethno-religious minorities such as Jews.

Although, arguably, Greater Romania was in many respects a new state, political life in the first post-war decade (1918–28) was largely dominated by the elites of the former Old Kingdom, grouped mainly within the National Liberal Party. Benefiting from the strong personality of their leader, Ion I. C. Brătianu (1864–1927), and his influence over King Ferdinand (1914–27), the liberals were able to implement their views concerning the country's development, in direct continuity with their pre-war strategy. Announced for the first time in 1913, Romania's 1921 land reform was the most radical expropriation in post-war Europe. It transferred 2,776,401 ha from large estates to small peasant properties, radically altering the structure of property ownership. (See Table 12.2.)

TABLE 12.2 *Distribution of the ownership of agrarian land in Romania, 1927*

Category	Changes (ha)	Total surface (ha)	Share of total (%)
Up to 10 ha	+ 2,776,401	6,508,596	81.43
10–100 ha	—	860,953	10.80
Above 100 ha	– 2,776,401	621,450	7.77

Source: Based on Mitrany, *The Land and the Peasant in Rumania*, 189. By permission of Oxford University Press.

Unlike in the Old Kingdom, the system of landownership in Greater Romania was overwhelmingly dominated by smallholders, who possessed 81.43 per cent of the total land. The interwar period thus put an end to the economic and political dominance of Romania's landed aristocracy. It is very telling in this respect that in 1920 the Conservative Party, the main port-parole of landlords' interests, disappeared from political life.

Although it declined as a distinct interest group, the Romanian aristocracy in the interwar period was far from extinct. Taking advantage of their political experience and connections, former conservative politicians—individually or in groups—joined new political parties. Some factions joined the newly established People's Party led by General Alexandru Averescu, while others became members of the Transylvanian National Party. With the exception of a few lower echelon 'technocrats', most of the former conservative politicians were, however, misfits in their new mass parties and tended towards reviving their own political party. In 1929, defecting from the People's Party, Grigore Filipescu—the son of an illustrious pre-war conservative politician—established the Vlad Țepes League, renamed the Conservative Party in 1932, but the new organization remained marginal. It is nevertheless important to note that Filipescu did not collaborate with radical parties, but adopted an anti-fascist attitude, thus continuing the pre-war conservatives' tradition of political moderation.

The case of the politician Constantin Argetoianu is representative of the political restlessness and frequent migrations of displaced aristocrats. Having been successively a member of all of Romania's major parties in the 1920s, from the National Liberal to the National Peasant and National Democrat parties, in 1932 he founded the Agrarian Union in an attempt to revive conservatism in a new form. While opposed to mass politics and universal suffrage, Argetoianu had no taste for radical politics. He was an adversary of the Legion and later discouraged General Cantacuzino from forging an alliance with the radical right.[15] Instead, Argetoianu supported King Carol II's plans to establish a personal regime.

By and large, however, the political orientation of Romanian aristocrats suffered significant changes in early 1930s. Having failed to make a significant impact on the post-1918 political system, a handful of aristocrats embraced radical politics in search of political visibility. Andrew Janos has pointed out that descendants of boyars represented 30.5 per cent of all parliamentary deputies in the first post-1918 decade, but that they fell to 15.2 per cent during the rightist National Union coalition government of 1930–1. While the parliamentary presence of aristocracy decreased, it is very telling that, during the 1930s, boyar descendants made up a significant proportion of radical right-wing organizations, accounting for 7.9 per cent of the deputies of the right-wing Romanian Front and 8 per cent of the Legionary deputies.[16] This change reflected the growing crisis of Romania's parliamentary system and the emergence of new personalized forms of politics. On the one hand, popular support for major 'old' parties began eroding gradually. On the other, a multitude of new radical political factions and groupings emerged. The Legion was to prove itself one of the most successful forces among the new parties. The second part of my essay focuses on its emergence and evolution, in an attempt to provide a sociological explanation for the Romanian aristocrats' participation in fascism.

II *Charisma and Mass Politics: The Legion of the Archangel Michael*

The Legion of the Archangel Michael has generally been considered one of the most complex and unusual 'varieties of fascism' in interwar East-Central Europe, for several reasons. First, it

[15] Arrested in November 1940 under the short-lived Iron Guard government, Constantin Argetoianu managed to escape death and was subsequently imprisoned under the Communist regime.

[16] Andrew C. Janos, *East Central Europe in the Modern World: The Politics of the Borderlands from Pre- to Postcommunism* (Stanford, Calif., 2000), 170–1. For details of his 'Elite Project' see 'Introduction', 2.

originated independently of Italian fascism and German National Socialism. Secondly, it was a vigorous political movement, and one of the few—along with the Ustasa Movement in Croatia and the Arrow Cross in Hungary—to assume a mass character. In 1937 it claimed an estimated 270,000 members and it received 478,000 votes in parliamentary elections.[17] Thirdly, it represented a fully fledged political movement, encompassing all 'five stages of fascism' identified by Robert Paxton.[18] In the case of the Legion, these five stages were: the creation of the movement in 1927; its emergence as a significant political player in 1931–3; a bid for power facilitated by the breakdown of the democratic regime at the end of 1937 and the subsequent failure of the authoritarian regime of Carol II in 1938–40; the exercise of power from September 1940 to January 1941; and, finally, the radicalization of the movement, its rebellion, and final ouster from power by General Ion Antonescu, with the support of the army. Most importantly, the Legion exhibited many peculiarities, combining, in a complex syncretism, general fascist characteristics with specific ideological features such as its religiosity and mysticism.

Elsewhere, I have reinterpreted the Legion as a totalitarian revolutionary movement of change based on the violent counter-culture of a radical youth.[19] I have argued that the Legionary ideology combined, in a heterogeneous but powerful synthesis, three main strategies of political mobilization. These included a charismatic type of legitimacy based on the millennialist cult of the Archangel Michael and the leadership of Corneliu Zelea Codreanu; the messianic mission of the interwar 'new generation'; and integral nationalism, including calls for 'cultural purification' and 'national regeneration' coupled with a rabid anti-Semitism.

Although it enrolled numerous priests, used the religious language of sacrifice, resurrection, and salvation, and attacked materialism and hedonism as signs of moral decay, the Legion was not a religious organization. In essence, it was a secular political movement of charismatic-revolutionary nationalism that,

---

[17] Armin Heinen, *Legiunea 'Arhanghelul Mihail': Mişcare socială şi organizaţie politică. O contribuţie la problema fascismului internaţional* (Bucharest, 1998), 17.

[18] Robert O. Paxton, 'Five Stages of Fascism', *Journal of Modern History*, 70 (Mar. 1998), 1–23.

[19] Constantin Iordachi, *Charisma, Politics and Violence: The Legion of the 'Archangel Michael' in Inter-war Romania* (Trondheim, 2004).

building on the tradition of mainstream Romanian nationalism, appropriated and adapted the vocabulary, symbols, and rituals of Eastern Christian Orthodoxy, as filtered by the Romantic Evangelical-nationalist revival in the first half of the nineteenth century and subsequently institutionalized in practices of sacralizing politics, to articulate its totalitarian political project of the renewal of Romanian society and the creation of the 'new man'. I argue that the Legion's revolutionary fervour and totalitarian orientation differentiate it from traditional anti-Semitic 'parliamentary' parties, placing it firmly within the spectrum of contemporary fascist movements.

As a charismatic movement, the Legion of the Archangel Michael put forward a formula for salvation based on the imminence of the apocalypse and encompassing strong millennialist overtones. In July 1927 Codreanu defined the leading principles of the Legion as 'faith in God', 'faith in our mission', 'love for one another', and 'song as the chief manifestation of our state of mind'. Instead of drafting a concrete plan of action, the Legion defined as its goal the salvation of the Romanian nation.

The messianic formula preached by the Legion shared most of the features of a millenarian salvation, but reinterpreted them in terms of Romanian national symbols and a specific socio-political context. Legionary writings were dominated by the effort of identifying and fighting the enemy. According to the Legion's ideologues, the main threat to Romania's national security was posed by the Jews, who occupied 'a special position', given their socio-political domination and their tendency to monopolize the liberal professions, and thus the country's political leadership.[20] They criticized the Minority Convention signed by Romania in 1919, arguing that 'minority status' was nothing but the legal consecration of privilege.[21]

Legionary publications were dominated by virulent anti-Semitic manifestos. In these writings, the imminent 'Jewish danger' allegedly threatening the national community was closely associated with the theory of universal conspiracy. The messianic formula proposed by the Legion was based on a 'double' conspiracy theory by lumping together the Jewish and

---

[20] Ion I. Moţa (alias Zyrax), 'Problema minoritară în România', *Axa*, 2/5 (22 Jan. 1933), p. ii.
[21] Ibid.

Communist dangers, a feature that accounted for its proselytizing power. This theory provided a psychologically acceptable explanation for the perceived precarious social status of urban Romanians, allegedly caused by the activities of 'privileged' minority groups which were able to influence—in an occult way—the political decision-making process.

The core of the Legionary ideology was the charismatic cult of Corneliu Zelea Codreanu, proclaimed as a 'new Messiah', the instrument sent by the Archangel to fulfil his commandments in order to bring salvation to the Romanian people. His biography displays the 'goal fixation' characteristic of charismatic leaders. Although he never held a position of power in the state apparatus, Codreanu succeeded in building a voluntary nucleus of faithful followers, becoming the object of a fanatical personality cult.

The Legion's party organization was shaped by the charisma principle. In August 1927 the Legion announced its first organizational structure, made up of four sections: the first and most important consisted of young people; the second section was composed of 'mature men'; the third section encompassed women; and the fourth was made up of Romanians living abroad.[22] Legion leadership was to be exercised in common by a council composed of former or current student leaders, the latter being granted only a consultative vote, and the Senate, made up of elected individuals over 50 years of age, a mixture of aristocratic figures and rightist intellectuals and politicians.[23] Originally conceived of as the highest authority within the Legion, the Senate assembled for the first time only in 1930. In fact, it had a merely decorative role, its members being appointed by Codreanu and not elected on a regional basis, as previously intended.[24] As a collegial body consisting of elder aristocratic figures, the Senate was meant to give the Legionary decision-making process symbolic legitimacy by formally guaranteeing 'that the law which is applied is really authentically traditional'.[25]

Despite its collective leading forums, the Legion had an authoritarian-militarist structure based on the undisputed leadership of

[22] 'Legiunea Arhanghelul Mihail', *Pământul Strămoşesc*, 1/2 (15 Aug. 1927), 3–4; and 'Organizarea Legiunii Arhanghelul Mihail', *Pământul Strămoşesc*, 1/5 (1 Oct. 1927), 3–4.

[23] Ibid.

[24] Heinen, *Legiunea 'Arhanghelului Mihail'*, 136.

[25] Max Weber, *Economy and Society: An Outline of Interpretative Sociology*, 2 vols. (Berkeley, 1978), i. 274.

'the Captain' and a hierarchical line of command. The main building blocks of the Legion's structure were its grass-roots cells called *cuiburi* (nests), defined as 'a group of people united under the command of a single man'. A nest was made up of three to thirteen members and led by a charismatic leader 'emerging naturally'.

The system of nests was very flexible, and assured an exponential expansion of the Legion's membership. After completing their training, members could leave their own nest and initiate a new cell by bringing in new converts who recognized their leadership. Cells stemming from a common original nest were considered part of a 'family' of nests. Such related nests were organized hierarchically, the original cell being the 'superior' one and its leader having authority over all other chiefs in that family. Territorially, nests were grouped in garrisons, sectors, counties, and regions led by chiefs appointed by Codreanu and directly responsible to him. In addition, at national level, above territorial regions, all Legionary sections had a general headquarters. These were led by chiefs appointed by Codreanu, as the Commander of the Legion (*Conducătorul*), and placed under his direct authority.

The hierarchical structure of the Legion was not democratic but military in character: the leader had to convene his subordinates 'as a commander of a regiment calls to order his subaltern officers'. Legionary chiefs at all levels had to file detailed monthly reports to their superiors, and their activities were attentively monitored. In order to prevent high Legionary leaders from becoming too independent and powerful, they could retain their posts for a maximum period of one year for regional leaders, and two years for political leaders. After being released from their function, Legionary chiefs were promoted, becoming part of the corpus of 'charismatic commanders'.

1. *The Legion and the Aristocracy*

On its establishment, the Legion functioned as a small male fraternity. In 1929 it boasted an estimated 400 to 1,000 members, the great majority young men of 20–5 years.[26] It was originally designed as an alternative elite organization, and not as a mass political party. Its 1927 Statute stipulated that the organization could not take part in parliamentary elections, and limited the

---

[26] Heinen, *Legiunea 'Arhanghelul Mihail'*, 139.

total number of legionaries to 3,000, with a maximum of 100 members per county.[27]

Although Codreanu demanded the abolition of the 'corrupt' and 'unrepresentative' parliamentary system, in 1929 he set 'going to the masses' as the Legion's strategic goal, mostly in the form of electoral marches organized in Moldova and Bessarabia.[28] In the first years, electoral gains remained rather modest, mainly because of the hostile attitude of the state administration. Soon, however, taking advantage of the social pauperization caused by the Great Depression (1929–33), the Legion enlarged its territorial basis and social composition. As a charismatic catch-all party, it incorporated diverse elements of society, among which the most important were students, blue- and white-collar workers, members of the lower rural and urban bourgeoisie, members of the rural and urban intelligentsia, ethnic Romanians from Macedonia colonized by the Romanian state in Dobrudja, and members of the aristocracy. While greatly affected by the post-war upheaval, these social strata were united by the feeling of being excluded from the full benefits of the social and political transformation. Codreanu's charisma, based on a compensatory salvational ideology, provided a unifying cement bringing these heterogeneous social strata together in a revolt of 'rising expectations'.

Although numerically they were not significant, aristocrats had a strong influence as part of the Legion's political leadership, the Legionary Senate, and the Friends of the Legion, an organization made up of about 1,000 people with the purpose of sponsoring the movement. The panoply of aristocrats attached to the Legion includes prominent figures such as Gheorghe Cantacuzino, Alexandru Cantacuzino, Mihail Sturdza, and Ilie-Vlad Sturdza, members of prestigious Wallachian or Moldavian princely families, as well as 'transient' sympathizers or collaborators such as Zoe Sturdza (the wife of Mihail Sturdza), painter Andronic Cantacuzino, architect G. M. Cantacuzino, and Prince Niculae, King Carol II's brother, excluded from the royal family in 1936.

Among them, the most prominent was General Gheorghe Cantacuzino. Born in 1869 in Paris, Cantacuzino received military

---

[27] 'Organizarea Legiunii Arhanghelul Mihail', 5.
[28] Cornelu Zelea Codreanu, 'Spre masele populare', in his *Pentru legionari* (3rd edn.; Bucharest, 1940), 331–78.

training in France and Romania, and had a successful career, attaining the rank of major and becoming chief of cabinet in the ministry of war (1910). His heroism during the First World War gained him the nickname *Grănicerul* (the Border-Guarder), the rank of general (in reserve), and the reputation of being a staunch anti-Communist.[29] After the war, capitalizing on his prestige, Cantacuzino engaged in politics as part of the nucleus of generals leading the People's Party. With the decline of that party, he defected to the Vlad Țepes League (later the Conservative Party).

According to Codreanu's own account, Cantacuzino 'converted' to the Legion in 1933 (at the age of 64) during a visit to the Legionary labour camp of Râpa Galbenă in Jassy. The old General's controversial decision can be partly explained by the political decline of the Conservative Party, leading to a potential blockage in his political career. The General was elected to parliament in 1920, 1926, and 1931 but he correctly anticipated that his new party would fail to gain parliamentary seats in the 1933 general elections. Cantacuzino's new political engagement was also due to the anti-Communist, ultranationalist, and (para)military character of the Legion, and its social discourse emphasizing discipline, obedience, and respect for hierarchy, which were all in line with the General's convictions. According to contemporary accounts, Cantacuzino used to emphasize the paradoxical implications of his political choice, which meant that he, 'the scion of a princely family descending from Byzantine emperors', voluntarily placed himself under the authority of Codreanu, 'the nephew of a forester'.[30] At times, however, the General regretted his association with the Legion, mostly because he was subsequently stigmatized as a 'black sheep' by the political establishment and by other aristocrats.

Upon his 'conversion', General Cantacuzino was appointed a member of the Legionary Senate, and took part in all major events that shaped the movement's evolution. His new political engagement was soon to become notorious. On 9 December 1933, convinced that the Legion's rapid development posed a major challenge to Romania's political establishment, Prime

---

[29] Lucian Predescu (ed.), *Enciclopedia Cugetarea* (Bucharest, 1940), 165.

[30] Horia Sima, 'Generalul Cantacuzino-Grănicerul', *Mari existenţe legionare*, 1/10 (1 Aug. 1965), available on-line at <http://miscarea.com/tara-exilul-mari-existente-gen-cantacuzino.htm>, accessed 25 Jan. 2007.

Minister Ion G. Duca, head of the National Liberal Party, signed a decree banning the political section of the Legion, the Iron Guard. Thousands of Legionaries were arrested all over the country and their organization was paralysed, just before the national elections.

In response, on 29 December 1933, Prime Minister Duca was assassinated by a death squad composed of three Legionaries. The three were captured by the police and charged with conspiracy and murder, along with prominent Legionary leaders or sympathizers including Codreanu and General Cantacuzino. After a short trial, the executioners were sentenced by a military tribunal to life imprisonment and forced labour while Codreanu and Cantacuzino, the moral instigators of the crimes, were acquitted. Cantacuzino's presence among the defendants was regarded by the Legionaries as 'a gift from God' because they were aware that the military jury would hesitate to convict a venerable war-hero general.

After serving a political ban of one year, Codreanu set up a new party called All for the Fatherland in December 1935. In order to mask its all too obvious continuity with the Legion, he entrusted the leadership of the party to Cantacuzino. The old General accepted the task only on condition 'that we all recognize Corneliu Zelea Codreanu as our superior chief'.[31] Cantacuzino's high contacts in the royal camarilla and his political influence allowed the general to act as a 'patron' of the movement, protecting it in relation to the royal palace or other state institutions and conferring on it public prestige. The wealthy General also supported the Legion financially, providing its first headquarters in Bucharest and the plot of land on which the Legionary centre, called the Green House, was built between 1936 and 1937.

Another highly prominent aristocratic leader of the Legion was Alexandru Cantacuzino (1901–39). The son of Alexandrina Pallady (1876–1944) and Grigore George Cantacuzino (1872–1930), and the grandson of the powerful George Gr. Cantacuzino (1832–1913)—former leader of the Conservative Party (1899–1907), prime minister of Romania (1899–1900, 1904–7), and one of the richest landowners of his time, nicknamed 'The Nabob'—Alexandru was thus the scion of two of the oldest boyar families,

---

[31] *Cuvântul Argeşului*, 1 (10 Aug. 1935), 5, cited in Zigu Ornea, *The Romanian Extreme Right: The Nineteen Thirties* (Boulder, Col., 1999), 282–3.

proudly bearing the title of 'Prince' to allude to his remote Byzantine imperial origins.

Alexandru received an elite education, studying law at the University of Bucharest (BA, Ph.D.), political science in Paris, and international relations at the innovative Hague Academy of International Law, established in 1923. He started a diplomatic career (1926–7), serving also as secretary of Romanian legations in The Hague and Warsaw.[32] In 1930 he engaged in journalism, collaborating with various right-wing journals such as *Convorbiri Literare*, *Axa*, *Cuvântul studenţesc*, and *Vestitorii*, and gradually became involved in the Legion as part of the first massive influx of intellectuals into its ranks.

A dynamic personality and leading ideologue, Alexandru rose rapidly within the Legion. He was one of the main organizers of the Legionary-dominated national student congresses in Craiova (April 1935) and Târgu Mureş (April 1936). Appointed 'Commander of the Annunciation', Alexandru was a member of the team led by General Cantacuzino which fought in Spain on the General Franco's side, and was decorated by Franco in 1937. In December 1937 he was elected to parliament, standing for the All for the Fatherland party. In January 1938, in recognition of his activities and the great prestige he had attained, Alexandru was named leader of the newly established paramilitary elite order 'Moţa and Marin', meant to glorify the memory of the two Legionary martyrs who died in the Spanish Civil War, and to preach the 'pedagogy of death and resurrection'.[33]

During Carol II's royal dictatorship (1938–40), Alexandru Cantacuzino fell victim to political repression along with other leading Legionaries. After Codreanu's arrest in April 1938, Alexandru was interned in a camp with other Legionary leaders and subsequently sentenced to nine years' imprisonment. He managed to escape from the camp and led the Legion clandestinely. Arrested again in January 1939, he was executed on 22 September 1939 with about 250 other leading Legionaries on the order of Carol II.

The elimination of the Legion's leadership ended a cycle in its history, bringing a new generation of activists to the forefront.

---

[32] Predescu (ed.), *Enciclopedia Cugetarea*, 937–8.

[33] 'O nouă unitate legionară în cadrul Partidului "Totul Pentru Ţară"', *Buna Vestire*, 270 (23 Jan. 1938), p. i.

The transformation of the Legion was concomitant with the sudden transition from a clandestine organization to a ruling party. On 6 September 1940 Carol II was forced to abdicate and General Ion Antonescu stepped in to fill the political void. Requiring a political mass movement to legitimize his authoritarian rule, the General invited the Legion to form a government with the army. At this stage, the most important aristocratic family supporting the Legion was the Sturdzas, represented by the diplomat Mihail Sturdza, his wife Zoe Sturdza, a member of the association Friends of the Legion, and their son Ilie-Vlad Sturdza. Descended from an old princely family, Mihail Sturdza embarked on a diplomatic career, serving in the Romanian Ministry of Foreign Affairs at embassies in Athens, Berne, Washington, Riga, and Copenhagen. His prestigious social origins, diplomatic experience, and opposition to former minister of foreign affairs Nicolae Titulescu's pro-Antante collective security approach (1927–8, 1932–6) meant that Mihail Sturdza was appointed minister of foreign affairs in the short-lived Legionary government that functioned between September 1940 and January 1941. In his memoirs, Sturdza puts forward an apologetic justification of the Legion's activities and defends the right of the aristocracy to act as Romania's traditional political elite.[34]

2. National Regeneration, the Aristocracy, and the New Charismatic Fascist Elite

Overall, according to available statistics, only 2–3 per cent of the total of 388 Legionary parliamentary candidates in the interwar period were of boyar descent.[35] Although there were not many aristocrats in the Legion, their participation was central to its discourse of political legitimization and social organization.

The Legionary ideology invested the native aristocracy with a paramount role in the regeneration of the Romanian nation. Ever since the nineteenth century palingenetic visions of Romanian nationalism had explained decadence in terms of the decline of traditional aristocracy and the loss of its militarist spirit. The writer and editor Ion Heliade Rădulescu (1802–72), initiator of the programme of national regeneration, blamed decadence on the harmful effect of upstarts or parvenus (*ciocoi*)

---

[34] Michael Sturzda, *The Suicide of Europe* (Boston, 1986).
[35] Janos, *East Central Europe*, 170–1.

who subverted the class of native boyars.[36] Along the same lines, the Romantic poet Mihai Eminescu (1850–89) attributed decadence to the disappearance of native boyars and their replacement by a 'superimposed' cosmopolitan urban class of foreigners who mercilessly exploited the peasantry.[37] The regeneration of the nation was possible only by reviving the patriarchal order of the Middle Ages characterized by an 'organic alliance' between the native boyar class and the peasantry. These ideas were emulated by the Legion, which put forward a manifold strategy of regeneration. On the one hand, the national body had to be cleansed of alien elements; if in the first half of the nineteenth century the main culprits had been the Greek Phanariots, in the second half of the century the agents of degeneration were the Jews, regarded as an invading foreign middle class. On the other hand, the political class needed to be radically renewed by fighting 'bourgeois politicianism' and reviving patriotic values and the militarist spirit under the leadership of the new fascist elites in alliance with the last representatives of the Romanian nobility.

In order to explain the link, this section explores the symbolic role assigned to the aristocracy in legitimizing the new fascist elite. The Legion had an elitist structure. Its organization combined charismatic leadership at grass-roots and top central levels with appointed officials named by Codreanu at intermediate levels; and the principle of geographical representation with that of central leadership. In its first phase of development, the Legion was dominated by a small inner group of former student activists led by Codreanu, which made up a charismatic nucleus and commonly endorsed major decisions. During this time the circle of 'charismatic aristocracy' was considerably enlarged. In 1933 Codreanu established the rank of Legionary Commander awarded to prominent new legionaries. In 1936 the Captain created the Knights of the Annunciation, a corpus of commanders selected on the basis of their combat merit, trust, and loyalty, and held in high esteem by Legionaries.

Both the Legionary Senate and the corpus of the Knights were conceived of as a fusion between the new charismatic elite and the old Romanian aristocracy. This fusion expressed the dual nature of the Legionary ideology. On the one hand it was revolutionary,

[36] Ion Heliade Rădulescu, *Opere*, 2 vols. (Bucharest, 2002), ii. 339.
[37] Dumitru Murărescu, *Naţionalismul lui Eminescu* (Bucharest, 1994), 68–81.

preaching radical renewal of the existing social order. On the other, while advocating the building of a totalitarian state, Codreanu looked backwards in history for models of a glorious medieval past, when the national community had been homogeneous and the Romanian aristocracy, allegedly, unmixed with foreigners. In this way Codreanu put forward a regressive utopia, a nativist reaction to social change and parliamentary democracy. In his *Pentru Legionari*, Codreanu contrasted the patriarchal order of the old Moldavian nobility (*vechea boierime moldovenească*) with the contemporary outlook of Moldavian cities, dominated by 'Jewish taverns throwing away their dirt, garbage, and slops'.[38]

The Legionary propaganda created and publicized the image of the patriotic and altruistic aristocrat, portrayed as a natural leader of the 'organic' rural community and thus embodying the main qualities of the charismatic Legionary elite. The prototype of the aristocratic father-figure was General Cantacuzino, whose patriarchal authority—supported by traditional law, Orthodox religious conviction, and his high military rank—was to serve as a 'hero model' in preparing the young Legionary elite. The Legionary press perpetuated 'the myth of the general', advocating a natural alliance between the new, heroic aristocracy of youth and the medieval, pre-Phanariot Romanian aristocracy. In an article written on the occasion of Cantacuzino's burial, Mircea Eliade points to the community of values shared by the alienated aristocracy and the Legionary elite, centred on the spirit of sacrifice, devotion, and militarism:

Embracing the ideals of the Legion, General Cantacuzino recognized in his new spiritual family that love of liberty, that feeling of honour and dignity, that courageous attitude in the face of death, suffering, and repression that he could not find in the soul of his contemporaries. General Cantacuzino found in the Legionary ideals his unspoiled credo. These youngsters who start their life preparing to die today make up the great Romanian family in which the pre-Phanariot virtue and masculinity embodied by General Cantacuzino illuminates the destiny of the entire century.[39]

In a eulogy published in 1969, Horia Sima—the Legion's post-Codreanu leader—argues that General Catacuzino was among the few aristocrats who understood their historical mission and

---

[38] Codreanu, 'Problema oraşelor', *Pentru legionari*, 91.
[39] Mircea Eliade, 'Mitul Generalului', *Buna Vestire*, 1 (14 Oct. 1937), 189.

'integrated perfectly into the legionary mentality', recognizing in Codreanu 'the leader of the new national elite, originating from the peasant masses, of the new Romanian aristocracy meant to replace the old boyars, exhausted and powerless'. In order to obscure the Byzantine origin of the Cantacuzino family, Sima claims that they were ethnically related to Romanians by their common antique Thracian roots, and by centuries of living together, in harmony with the peasantry.[40] Sima's attempt to prove the national character of the Cantacuzinos and their pre-eighteenth-century assimilation was a response to the emergence of an anti-Phanariot discourse within the Legion, promoted mostly by Macedonian Romanians of anti-Greek orientation. In reaction to the increasingly factional competition within the organization in the late 1930s, the 'Macedonians' used the anti-Phanariot rhetoric, discrediting their competitors as anti-national.

If General Cantacuzino served as a patriarchal father-figure of the new man, Alexandru Cantacuzino was a prototype of the young generation of fascist aristocrats. Alexandru's political views were influenced by those of his mother, 'Princess' Alexandrina, although his political engagement was certainly more radical. One of the co-founders of the National Orthodox Society of Romanian Women (1910) and its interwar president, Alexandrina combined nationalism with Orthodox ethics and conservative feminism.[41] She was one of the most combative activists for women's social and political emancipation, mostly through the charitable work of well-to-do women, being convinced that the upper aristocratic classes had a historical duty to 'emancipate' the masses.

Alexandru shared many of these concerns, but reinterpreted them from a fascist perspective. Imbued with an anti-Communist and militant fervour, his writings attempted to reconcile nationalism with Orthodox ethics and the fascist revolutionary spirit. Like George Sorel, Alexandru Cantacuzino hailed violence for its 'purifying' effect, and pleaded for a form of 'heroic Christianity' based on a peculiar road to collective salvation through fascist combat and sacrifice for the national cause. He was primarily concerned with the creation of the Legionary 'new man', defined as a superior type of 'human

[40] Sima, 'Generalul Cantacuzino-Grănicerul'.
[41] Predescu (ed.), *Enciclopedia Cugetarea*, 162.

being' shaped by 'Christian conceptions and a new philosophy of life'.[42]

Nevertheless, the 'aristo-fascist' discourse was not always in tune with the Legionary ideology. The aristocracy perpetuated an image of itself that underlined its natural superiority and reclaimed its lost privileges on the basis of its traditional legitimacy. At a time of decline in patronage and growth in professionalism in society, Romanian aristocrats tried to capitalize on their paternalistic treatment of peasants and their role in keeping traditional rural communities together. In its struggle with the bourgeoisie for social, cultural, and economic predominance, the aristocracy depicted itself as the bearer of tradition and religion in sharp contrast to bourgeois materialism and egotism.

In his memoirs covering the period 1937–49, Ilie-Vlad Sturdza compares the 'Romania of the boyars' with the post-1918 bourgeois Romania, emphasizing the contrast between the patriarchal order of aristocratic rule and the dictatorial drive of Ion Antonescu's military regime (1940–4), regarded as the political victory of the bourgeoisie.[43] Allegedly, many of the micro-practices of power that he employed during the short Legionary rule emulated those traditionally used on boyar's estates, such as ad hoc courts of justice for poor peasants, which Sturdza also used in judging litigation between Romanian peasants and Jews.[44] Significantly, Ilie-Vlad Sturdza postulates an 'accommodating' and issue-oriented anti-Semitism which he sees more as a strategy for the manipulation of elites than as justified on racial or religious grounds. Sturdza also denounces the violence of Antonescu's regime, comparing it unfavourably with paternalistic practices of negotiation in his view characterizing aristocratic rule.

This distinction departs from the Legion's radical anti-Semitism as an indication of the aristocracy's more tolerant attitude towards the Jews. As such, it illustrates social-ideological divisions clearly evident among the heterogeneous Legionary membership. Discourses of legitimization put forward by the Legion and the aristocracy coincided in their harsh criticism of

[42] See Alexandru Cantacuzino, *Opere complete* (Munich, 1969).
[43] See Ilie-Vlad Sturdza, *Pribeag printr-un secol nebun: De la Legiunea Arhangelului Mihail la Legiunea Străină* (Bucharest, 2002).
[44] Ibid. 40.

the bourgeoisie, their rejection of parliamentary democracy, and their endorsement of an elitist social structure based on military hierarchical subordination. Both discourses called for the revival of the glorious, pre-Phanariot, 'national' past.

Although they had this much in common, there were nevertheless significant differences between these two 'related' political projects. The aristocracy was not committed to mass politics, but argued for a return to the traditional order of the Estates. Representing the economic interests of large landowners, it favoured free trade and the development of a cosmopolitan middle class made up of foreign elements. Although it adhered to the nationalist discourse, the traditional aristocratic representation of the peasantry was that of a poor, 'dirty', and ignorant class unable to manage itself. In its turn, the Legion advocated building a modern, totalitarian, political order based on a homogeneous ethnic community purged of foreign elements. Its ultra-nationalist discourse idealized the peasantry as the authentic repository of the Romanian national character. Although it endorsed a corporatist organization that would apparently revive the Estates and guilds of the Middle Ages, the Legion called for a strong centralized economy, protectionism, and state intervention in the economy, expressing the interests of the native middle class. In the long run, the aristocracy's specific interests were thus not only subordinated, but in fact also largely divergent.

III *Conclusion*

As in other Central and Eastern European countries, in Romania the history of the nobility can be written as a story of decline from medieval 'glory', via a gradual loss of influence in the era of mass politics, to its final downfall under Communist repression. In the Middle Ages Moldova and Wallachia boasted a virile nobility that managed to preserve its domestic privileges and the internal autonomy of its principalities in the face of the Ottoman invasion, and to assimilate numerous Byzantine and Balkan immigrant nobles. However, starting with the early modern period the Romanian aristocracy lost all its major political battles. During the seventeenth and the eighteenth centuries it lost its internal cohesion as it was infiltrated by Phanariot

Greeks in the service of the Ottoman Empire, leading to a genuine 'Greek–Romanian symbiosis'.[45] With the creation of the Romanian nation-state in 1858, the aristocracy was stripped of its legal privileges in favour of full civil equality under a modern civil code. Politically, the aristocracy gradually lost its electoral dominance to urban strata in the second half of the nineteenth century, and to mass political participation in the interwar period. From an economic point of view, the aristocracy suffered two major land expropriations, in 1864 and 1921, which on aggregate stripped it of 80 per cent of its lands.

The dramatic economic and political decline of the aristocracy in the interwar years accounts for the lack of research on the topic. To date, there are no monographs on the aristocracy, syntheses of Romanian history simply recording the fact that aristocracy 'disintegrated' both as a distinct socio-legal category and as a useful analytical concept. Written from a teleological perspective, such works obscure the important role which aristocrats continued to play in Romanian politics and the significant social and economic influence they exercised in the first half of the twentieth century. In fact, through various mechanisms of elite reproduction such as matrimonial alliances and economic and professional diversification, the aristocracy managed to preserve its socio-cultural prestige, mixing with new leading social categories. On the one hand aristocrats underwent a process of urbanization and *embourgeoisment*; on the other, leading capitalists bought manorial estates and emulated the aristocratic way of life. In the cultural field, the aristocracy managed to preserve and even enhance its prestige, associating the country's major intellectual figures with its discourse.

Attempting to reassess the importance of studying the aristocrats as social and political actors in their own right, this essay has argued that traditionally the Romanian aristocracy was not associated with radical politics. While staunchly defending its landed property and class privileges, the aristocracy endorsed an inclusive policy of ethnic immigration and collaboration with foreign capital. The significant—if partial—participation of aristocrats in the fascism of the 1930s can be explained in terms both of sociological factors and psychological motivation. On the one

---

[45] Paul Cornea, *Originile romantismului românesc* (Bucharest, 1972), 61–4.

hand, the aristocracy lost its socio-economic and political predominance as a result of the radical land reform; in the 1930s it was also heavily taxed in order to finance the state programme of industrialization. On the other hand, having lost its political influence and the electoral machinery represented by the Conservative Party, many aristocrats looked for other political forces that could grant them access to power. In this context, the Legion offered certain déclassé aristocrats the prospect of becoming part of an alternative national elite in the making, based on an ad hoc coalition between lower status 'would-be' elites and the former aristocracy. Although presented by fascist propaganda as a 'perfect union', this marriage of convenience did not lack tension, as the aristocracy dreamt of the revival of the old patriarchal order of the Old Regime, while the Legion attempted to build a fascist totalitarian state.

Notes on Contributors

CARLOS COLLADO SEIDEL is a member of the Department of Modern History at the University of Marburg and was a Visiting Fellow at the London School of Economics and Political Science in 2006. His main areas of interest are the history of Spain in the twentieth century and Nazi Germany. His most recent publications are *España, refugio nazi* (2005) and *Der Spanische Bürgerkrieg: Geschichte eines europäischen Konflikts* (2006).

ECKART CONZE has been Professor of Modern History at the University of Marburg since 2003, and has been Guest Professor at the Universities of Toronto and Bologna. In 2007 he was a Visiting Fellow of Sidney Sussex College Cambridge. In addition to the history of German and European aristocracies and elites, his research interests include the history of international relations from the eighteenth to the twentieth century and the history of the Federal Republic of Germany. His most recent publications on the history of the aristocracy are *Von deutschem Adel: Die Grafen von Bernstorff im 20. Jahrhundert* (2000); *Adel und Moderne: Deutschland im europäischen Vergleich im 19. und 20. Jahrhundert* (2004); and *Kleines Lexikon des Adels* (2005).

EAGLE GLASSHEIM is Assistant Professor of History at the University of British Columbia, Canada. He is the author of *Noble Nationalists: The Transformation of the Bohemian Aristocracy* (2005); 'Ethnic Cleansing, Communism, and Environmental Devastation in Czechoslovakia's Borderlands, 1945–1989', *Journal of Modern History*, 78 (2006), 65–92; and 'Between Empire and Nation: The Bohemian Nobility, 1880–1918', in Pieter Judson and Marsha Rozenblit (eds.), *Constructing Nationalities in East Central Europe* (2004).

LOTHAR HÖBELT is Associate Professor of Modern History at the University of Vienna and since 2001 also Lecturer at the Military Academy Wiener Neustadt. In 1992 he was Visiting Professor at the University of Chicago. His most recent publications include

Von der Vierten Partei zur Dritten Kraft: Die Geschichte des VdU (1999); *Defiant Populist: Jörg Haider and the Politics of Austria* (2003); and *Landschaft und Politik im Sudetenland* (2004). He is the editor of, among many others (with Wilhelm Brauneder) *Sacrum Imperium: Reich und Österreich 996–1806* (1996); and *Republik im Wandel: Die große Koalition und der Aufstieg der Haider-FPÖ* (2001).

CONSTANTIN IORDACHI is Assistant Professor in the History Department, Central European University, Budapest, Co-Director of Pasts, Centre for Historical Studies, and Associate Editor of the journal *East Central Europe/L'Europe du Centre Est.* He has published widely on citizenship, nationalism, and religion in Central and South Eastern Europe. His many publications include *Charisma, Politics and Violence: The Legion of the 'Archangel Michael' in Inter-War Romania* (2004); and *Citizenship, Nation- and State-Building: The Integration of Northern Dobrogea into Romania, 1878–1913* (2002); and he is co-editor of *Nationalism and Contested Identities: Romanian and Hungarian Case Studies* (2001).

JAN DE MAEYER is Professor at the University of Leuven (Belgium) and the Director of KADOC (Documentation and Research Centre on Religion, Culture and Society, 1750–). His publications and research are on religion, society, and art in the nineteenth and twentieth centuries.

STEPHAN MALINOWSKI is Assistant Professor at the Free University Berlin, where he teaches courses on Modern Western European History. In 2001 he received his Ph.D. from the Technical University Berlin for a dissertation on the social decline and political radicalization of the German aristocracy between 1871 and 1945 which was awarded the Hans Rosenberg Prize and published in 2003 as *Vom König zum Führer: Deutscher Adel und Nationalsozialismus*. He was a Kennedy Fellow at the Center for European Studies at Harvard University in 2005/6 and is currently preparing a book with the working title *Fighting Backwardness: Late Colonial Wars and Early Development Aid in Kenya and Algeria (1940s–1960s)*.

JENS PETERSEN was Deputy Director of the German Historical Institute in Rome and has published widely on political and cultural subjects. He is an acknowledged expert on fascism. His many publications include *Quo vadis, Italia? Ein Staat in der Krise* (1995).

IGNÁC ROMSICS is Professor of Modern Hungarian History at the University of Budapest (ELTE), a Member of the Hungarian Academy of Sciences, and General Secretary of the Hungarian Historical Society. Between 1993 and 1998 and for the academic year 2002/3 he held the Hungarian Chair at Indiana University, Bloomington (USA). He is the author of several books including *Wartime American Plans for a New Hungary* (1992); *István Bethlen* (1995); *Hungary in the Twentieth Century* (1999); and *The Dismantling of Historic Hungary* (2002).

KARINA URBACH is a Research Fellow at the German Historical Institute London. Her Cambridge Ph.D. was published as *Bismarck's Favourite Englishman: Lord Odo Russell's Mission to Berlin* (1999). She is editor of *Royal Cousinhood: Anglo-German Family Networks 1832–1918* (forthcoming 2008) and co-editor of *Birth or Talent? The Formation of Elites in a British–German Comparison* (2003). She is completing a monograph on the European ties of the German aristocracy 1914–39 and is commissioned to write a biography of Queen Victoria.

HANS DE VALK is Senior Researcher at the Institute of Netherlands History (ING), The Hague, where he has published text editions of historical sources, analytical inventories, and research guides. He is the author of books and articles on Dutch political history, the history of Dutch Catholicism, and the Roman Curia in the nineteenth and twentieth centuries.

Index

abdication 106, 136, 164, 225
Acción Española 113–17
Acoz, Marie-Pierre d'Udekem d' (née
    Verhaegen) 36, 48, 51
Action française 26–8, 30, 46
Agnelli, Giovanni 110
agriculture 44–5, 58, 68n., 96–7, 107, 111,
    114, 120, 135, 142–4, 151, 155, 171, 175,
    184n., 188, 191, 197, 203–4, 211–13,
    215
Alba, Duke of 63–4, 122, 124
Albert I, King of Belgium 37, 45
Alexander, Tsar 61
Alfieri, Dino 103
Alfonso XIII, King of Spain 114–15, 120,
    124–5
Alfonso of Orleans, Infante 123–5
Andes, Count of the 114
Annunzio, Gabriele d' 99–100
Ansaldo, Juan Antonio 116
Ansembourg, Maximilien de Marchant et
    d' 83–6
anti-Bolshevism/anti-Communism 8, 11,
    26, 31, 42, 45, 47–8, 59–63, 64n., 65,
    67, 76, 81, 98, 106, 123, 135, 144, 159,
    176, 179–81, 183–4, 192–3, 203, 218,
    222, 228, 230
anti-parliamentarianism 8–9, 20, 27,
    29–30, 45, 55, 60, 63, 68, 76–7, 82–3,
    98–9, 103, 113, 116, 118, 120, 124, 130,
    133–5, 141–2, 146, 151-3, 155–9, 162,
    167, 170, 174, 176, 191–3, 195–6, 198,
    202–5, 208, 214, 217, 220–1, 227, 230
anti-Semitism see also: Jewish population
    8, 9, 23–6, 29, 48, 67–8, 83, 87, 134,
    139–41, 159, 170, 192–4, 196, 198,
    217–18, 226, 229
Antonescu, Ion 217, 225, 229
appeasement 53, 55–6
Arendt, Hannah 25
Argetoianu, Constantin 215–16

Arriluce de Ibarra, Marquess of 114
Arrow Cross movement 196–9
Athlone, Countess of 66
Atholl, Duchess of 69
Attems, Anton 174n.
Auersperg, Alois 177
Auersperg, Karl 162n.
Averescu, Alexandru 215
Azaña, Manuel 113

Badoglio, Pietro (later Ducca di Addis
    Abeba) 93, 102–3
Baernreither, Joseph M. 164
Balfour, Arthur 62
Bandinelli, Count Ranuccio Bianchi
    106–7
Bardolff, Karl von 182
Barrès, Maurice 22
Barzini, Luigi 6
Beaufort, Henriette Laman Trip de 79
Becket, John 58
Bedford, Duke of see: Tavistock
Belcredi, Karel 158n.
Belder, Jos de 35
Beneduce, Alberto 102
Benes, Edward 178
Berchtold, Leopold Count 181
Berger-Waldenegg, Egon 179n.
Berl, Emmanuel 29n.
Bernstoff, Andreas Graf von 132, 136–7,
    139–40
Berstein, Serge 25
Bethlen, István 191–5
Bettino, Ricarsoli 91
blood (as a metaphor) 6, 61, 67, 88, 101,
    134, 143, 207–8
Bocchini, Arturo 102
Bolshevism see: anti-Bolshevism/anti-
    Communism
Borletti 95
Boulanger, Georges 22–3

bourgeoisie/*Bürgertum see also*: middle
classes 2–3, 5, 19, 20, 23, 38, 45, 75,
92–4, 105, 107–8, 110, 113, 116, 155,
168, 171, 175, 203, 221, 226, 229–31
Brătianu, Ion Constantin 210, 213–14
British Union of Fascists 56, 68
Brocket, Lord 70
Buccleuch, Duke 70
Burch, Count Alexandre von der 48
Burrin, Philippe 25

Cadogan, 5th Earl of 53n.
Cadogan, Alexander 53
Calvo Sotelo, José 117
Cantacuzino, Alexandru 221, 223–4, 228
Cantacuzino, Andronic 221
Cantacuzino, Grigore George 223
Cantacuzino-Grianicerul (General) 201–2,
216, 221–4, 227–8
Caracciolo, Marella 110
Carlos of Borbón y Orleans, Infante 120
Carol II, King of Romania 216–17, 224–5
castles (chateaux/country houses) 7, 12,
23, 30, 44, 59–61, 64n., 66–7, 70,
83–5, 95, 107, 175, 184, 188
Cavour, Camillo Benso Count di 91
Cecil family 67
Chamberlain, Houston Stewart 67, 181
Chambrun, René Count de 31–2
Channon, Chips 66
Chapelle, Fernand Bonnier de la 31n.
charisma/charismatic leader 9–10, 28, 54,
118, 136–7, 139, 201–2, 216–21, 225–7
charity work 228
Charles I, Emperor of Austria–Hungary
168, 189, 191
Charles II, King of Great Britain 22n.
Chateaubriand, François René vicomte de
17
Chelwood, Cecil Viscount of 60, 62, 68
Chiavolini, Alesssandro 103
Churchill, Arabella 63
Churchill, Winston 63–4, 67
Ciano, Costanzo 102
Ciano, Galeazzo 103
Cini, Vittorio 95
civil service 7, 18–19, 40–1, 74, 78, 81,
84–6, 91, 93–4, 101–3, 105, 123, 130,

149, 161–2, 171–2, 183, 189, 191–2,
196, 206–8
civil war 99–100, 144, 171, 174, 181, 194,
199
Clam, Heinrich 168
Coburg, Duchess of *see*: Romanova
Coburg, Duke of 65–6
Codreanu, Corneliu Zelea 201, 217–24,
226–8
Colijn, Hendrik 82
collaboration 30–2, 51, 75, 77
Colloredo-Mannsfeld, Rudolf 184n.
Colombi, Marchesa 108
colonies 27, 30, 37, 59, 62, 67, 70, 81, 86,
181, 188
Communism *see*: anti-Bolshevism/anti-
Communism
conservatism 8–9, 17, 20, 25, 28, 39, 45,
56, 57n. 63, 68, 73, 76–7, 82, 86, 99,
114–15, 123, 136, 137–8, 141–2, 150,
152–7, 162, 167–8, 172, 180–1, 192–7,
199, 201–2, 204, 207, 209–13, 215,
222–3, 228, 232
constitution:
Austria 166–7, 170, 173–4, 177
Belgium 37–9, 45
Britain 55, 69, 118
Germany 134
Italy 98, 100, 110
Netherlands 74–5, 82
Romania 207–9, 211
Spain 124
Coreth, Botho 179n.
corporatism 46, 48, 56, 77, 82, 86, 95, 118,
121–2, 151, 153, 155–6, 159, 174–80,
183–4, 190, 195, 230
Coudenhove, Gerulf Count 181n.
Coudenhove-Kalergi, Richard Count 163
countryside 70, 95, 97, 106, 175, 207
coup d'état 23, 28–9, 109, 114, 120, 133, 137,
170, 172–5, 183–4, 210
court 57, 64, 81, 85n., 112, 162, 207
Crespi, Silvio Benigno 95
Cripps, Sir Stafford 68
Crispi, Francesco 92
criticism of aristocracy 68, 98, 107
Cromwell, Oliver 22
culture 6, 9, 12, 19, 21, 32, 36, 38, 57, 75,

91, 95, 99, 131, 140, 144–6, 152, 212, 214, 217, 229, 231
Curzon, Lord 62
Cuza, Alexandru Ioan Prince 210–11
Czernin, Ottokar Count 164, 181
Czernin, Peter Count 184
Czernin, Rudolf 158n.
DAG (Deutsche Adelsgenossenschaft) 69, 140n., 141, 145
Dankl, Viktor 168
Darlan, Admiral François 31n.
Darré, Walther 88
death rate 21, 57
Degrelle, Léon 10, 48–51
Depretis, Agostino 92
Deterding, Henry 82
Diaz (later Duca della Vittoria) 93, 103
diehards 57, 62, 64n.
diplomatic service 11, 18, 31n., 32, 53, 62, 64, 74, 93–4, 102–4, 112, 164–5, 169n., 177–8, 190–1, 197, 199, 224–5
Dobrzensky, Jindřich 158n.
Dollfuß, Engelbert 174–6, 178
Dönhoff, Marion Gräfin 129n.
Downe, Lady Dorothy 70
Dreyfus affair 17, 23–4, 26, 29
Drumont, Edouard 23
Dubsky, Adolph Count 163, 184–5
Duca, Ion G. 223
Dulles, Allen 66n.
Dumba, Nikolaus 164
Durloo, Luc 36
dynasty see: monarchy

economy see also: inflation 7, 12, 15, 20, 35, 38, 42, 45, 48, 56–9, 60n., 77, 82, 86, 96, 105–6, 111, 113, 131, 140, 145–6, 149, 151, 154–5, 162, 167, 171–2, 177, 183, 189, 196–7, 203–4, 209–15, 221, 229–32
education, aristocratic 19, 22, 30, 36, 45, 47–8, 53–4, 65n., 78–81, 83, 86, 102, 105, 107, 118, 143, 165, 189, 191, 194–5, 197, 199, 211–12, 214, 224
Edward VII, King of Great Britain 57
Eenoo, Romain van 35
elections 39, 45, 48–9, 75–7, 82, 85, 98, 118, 140, 154, 162, 170, 173, 174n., 193,

195, 197–99, 201–2, 209–11, 213–14, 216–22, 224, 231–2
Eliade, Mircea 227
Eliseda, Marquess of the 113–14, 116–18, 120, 122
elite, aristocratic concept of 22, 67, 76, 111, 141–2, 156–7, 192, 202, 220, 226–7, 230, 232
emigration/exile 16–17, 27, 30, 61n., 66, 104, 109, 114–15
Eminescu, Mihai 226
ennoblement 19, 37–8, 42, 64, 73–4, 95, 102–4, 110–11, 120, 161, 183, 188, 206–8
entrepreneurs 86, 95, 97, 189
Esher, Viscount 68
estates see: landowners
Estella, Marquess of 115
Esterházy, Duke Pál 189
Eugene, Archduke 178, 182
Europe 52, 59, 61, 163, 184

Falange 114–21, 123, 125
family, concept of 1, 6, 29, 32, 64, 76, 112, 143, 156, 159, 166
farming see: agriculture
Farneti, Paolo 91
Fayette family 31
Fedele, Pietro 103
Federzoni, Luigi 103
Ferdinand, King of Romania 214
Festetics, Sándor Count 197–8
feudalism 38, 70, 84, 111, 118, 149, 154–5, 160, 181n.
Fey, Emil 175, 177, 179n.
Filipescu, Grigore 215
finance/banking 19, 36, 38, 41, 43, 75, 78, 81–2, 84, 105, 111, 149, 204
First World War 7, 11, 21–2, 31n., 38, 42, 44–6, 57, 60, 81, 83, 96–9, 103, 114, 131, 133–4, 138, 149, 163, 168, 178, 181, 197, 201–2, 204, 214, 222
Florio, Vincenzo 95
forests, ownership of 50, 167–8, 184
Fortunato, Giustino 99
Foscari 106
Foxá, Count of 116
Franckenstein, George 165

Franco Bahamonde, Francisco 4, 8, 11,
    47–8, 63–4, 119, 121–5, 179, 224
French Revolution 16, 19, 20, 37, 45, 59,
    154, 156–7
Furet, François 18
Fürstenberg, Karl Emil Prince 178n.
Fürstenberg, Max Egon Prince 166

Garibaldi, Guiseppe 99–100
Gasperi, de 104
Gaulle, Charles de 29–31
generations (conflicts, debates) 9, 46, 130,
    136–7, 183, 228
gentry *see*: lower nobility
George V, King of Great Britain 61, 178
German revolution 1918 134–5, 140–1,
    181n.
Giménez Caballero, Ernesto 115
Giolitti, Giovanni 92, 100
Giraudoux, Jean 32
Goad, Harold 118
Goebbels, Josef 65
Goering, Hermann 53, 66, 69n., 71, 179,
    181, 183
Goicoechea, Antonio 117, 124
Gonzáles Cuevas, Pedro Carlos 113–14
Gotha (Almanach) 171
Graham, Marquis of 54, 70–1
Grandes/grand seigneurs see: higher nobility
Grandi, Dino 102
Gregory, Berndt von 183n.
Grunne (senator), Xavier de Hemricourt
    de 51
Grunne, Eugéne de Hemricourt de 50–1
Guarneri, Felice 102
Guérin, Jules 23
Guermantes, Duc de 24

Habicht, Theo 176
Habsburg, Francis Joseph, Emperor of
    Austria–Hungary 189
Habsburg, Otto von 169, 178, 179n., 191
Halifax, Lord 53, 70
Hanfstaengel, Ernst ('Putzi') 54n.
Hartig, Edmund 179n.
Haushofer, Albrecht 65
Hauteclocque-Leclerc, Philippe de 30
Hayes, Carlton 123

Heimwehr (home guard movement)
    169–76, 177n., 178–80, 182, 184n.
Heine, Heinrich 6
Helldorff, Wolf Heinrich, Graf von 130
Heller, Hermann 102
Henlein, Konrad 182n., 184–5
Henry, Colonel 24
Hess, Rudolf 65
Hesse family 66
Hessen, Philip von 10
Heydrich, Reinhard 181n.
higher nobility 1, 2, 4–5, 6n., 10–11, 15,
    53–4, 56–7, 63n., 65, 68–9, 71, 74, 94,
    120, 123, 145n., 149, 166, 168, 171,
    187–8, 191, 207
Hindenburg, Paul von 8, 139–40
Hitler, Adolf 8, 10–11, 54–6, 64–7, 69, 70,
    87, 100, 106, 116, 138, 150, 153, 157–9,
    176, 177n., 178–81, 182n., 195–6
Hoare, Sir Samuel 121, 125
Hofmannsthal, Hugo von 7, 156
Hohenberg family 182
Hohenlohe-Langenburg, Ernst II 6n.
Hohenlohe-Langenburg, Max Prince 11,
    66, 185n.
Hohenlohe-Langenburg, Victoria 65
Hohenlohe-Waldenburg-Schillingsfürst,
    Stephanie 66n.
Hohenzollern *see*: William II
Hohenzollern-Sigmaringen, Karl Ludwig
    of 211
honour, aristocratic concept of 6, 8, 106,
    130, 144, 177, 227
Horthy, Miklos 8–10, 54, 61n., 67, 191,
    193, 197–8
Hoyos, Rudolph Count 166, 176, 177–9n.,
    180, 182, 184n.
Hugenberg, Alfred 170–2
hunting 12, 66, 188
Huyn, Count von 84

industry 19–20, 38, 42–3, 55, 70, 75, 78,
    81–2, 84, 97, 101–2, 105, 111–12, 143,
    149, 154, 156, 168, 171–2, 174n., 189,
    193, 195, 197, 199–200, 203–4, 212,
    232
inflation 96–7, 107
Irish question 57, 59–60, 69

Iron Guard movement 9, 201–2, 216, 230, 232
Irvine, William 25
Ishiguro, Kazuo 55

Janos, Andrew 216
Janssens, Paul 36
Jenks, Jorian E. F. 68
Jewish population *see also*: anti-Semitism 21, 54, 67, 79, 83, 133, 140, 167, 170, 178, 182n., 184, 189, 194, 196, 198, 200, 204, 212, 214, 218, 226–7, 229
Jones, Larry 138
Joseph, Francis 164
Juan of Borbón, heir to the throne of Spain 120–5
Junker 1, 143
Juntas de Ofensiva Nacional-Sindicalista (JONS) *see also*: Falange 114–17, 19

Kellogg, Michael 11
Kemény, Gábor Baron 199
Kerckering zur Borg, Maximilian 139
Khuen-Belasi, Karl 184–5
Kindelán, Alfredo 122n.
Kinnoull, Earl 56, 68
Kinský, František 158n.
Kinsky, Ulrich 182–3n.
Kinský, Zdeněk Radislav 158n.
Kleist-Schmenzin, Ewald von 142
Kolowrat, Leopold Count 162
Kolowrat, Zdeněk 158n.
Kun, Bela 61

Labour Party *see*: socialism
Lamberty, Max 50
Lamennais, Robert de 210
Lampedusa, Tomasi di 7, 75
Lanaro, Silvio 95
land reform 114, 120, 149–51, 159, 162, 168, 191, 193, 197–8, 210–11, 213–14, 231–2
landowners 5, 7, 12, 19, 55–6, 58–9, 83, 91–2, 97, 103, 120, 135, 142–3, 149–51, 153, 155, 159–61, 165–6, 181, 184, 187–9, 196–9, 203–6, 208–15, 223, 229–31
language 20, 26, 69, 217–18

Laval, Josée 31
Laval, Pierre 31
leadership. aristocratic concept of 6, 56, 67–8, 79, 83, 85, 99, 101, 111, 121, 134, 136, 142–3, 195, 219, 226–7
League of Nations 150–1
Ledebur, Eugen 152
Ledesma Ramos, Ramiro 115–17
Ledóchowski, Count 84
Leo XIII, Pope 20
Leopold I, II, III, kings of Belgium 37
liberalism 37, 39, 48, 74, 76, 81–2, 82, 85, 93, 95, 98–99, 104, 106, 108, 111, 113, 116, 118, 120, 130, 133, 146, 153–7, 159, 167, 170, 176, 192–6, 201n., 204, 207, 209–15, 223
Lichtenstein, Aloys Prince 161, 162n., 165, 167
Lippowitz, Jacob 170n.
Lloyd, Sir George 62
Lobkowicz, Jan 158n., 181n.
Londonderry, Lady 59, 60
Londonderry, Lord 55
Louis XIV 66
Louis, Eugéne 27
lower nobility 4, 5, 58n., 67n., 74, 191–3, 204, 207
Ludendorff, Erich 66
Ludovici, Anthony 68
Lueger, Karl 167
Luigi, Federico 91
Lymington, Viscount (later Earl of Portsmouth) 54, 61, 66n., 68, 70

Maeztu, Ramiro de 113
Mandl, Fritz 170n.
Mar, Earl of 70
March on Rome *see also*: Mussolini, Benito 28, 63, 101–2, 105
Marismas del Guadalquivir, Marquess 113–14
Marlborough, 9th Duke of 12
Marmora, Alfonso 91
marriages (aristocratic) 2, 11–12, 31, 36, 38, 61, 65, 66n., 76, 79–81, 86–7, 95, 105, 107, 110, 143, 162, 171n., 183–4, 187, 189
Marzotto 95

Masaryk, Tomáš 166
Matteotti, Giacomo 100
Maurras, Charles 22, 26, 46, 114
Mazzonis, Guido 95, 105
Medinger, Wilhelm 151
Meester, Antoine de 50
memoirs 12, 169n., 182n., 225, 229
Menabrea, Count 91
meritocracy 17, 19, 22, 195
Michelet, Jules 210
middle class 3, 9, 22, 45, 75, 77, 79, 81,
    85–6, 91, 161, 167–8, 172, 174–5, 181,
    196, 204, 209, 212, 226, 230
military 2, 7, 9, 18–19, 21, 26–7, 29–32,
    41–2, 44, 46, 56–7, 74, 84, 86, 91–3,
    97, 100–3, 112, 114, 117, 119–24,
    132–4, 139, 149, 158–9, 161–2, 165,
    169, 171, 174, 177–8, 183, 189, 196–7,
    201, 205–7, 212, 217, 221–3, 225, 227,
    229–30
Milza, Pierre 25
Mirabeau, Sibylle-Gabrielle Marie-
    Antoinette de Riqueti, comtesse de
    Martel de Janville (*nom de guerre*:
    'Gyp') 24
Missori, Mario 102
Misurata, Volpi di 102
Mitford, Diana (later Lady Diana Mosley)
    9, 65, 69
Mitford, Nancy 15–16, 69
modernity/anti-modernism 2, 9, 15, 19,
    31, 37, 50, 54, 57n., 79, 84, 99, 113,
    140, 143, 146, 192, 203, 207, 209, 230
Modráček, František 149
Mola, Emilio 120
monarchy 16, 26, 29, 108
    Belgium 37–8, 44–5, 50–1
    Britain 61, 65
    France 16, 18, 23, 27, 29
    Germany 133–4, 136–7, 139, 142
    Habsburg 109, 149–50, 152, 154, 156,
        161–5, 176, 178, 182, 184, 185n., 189,
        191
    Hungary 67n.
    Italy 10, 92, 94–5, 98–101, 104, 109–10,
        137
    Netherlands 73–4, 81

Romania 202
monarchist movements:
    Austria 168, 169n., 179
    Belgium 48
    Britain 66n.
    France 22, 27–8, 31n.
    Germany 10, 136–7, 141, 146
    Hungary 191, 195
    Italy 100, 109
    Romania 204
    Spain 73, 113–17, 120–1, 123–5
Monasterio, José 122n.
Monck, George 22
Montelera, Rossi di 105
Moore, Barrington 202–5
Morés, Marquis de 23
Mosley, Oswald 55–6, 68–9
Mun, Albert de 20
Musiedlak, Didier 93, 103
Mussert, Anton 84
Mussolini, Benito 10, 28, 51, 63, 64n., 67,
    81, 98–105, 109, 136–7, 174, 179, 182n.

Napoleon I 17, 37
Nassau-Siegen, Karl Heinrich Nikolaus
    Otto Prinz von 2
National Socialism 9–12, 35, 51, 53–5,
    56n., 61, 64–5, 67–8, 70, 77, 79–80,
    84–8, 101–2, 118, 121, 129–30, 134–5,
    137–8, 141–2, 144–5, 150, 153, 157,
    163, 172–7, 178n., 179–85, 195–8, 217
nationalism 8, 46–7, 49–50, 57, 98, 115,
    119, 139–40, 149–53, 155, 158–9, 181,
    204, 207, 217–18, 225, 228, 230
networks (aristocratic) 6, 8, 11, 28, 30, 56,
    60–1, 64–6, 75, 84, 182, 188
Neustädter-Stürmer, Odo 179n., 184n.
new nobilty *see*: ennoblement
Niculae, Prince (King Carol II's brother)
    221
Nitti, Francesco Gaverio 98
Northumberland, 8th Duke of 62, 67
novels about the aristocracy 7, 21, 55, 75,
    79, 183n.

occupation 29, 30, 45, 51, 75, 82, 85, 87,
    158–9, 192, 207–8
Ophul, Marcel 32

Orgaz, Luis 122n.
Orléans, Duc d' (later Compte de Paris)
    23, 27
Orsini-Rosenberg, Prince 165

Pálffy, Fidel Count 196–9
Pallady, Alexandrina 223, 228
Parish, Karel 158n.
parliamentarism see: anti-parliamentari-
    anism
parliaments 38–40, 42, 48–9, 56–7, 62,
    65, 68–9, 74–5, 82, 85, 92–3, 98, 100,
    103–4, 118, 122, 149, 161–2, 166, 190,
    195, 208, 211, 221–2, 226
patriotism see also: nationalism 21, 30, 48,
    57, 81, 83, 87, 112, 133, 136, 151, 153,
    180, 226–7
patronage 118, 223, 229
peasants see also: agriculture 59, 97,
    149–50, 154, 203, 210–15, 226, 228–30
pedigree 5, 54, 56, 143
peerage see: higher nobility
Pelloux, Luigi 92
Petain, Marshal 29n., 32
Pfrimer, Walter 174
Pollio, Alberto 93
Polzer-Hoditz, Arthur 168
Ponte, Miguel 122n.
Popular Front 47, 179, 181
Portland, Duchess of 53
Portland, Duke of 58
press (newspapers) 31, 47, 51, 54, 58–9, 62,
    63n., 81, 92, 94, 99, 101, 104, 113, 119,
    153, 155, 161, 170n., 179n., 184n., 192,
    199, 218, 224
Primo de Rivera, General Miguel 115
Primo de Rivera, José Antonio 115,
    117–19
privileges 16, 37, 73–5, 80, 93, 134, 142,
    155, 193, 206, 208–9, 218–19, 229–31
Proust, Marcel 6, 23

Queensborough, Lord 70
Quinet, Edgar 210
Quintanar, Marquess of 114

Rădulescu, Ion Heliade 225
Ramanones, Count 111

Rappard, Ernst van 86–8
Redesdale, Lord 67
Reinsdorff, Helmut von 183n.
Reither 184n.
religion 8–10, 77, 82, 98, 115, 117, 138–9,
    146, 149, 153–4, 157, 162, 167–8,
    173–5, 180, 194, 205, 217, 228–9
    Catholicism 7, 10, 20, 35, 39, 44–8,
    50–1, 74, 76, 83–5, 95–6, 98, 101, 109,
    112–13, 118, 120, 125, 138–9, 145,
    153–5, 163, 166–7, 177, 180, 189
    Protestantism 10, 74, 76, 82, 138–9
    others 10, 70, 189, 191, 227–8
Rémond, René 25, 27
renegades 10n., 69, 106
Renner, Karl 165, 171
Renoir, Jean 21
resistance movement 30–2, 37, 51–2, 83,
    109, 129–31
restoration 29, 37, 111, 113–14, 116, 119,
    121–5, 136–7, 141, 163, 165, 178
Revertera, Peter 179
Rexism see: Degrelle, Leon
Ribbentrop, Joachim von 64
Ricasoli, Baron 91
Robilant 106
Rocca Muzzatti, E. Morozzo della 108
Rocco, Alfredo 103
Rocque, Count de la 27, 29
Rodezno, Count of 114, 120
Roey, Cardinal van 51
Rohan, Alain 153n.
Rohan, Karl Anton 61, 153, 155–8, 163,
    181, 182n., 184–5
Romano, Sergio 94
Romanov, Grand Duke Cyril 65
Romanova, Maria Alexandrovna (later
    Duchess of Coburg) 61
Romney, Earl of 57
Ronald, Lord 54
Roque, Count François de la 26, 29
Rosenberg, Alfred 177n.
Rosetti, C. A. 210
Ross, Lady Una 59
Rossi, Ernesto 95
Rothschild, Baron 173, 181
royalists see: monarchist movements
Rudini, Marchese di 92

Rupprecht, Bavarian Crown Prince 10, 58
Russian revolution (1917) 45, 47, 59, 98,
   135

SA (Storm Troopers) 130, 184–5
Saint-Loup, Marquis de 24
Sainz Rodríguez, Pedro 115, 120
Salazar, Antonio de Oliveira 195
Saliquet, Andrés 122n.
Saltillo, Marquess of 113
Sanjurjo, José 114
Sargent, John 12
Savoyard family 95
Schober, Johannes 172–3
Schönborn, Friedrich Karl 174n.
Schönburg-Hartenstein, Alois Prince
   165–6
Schuschnigg, Kurt 176, 178–9, 181
Schwarzenberg, Adolph Prince 180–1,
   185
Schwarzenberg, Bedřich 151
Schwarzenberg, František 152
Schwarzenberg, Karel 153–8
Scott, William Lord 70
Second World War 29–31, 37, 51–2, 64,
   71, 75, 77, 79, 121–3, 159, 183, 197–9
Segonzac, Pierre Dunoyer de 30
Seipel, Ignaz 162–3, 168–9, 172–3
Serényi, Miklós Count 199
Serpieri, Arrigo 97
Serrano Suñer, Ramón 121
Severen, Joris van 49
Sforza, Carlo Count 104
Sieghart, Rudolf 170n.
Sima, Horia 227–8
Sirinelli, Jean-François 16
Snoy et d'Oppuser, Jean-Charles Baron
   50–1
social life 81, 106, 108, 112, 188
socialism 20, 26, 39, 45–8, 50, 55, 57, 60,
   62n., 76, 81–2, 97–9, 133, 154–8, 162,
   167–70, 172–6, 179, 192–3
Solchaga, José 122n.
Sorel, George 228
Soucy, Robert 25, 27
Spanish Civil War 47, 118–20, 123–4, 179,
   181, 224
Spanish Republic 114–17, 119–20

Spann, Othmar 177
SS 23, 86–7, 130, 143n., 184–5
stab-in-the-back myth (Dolchstoßlegende) 22,
   132–4
Stalin, Joseph 181
Ständestaat/corporate state see: corpo-
   ratism
Starabba, Antonio 92
Starhemberg, Ernst Rüdiger Prince 163,
   173–5, 178–9, 183
Sternberg, 'Montschi' 168
Sternberg, Cecilia 182–3n.
Sternberg, Leopold 158n.
Sternhell, Zeev 25–6
Stokes, Gale 203–5
Strachwitz, Hugo 158n.
Stresemann, Gustav 172
Sturdza, Ilie-Vlad 221, 225, 229
Sturdza, Mihail 221, 225
Sturdza, Zoe 225
Sturdzas family 202, 225
Sudeten German Party 158, 184–5
Sudeten German 151–2, 158–9, 162, 167,
   184–5
Szálasi, Ferenc 196–9
Széchenyi, Ljos Count 199

Tassigny, Jean de Lattre de 30
Tavistock, Marquis of (later Duke of
   Bedford) 55, 56n., 70–1
taxation 45, 48, 96, 98, 208, 232
Teleki, Pál 191, 194–5
Temesváry, Ede Baron 199
Terlinden, Viscount Charles 48
Thienen, Wolfgang Baron 184
Third Reich see: National Socialism
Third Republic 18–26, 33
Thun, Franz Prince 184
Thurn-Valsassina, Maximilian Count
   170n., 179n.
Tinti, Friedrich 179n.
Titulescu, Nicolae 225
Toncic-Sorinj, Lujo von 177
Tour du Pin de la Charce, Marquis de la
   20
Trapp, Georg von 182
Traun, Rudolf 184
Trianon, treaty of 66n., 187, 197

Trollope, Anthony 55
Turnatori, Gabriela 108

Umberto II, King of Italy 109–10
universal suffrage: *see* elections
university *see*: education
Uzés, duchess d' 23

Vanderbilt, Consuelo 12
Varela, José Enrique 121–2
Vecchi, Cesare Maria de 102
Vereinigung katholischer Edelleute
    (Association of Catholic Nobles)
    165–6
Versailles, treaty of 144, 165, 169
Vichy 25, 29–31
Victor Emanuel III 100, 109
Vigerie, Emmanuel d'Astier de la 31
Vigerie, Henri d'Astier de la 31n.
Volpi, Guiseppe 95
Vos, Louis 35
Vroylande, Robert du Bois de 51

Wächter, Otto von 183n.
Waugh, Evelyn 7
wealth *see also*: estates 6, 54–7, 59, 68n.,
    69, 97, 106–7, 112, 138, 155, 187, 189,
    191, 197–8, 200, 221, 223

Weimar Republic 22, 101, 130, 133–7,
    139–43, 145n., 176
Wense, Baron 168
Westminster, (Loelia) Duchess of 5, 60n.,
    67
Westminster, Duke of 67, 70
Westphalen, Count Ferdinand 177
Wied family 66
Wiesener, Friedrich von 169n., 178, 182
Wilhelm, Crown Prince (Germany) 136
William I, King of the Netherlands 37, 74
William II, German Emperor 57, 136
Wils, Lode 49
Wittelsbach *see*: Rupprecht
Wittgenstein, Ludwig 1, 11
Wolff, Gustav 168–9, 182
women 42, 49, 80, 108, 154, 228
working class 2, 20–1, 23, 45, 56, 63, 112,
    145, 170, 180

Ydewalle, Hubert d' 51

Zayas, Marquess of 116
Zessner-Spitzenberg, Hans Karl Freiherr
    von 178
Zita, Empress of Austria–Hungary 165
Zoelen, Robert Groeninx van 80–3